THE ULTIMATE GUIDE TO
DOGS

THE ULTIMATE GUIDE TO
DOGS

David Alderton

Bath · New York · Singapore · Hong Kong · Cologne · Delhi · Melbourne

This edition published by Parragon in 2010

Parragon
Queen Street House
4 Queen Street
Bath BA1 1HE, UK

Created and produced by

 studio **cactus** Ⓒ

13 SOUTHGATE STREET   WINCHESTER   HAMPSHIRE   SO23 9DZ

DESIGN Laura Watson, Sharon Rudd
EDITORIAL Jennifer Close

ISBN: 978-1-4454-1565-9

Printed in China

STUDIO CACTUS WOULD LIKE TO THANK
Sharon Cluett for original styling; Jo Weeks for proofreading;
Penelope Kent for indexing; and Candida Frith-MacDonald for
additional text

PICTURE CREDITS
All images © Tracy Morgan Animal Photography, except:
Abramova Kseniya 4 l; Aleksander Bochenek 78 b r; Aleksey Ignatenko 76 b l;
alexan55 49 t r, 49 b l; Andrew Williams 58 b; Animal Photography 53 b, 61 b r;
Annette 35 t l; Artur Zinatullin 49 b r; Corbis Images 52 t, 61 t l; cynoclub 37 b r,
82 t r; Studio Cactus 33 b l, 33 b r, 38 t l, 38 b r, 39 t, 41 b, 47 t l, 47 r, 47 b l, 52 b
l, 52 b r, 53 t, 59 b, 60 t, 60 b, 62 t r, 62 b l, 64 t, 64 b, 65 t l, 65 b r, 67 b, 68 t l, 68 b
l, 69 t r, 70 b l, 70 b r, 71 c r, 72 b, 78 t l, 78 t l, 81 b l, 85 t, 87 b l, 90 t r, 92 b l, 92
b r, 94 b l; Diane Critelli 10 t r; DK Images 84 b l; Eline Spek 14; Eric Isselée 23 b,
33 t, 37 b l, 45 b , 46 t r, 73 t r, 80 t, 80 b l, 81 t r, 83 b r, 85 b, 92 t r; Erik Lam 21 t
l, 66 t r, 87 t l, 87 t r; Gemmav D. Stokes 40 b; Getty Images 32 b, 35 b l, 42 t r, 46
b l, 56 b, 71 b l, 79 t; Hedser van Brug 11 t r, 54 b; ingret 21 b l; Ingvald
Kaldhussater 86 b; iofoto 28 t r; iofoto 35 t r, 39 b r; istock 44 b; Iztok Noc 73 b r;
Jacqueline Abromeit 42 t l; James Klotz 54 t l; Jay Crihfield 34 b l; Jeffrey Ong
Guo Xiong 77 b l; Joy Brown 23 t r; Kirk Geisler 12 b l, 66 b l; Kristian Sekulic 2–3;
Laurie Lindstrom 48; Marc Henrie, ASC 82 b, 89 t, 89 b; Mary E. Cioffi 9 t r;
Matthew Collingwood 78 b l; Michael Ledray 17 t; Michal Napartowicz 43 t r; N
Joy Neish 13 c r; NHPA 6, 12 b, 24 t; Nicholas James Homrich 94 b r; Nicholas
Peter Gavin Davies 25 t; Pavel Bortel 20 t r, 20 b; Pedro Jorge Henriques
Monteiro 8 b; photos.com 62 b r, 88 b r, 90 b, 91 c l, 94 t; pixshots 65 b l;
Rebecca Schulz 91 t r; Rhonda ODonnell 29 t r, 91 b; Rolf Klebsattel 74 t r;
Sergey I 9 b l; Shutterstock.com 13 t, 95 t r; Sklep Spozywczy 21 b r; Sonja Foos
31 t r; Steven Pepple 42 b; stoupa 66 b r; Susan Harris 9 b l; Tad Denson 11 b r,
87 b r; vnlit 32 t l, 32 t r; Waldemar Dabrowski 26 b l, 35 b r, 57 b, 74 b l; Werner
Stoffberg 10 b l; WizData, inc. 28 b; wojciechpusz 43 b; zimmytws 69 b.

COVER IMAGES: Main Image: Yellow Labrador Retriever © Mark Raycroft/
Minden Pictures/Gettyimages. Right hand side/back image: Grassland ©
Corbis. Bottom left to right: West Highland White Terrier © Steven Pepple;
Basset Hound © Sean MacLeay; British Bulldog © Claudia Steininger

CONTENTS

ABOUT THIS BOOK

There is no universal system of breed classification for dogs but, generally, they are divided on the basis of their original function. Some categories such as the hound group are more natural than others, which may simply consist of breeds with diverse working ancestries. Not all breeds are recognized for show purposes, and recognition can vary between different organizations and countries.

BREED RECOGNITION

The divisions used in this book are linked to those employed by kennel clubs around the world, with acceptance by the UK's Kennel Club (KC), the Fédération Cynologique Internationale (FCI), and the various American Kennel Clubs (AKCs) being listed under the individual entries.

This is not to say that judging standards are the same in each case, however, because these do vary between organizations, and in turn affect the judging process itself. In some instances, although dogs may exist in a wide range of colours, this does not mean that all varieties are universally accepted for show purposes.

COAT COLOURS

The coat colour swatches that accompany the individual entries give a guide to the colours and colour combinations linked with particular breeds, but should not be interpreted literally in all cases. The cream swatch, as an example, describes breeds with very pale coats, whose coloration may range from white through to a dark shade of cream. More precise individual information about the colours associated with a particular breed can be found in the fact box accompanying the entry, although bear in mind that not all colours or coat variants are equally common within a breed. On the other hand, in some cases, as with the Golden Retriever, coat coloration can actually be a defining feature of the breed.

SYMBOLS IN THE BOOK

At-a-glance symbols are used to provide information such the size to which a dog of a particular breed will grow, its coat type, and its level of activity; these symbols can assist in choosing a breed that will match your requirements. The height of most breeds is standard, but bear in mind that in the case of bigger breeds, bitches usually grow to a slightly smaller size than male dogs. Also, the level of exercise that an individual dog requires will be affected both by its age and its overall state of health.

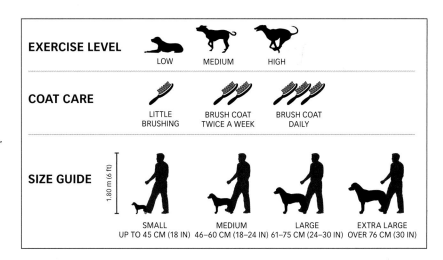

| EXERCISE LEVEL | LOW | MEDIUM | HIGH |

| COAT CARE | LITTLE BRUSHING | BRUSH COAT TWICE A WEEK | BRUSH COAT DAILY |

| SIZE GUIDE | SMALL UP TO 45 CM (18 IN) | MEDIUM 46–60 CM (18–24 IN) | LARGE 61–75 CM (24–30 IN) | EXTRA LARGE OVER 76 CM (30 IN) |

1.80 m (6 ft)

COAT COLOURS

 BLACK

 CREAM

 GREY

 BLUE

 RED/TAN

 GOLD

DARK BROWN

 GOLD AND WHITE

 BLACK AND WHITE

 TAN AND WHITE

 BLACK AND TAN

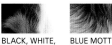 BLACK, WHITE, AND TAN

 BLUE MOTTLED WITH TAN

 BLACK BRINDLE

THE ORIGINS OF BREEDS

What sets the dog apart from all other domestic animals is the way it has adapted, in terms of its association with us. Dogs have performed a very wide range of roles through history, mirroring the changes that have taken place in human society down through the millennia, and have been bred to fit these different niches. This is an ongoing process, as reflected by the growing number of so-called 'designer dogs' now being created.

HUNTERS AND GUARDIANS

At the outset, dogs were kept as hunting companions, helping to provide food, in addition to acting as guardians around settlements. Then, once agriculture started to develop, dogs were used to herd and guard livestock. Their role as hunting companions continued to diversify, and when shooting became a fashionable pastime in the 1800s, breeds of dog were created specially as gundogs. It is the adaptability of the dog that has seen their skills being used in a wide range of different activities.

The most significant change to date started in the late 1800s. The increasing mechanization that was taking place in Europe and North America gave many people more leisure time and greater wealth, as reflected by a growing middle class. This was a time of evolutionary theory, and people were embarking on selective breeding of a wide range of plants and animals, which became known as 'fancying'. The results of such endeavours were seen at shows.

THE SHOW SCENE

Up until this stage, there had been no breeds as such but, rather, dogs had developed recognizable characteristics linked to their work. The breed concept of today arose in conjunction with the show scene.

Dogs are categorized at shows according to a clear format. The breeds are divided up into different breed groups, such as hounds, that reflect their origins. Then within each breed division, there will be various 'classes' depending on the size of the show and its popularity. Class winners compete for the best of breed title, and each of these then progress to best in group. Finally, these winners compete for the best in show award, each being judged against their individual breed standard.

SPANIEL Extremely versatile and generally very friendly, working spaniels track down prey and flush it out for the waiting hunters. They then use scent to find the fallen quarry and retrieve it.

SETTING THE STANDARD

The ideal example of each breed is encapsulated in the breed standard, which is laid down by the registration body, such as the Kennel Club (KC) in the United Kingdom, or the Fédération Cynologique Internationale (FCI) in mainland Europe. The situation is more confused in the United States as there are a number of separate registration bodies, of which the best known is the American Kennel Club. The standard is an attempt to portray in words a description of what the breed should look like, in all respects, including coloration.

DESIGNER DOGS

A popular growing trend in dog breeding is what are now being called 'designer dogs', the result of crosses between existing purebreds with the aim of capturing the most desirable traits of both parents. Designer dogs may represent a new breed category for show purposes in the future. Although this type of breeding has a novelty value, it is simply a continuation of the same trend that has taken place since the very start of the domestication of the dog.

Breeders creating true designer dogs are usually aiming to refine the personalities and characteristics of these dogs so as to make them better companions, which is the main role of the dog today. Quiet, cute, small, and trainable are just some of the characteristics that are usually favoured. The range of designer dogs continues to increase, with over 75 such crosses having been named to date. The trend is now firmly established to combine parts of the name of both ancestral breeds in that of the designer dog. Hence Labradoodle, reflecting a cross

PUGGLE The increasingly popular Puggle is a designer crossbreed created by crossing the Pug and the Beagle. The result is a good-natured, active, and playful companion breed with a distinctive and endearing expression.

between a Labrador Retriever and a Poodle, a Cock-a-poo, which is the result of a Cocker Spaniel–Poodle ancestry, or a Puggle, a cross between a Pug and a Beagle.

Poodles have played the most significant role so far in the ancestry of designer dogs, partly because they do not shed their fur, so seem to be less likely to trigger an allergic reaction in people who are sensitive. This hypoallergenic aspect can be critical especially for disabled people, who may otherwise be deprived of canine assistance. In fact, Labradoodles – currently the best known of the designer dogs – were originally created for this reason to aid those with impaired sight.

SHOWING THE SAME BREED Depending on the size of the show, there will be various classes within each actual breed division, such as classes for puppies, or for older, 'veteran' dogs.

LABRADOODLE The general aim with crosses of this type is to create a dog with a fairly individual appearance, while selecting for desirable traits and behaviour.

COMPANION DOGS, TERRIERS, AND HOUNDS

These three groups of dogs cover a wide diversity from tiny companions to independent terriers and gregarious hounds, and range from the oldest sighthound breeds in the world to newly created and refined canine companions. What they all share is popularity with pet owners, and a relatively easy adaptation to modern lifestyles and new roles.

COMPANION DOGS

Today, many breeds created for a working purpose are kept simply as companions, but for thousands of years humans have bred dogs purely for that role. In a number of cases, companion dogs were effectively smaller examples of larger breeds, often referred to as toy breeds, but miniaturization can lead to a decline in the breed's soundness. They have been bred for submissive docility and affection, while aggression, hunting instincts, and other 'awkward' traits have been quietly sidelined.

BICHON It is possible to track the Bichon lineage back thousands of years, with these small companion dogs all being distinguished by their white, fluffy coats. They are today's most popular companion breed.

MODERN COMPANIONS

Having been bred over the course of centuries to act as companions, the toy breeds are ideally suited to domestic living. They are generally very intelligent and responsive by nature, making them easier to train than larger dogs created for working purposes. Their exercise needs are modest and so they are ideally suited to modern-day urban life. They are a good choice for older owners, because their size means they are easy to pick up when necessary. Their lifespan is also likely to be longer than that of larger breeds.

TERRIERS

Dogs have always had a natural tendency to hunt, and this instinct remains strong in the case of the terrier breeds. They were created as industrious, hardy farm dogs, and still display great stamina. These little dogs were miniaturized from hounds to follow prey underground – their name comes from *terre*, French for 'earth' – and kill it or drag it out. This work required dogs small in size but big in spirit. Some are still kept on farms for their working abilities.

Most terriers are versatile hunters, capable of ambushing unwary rabbits, although being employed more commonly to hunt down and kill rodents around the farm. In the 19th century, public ratting contests showcased this ability. Other even more macabre forms of entertainment were developed in the growing industrial cities. Dog-fighting became popular, with the tenacity and bravery

ACTIVE It is important not to be fooled by their size, because terriers generally need plenty of exercise, possessing great stamina. They can also prove to be rather obstinate by nature, and need sound training.

of terriers putting them in the front-line of such contests. Breeds that were developed for this purpose include the Staffordshire Bull Terrier.

MODERN TERRIERS

As there has been less need for working terriers over recent years, their numbers have fallen to the extent that some breeds now face an uncertain future. Others, notably those that have been miniaturized even further, such as the Yorkshire Terrier, often tend to be considered more as companion dogs today.

Terriers are very hardy, long-lived dogs, which thrive in a rural environment. They are generally small in size, and their lively personalities mean they make good companions, especially for older owners. They will also prove alert guardians around the home. However, their rather impatient and often dominant natures mean they are probably not the ideal choice for a home alongside young children, and need sound training to reduce their innate pugnaciousness towards other dogs.

HOUNDS

Hounds represent the oldest group of dogs, having been developed primarily for hunting purposes. They are broadly divided today into sighthounds and scenthounds, reflecting the way in which they pursue their quarry. Most countries have their own breeds of hound, although some of these still remain very localized in their distribution.

Lightly built sighthounds were among the early types to develop, principally in North Africa and the Middle East. Sighthounds have a narrow nose, with their eyes being well positioned towards the sides of the head to help them to identify movement in their vicinity. Most sighthounds tend to hunt individually, or in couples, pursuing their quarry through open countryside where they can maintain visual contact.

The ability to track quarry by scent is required in wooded areas of northern Europe. The development of scenthounds reached its greatest diversity in France, prior to the French Revolution of 1789, when most of the country's châteaux had their own packs of these hounds. A further change occurred with the emergence of the basset forms of many of these breeds. This name originates from the French word *bas*, meaning 'low', reflecting the stature of such dogs with their characteristic short-legged appearance.

MODERN HOUNDS

Hounds are lively, friendly, and responsive dogs by nature, ideal for

RACERS Greyhounds are popular today as racing dogs, but they are an ancient type and images of dogs bearing an unmistakable similarity to Greyhounds have been discovered among the artefacts of ancient Egypt.

a home with children. The social nature of most hounds means that they tend to agree well together if you want to keep more than one dog at home. Not all hounds require long walks – Greyhounds, for example, need little more than an opportunity to run in an open field or park for a relatively short time. However, training hounds not to run off when out walking is often difficult, particularly in the case of scenthounds, as they will be instinctively inclined to set off on a trail.

HOUNDS Pack hounds tend to be bi-coloured or tri-coloured, usually in a combination of black, white, and tan.

GUNDOGS, HERDING DOGS, AND WORKING DOGS

From highly specialized gundogs, bred to work on a one-to-one basis with handlers, to jack-of-all-trade farm dogs, capable of herding, guarding, and pest control, these three groups of dogs cover a wide variety of sizes, shapes, and functions. As changes in lifestyle and agriculture have reduced the demand for some of their traditional roles, many breeds are finding new roles in the show ring and as companions.

GUNDOGS

As hunting developed, so did a need for dogs that could carry out actions quite against their nature: pointers and setters that could find quarry but then hold back from pursuit and freeze or crouch to leave an open shot, spaniels to flush game out from cover, and retrievers to find the fallen bodies and gently carry them back. All these tasks needed highly trainable, obedient, and patient dogs, and so many gundog breeds are also excellent family companions and assistance dogs. They settle well in the domestic environment, although their level of activity is such that they really need the opportunity to exercise in a rural area on a daily basis. There is often a divergence now in type between working gundogs and those seen in the show ring.

TYPES

Retrievers were developed to retrieve shot game, working effectively in a wide range of terrain, and not being afraid to enter water to obtain shot waterfowl. Spaniels locate and flush quarry, particularly birds, for the waiting guns, picking up scents readily and making able retrievers too. Pointer breeds have been in existence for 500 years or more. They indicate the presence of quarry by adopting their characteristic pointing stance, leaning forward with one of their front legs raised off the ground. Subsequently, they can retrieve the shot game. Setters represent another older division within the gundog category, with their name deriving from the old English verb 'set', meaning 'to sit'. They sit down or crouch low when they detect game.

HERDING DOGS

Once people gave up a nomadic lifestyle dependent on hunting and started to farm, new types of dog were developed. Dogs assisted humans in controlling the movements of goats, sheep, and other livestock, as well as guarding these animals from predators. A number of herding breeds are still kept primarily for working purposes and are rarely seen in the show ring or, indeed, anywhere outside of their native lands.

CHOCOLATE LABRADOR
Labradors should have 'soft' mouths, meaning that they are able to retrieve shot game, such as the duck seen here, without breaking the skin.

HERDING DEER Dogs will herd a wide variety of animals including deer and even geese. A dog's herding instinct derives from its wolf ancestor, which drives its prey towards other pack members during the hunt.

TYPES

Breeds of herding dog have been developed in most parts of the world, and their appearance is influenced to a large extent by the terrain in which they have evolved, usually over the course of centuries. In many instances, they have a dense and often quite long water-resistant coat, which serves to protect them from the worst of the weather.

The dogs in this group are quite variable in size, reflecting their functions. Cattle dogs tend to be small in size, as typified by the Welsh Corgis. This is because they had to be nimble, darting in amongst herds of cattle to nip at the backs of their feet.

In areas where wolves menaced livestock, herd guardians were developed. Not all areas of the world could support a number of different breeds to work with farmstock. This resulted in the development of dogs that could not only herd but also undertake other tasks around the farm.

WORKING DOGS

The description of working dogs is really a catch-all, because with the exception of the companion dogs, all of today's breeds were originally created to undertake specific tasks. Working dogs are friendly and affectionate by nature towards their family circle, and usually prove amenable to training. The large size and strength of many working breeds means that controlling them on a lead may be difficult. They also have large appetites, making them relatively costly to keep. Their maximum lifespan is likely to be shorter than that of smaller breeds, rarely exceeding ten years.

SLED DOGS Siberian Huskies have been replaced in arctic races by the faster Alaskan Husky, but are excellent dogs for moderate loads over long distances.

MASTIFF Recognizable by their large size, stocky bodies, and a wide head with powerful jaws, mastiffs have an overhang of skin around the lips, known as jowls, while the skin on the forehead is wrinkled.

TYPES

This group name covers guarding and rescue breeds, and includes sled-pulling dogs, which had a vital role in moving supplies and people between remote isolated communities before mechanized transportation. Many members of this group owe their origins to mastiff-type stock – formidable animals with huge heads and powerful jaws that are the ultimate guard dogs. The ancient mastiff bloodline is thought to have begun in the vicinity of China thousands of years ago, and reached Europe along the Old Silk Road. These early mastiffs soon spread widely through Europe, often being used in battle. The overall impression of mastiff breeds is one of tremendous strength.

BREED CATALOGUE

Dogs today are being kept increasingly as companions, rather than for their working abilities. Over the course of little more than a century, their role has altered dramatically, with this change being triggered initially by a growing interest in competitive showing. The original working abilities of breeds have not been neglected though, and there are still field trials where dogs are assessed on these traits rather than on their appearance, which is the case in the show ring. Some dogs compete with equal success in both areas but, increasingly, there has been a divergence in appearance or 'type' between working and show dogs of the same breed.

SHETLAND SHEEPDOG Some herding and gundog breeds have separated into down-to-earth working lines and show dogs with features like fuller coats. But many a show Sheltie still combines brains and beauty, scoring well in trials.

Australian Shepherd (Miniature)

ORIGIN United States

HEIGHT 33–45 cm (13–18 in)

WEIGHT 6.8–13.6 kg (15–30 lb)

EXERCISE LEVEL

COAT CARE

REGISTERED None

COLOURS Blue or red merle, black, red, may have white and tan markings

Among variations on this breed's name are the North American Miniature Australian Shepherd, once the North American Shepherd, reflecting the fact that its name and its nationality are at odds.

 BLACK RED/TAN BLUE MOTTLED WITH TAN

BREED ORIGINS

This breed is descended from the Australian Shepherd, a breed created entirely in the United States using dogs from Australia and New Zealand. That breed was noted for its friendly personality, and so creating a smaller breed that would fit in better with urban lifestyles was a natural step. The smallest of the big breed were selected as breeding stock, the aim being to produce a perfect miniature in all physical respects, with the same lively and engaging character as the parent. Intelligent and trainable, this is a wonderful dog for an active family, and will relish being allowed to show off in trials.

CITY SLICKER This breed's size means it can be kept comfortably in urban confines, its trainability means it can be well behaved, and it has a low inclination to bark.

Australian Silky Terrier

ORIGIN Australia

HEIGHT 25–28 cm (10–11 in)

WEIGHT 5.5–6.3 kg (12–14 lbs)

EXERCISE LEVEL

COAT CARE

REGISTERED KC, FCI, AKCs

COLOURS Blue and tan

As much terrier as toy, this breed is similar in appearance to the Yorkshire Terrier, but not quite so diminutive. Although created as a companion breed, it is more than capable of despatching small vermin, and quite feisty when it comes to declaring and defending its interests.

BREED ORIGINS

Although the Australian Silky Terrier only appeared at the turn of the 20th century, its origins are not clearly known. It is probably a cross of the Australian Terrier and the Yorkshire Terrier, possibly with some Skye Terrier thrown in. It can be territorial and independent, so early socialization and obedience training are essential. Given these, this lively and inquisitive breed makes a cheering companion.

STRICTLY DECORATIVE The long coat is fine and silky, and matts easily, so does require daily grooming. Despite its length, it is not insulating, because it lacks an undercoat, so this is a warm-weather breed.

Bichon Frisé

ORIGIN Tenerife
HEIGHT 23–30 cm (9–12 in)
WEIGHT 4.5–7.2 kg (10–16 lb)
EXERCISE LEVEL
COAT CARE
REGISTERED KC, FCI, AKCs
COLOURS White

These playful dogs have been popular companions for centuries, and make excellent family pets. The breed's fluffy appearance stems from its distinctive double-layered silky coat.

BREED ORIGINS

It is thought that the Bichon Frisé is descended from the ancient European water spaniel called the Barbet. This is reflected by its name, which is an abbreviated form of Barbichon, translating as 'Little Barbet'. The breed is also called the Tenerife Dog, and also the Bichon Tenerife, reflecting the fact that its development took place on this island, part of the Canaries group off the northwest coast of Africa. Its ancestors were probably introduced here from Spain over 500 years ago. They became highly sought-after pets at the royal courts of Europe, before gradually falling out of favour and ending up as circus performers. The breed's name is pronounced 'Beeshon Freezay'.

SNOW WHITE The coat of this breed is naturally curly. It is trimmed back on the face, and this serves to emphasize the round, dark eyes.

Bolognese

ORIGIN Italy
HEIGHT 25–30 cm (10–12 in)
WEIGHT 2.7–4.1 kg (6–9 lb)
EXERCISE LEVEL
COAT CARE
REGISTERED FCI
COLOURS White

Although closely related to the Bichon Frisé, the Bolognese differs significantly because its coat is not double-layered, although it does stick up rather than lie flat. This is described as 'flocking', and gives the breed its fluffy appearance.

BREED ORIGINS

The precise ancestry of the Bolognese is something of a mystery. Its closest relative within the Bichon group is the Maltese, but it is unclear as to whether the Maltese is its direct ancestor or descendant. The Bolognese's origins date back to around 1000AD, with the breed then evolving in the Italian city of Bologna, from which its name is derived. The Medici family in Italy gave these dogs as gifts to obtain favours and many European rulers fell under their charm.

Part of the Bolognese's undoubted appeal, aside from its attractive appearance, is the very strong bond that these dogs form with their owners.

ONLY WHITE While today, only white examples of the Bolognese are known, both black and piebald examples were recorded at an earlier stage in its history.

Cavalier King Charles Spaniel

ORIGIN United Kingdom

HEIGHT 30 cm (12 in)

WEIGHT 5.5–8.1 kg (12–18 lb)

EXERCISE LEVEL

COAT CARE

REGISTERED KC, FCI, AKCs

COLOURS Black and tan, Blenheim (white and tan), ruby, tri-colour

This breed has an attractive appearance and pleasant disposition. They are not particularly energetic dogs, so they are suited to city life, and ideal for a home with children.

RED/TAN   TAN AND WHITE   BLACK AND TAN   BLACK, WHITE, AND TAN

BREED ORIGINS

Small spaniel-type dogs became very fashionable in Britain during the late 1600s, being favourites of King Charles II, as is clear from contemporary paintings. Subsequently, however, their appearance began to change. The modern breed owes its existence to a rich American called Roswell Eldridge. During the 1920s, he put up substantial prize money at Crufts for examples of the King Charles Spaniel or English Toy Spaniel, which resembled the original 17th-century type. Over the five years of Roswell's involvement with the show, the number of such dogs being exhibited increased, and gradually this type of spaniel became more popular. It was then recognized as the Cavalier King Charles Spaniel, to separate it from its now relatively scarce close relative. The most evident distinguishing feature between the breeds is the longer nose displayed by the Cavalier.

TRI-COLOUR Black and white is predominant in this colouring, with these colours being evenly distributed. Tan markings show above the eyes, on the cheeks, and in the ears.

BLENHEIM This colouring is the most popular variety, having been originally created on and named after the Duke of Marlborough's estate. Rich chestnut colouring is separated by individual white markings, with a white central area usually evident on the centre of the head.

BLACK AND TAN These puppies display their raven-black colouring, offset with tan markings. The other variety is ruby – a rich red shade.

Chihuahua

ORIGIN Mexico

HEIGHT 15–23 cm (6–9 in)

WEIGHT 1.0–2.7 kg (2–6 lb)

EXERCISE LEVEL

COAT CARE (sh) (lh)

REGISTERED KC, FCI, AKCs

COLOURS No restrictions on colour or patterning

The smallest breed in the world, the distinctive-looking Chihuahua possesses the character and bark of a much larger dog. They are noisy by nature, and have a fearless temperament.

 BLACK CREAM GREY BLUE RED/TAN

BREED ORIGINS

The Chihuahua is named after the province in Mexico where it originated, but its ancestry remains mysterious. It may be a descendant of a range of companion breeds which were kept throughout the Americas in the pre-Colombian era. Others suggest that its ancestors might have been brought from Spain by the early settlers, and may have

SMOOTH-COATED This is the traditional form of the breed, which is characterized by a domed, apple-shaped head. Its large ears are positioned at an angle of about 45 degrees to the head.

interbred with local dogs, to create the breed of today. Chihuahuas first started to attract attention outside Mexico during the 1850s, when they became fashionable companions for wealthy US women, and even today, the breed enjoys celebrity status.

LONG-COATED The coat is soft, with the hair forming a very evident plume on the tail. Longer fur is evident too on the sides of the face, and on the underparts of the body, with feathering on the legs. The coat itself lies flat.

Coton de Tuléar

ORIGIN Madagascar
HEIGHT 25–30 cm (10–12 in)
WEIGHT 5.5–6.8 kg (12–15 lb)
EXERCISE LEVEL
COAT CARE
REGISTERED FCI
COLOURS White

This breed is one of relatively few to have originated in Africa, and has grown rapidly in popularity over recent years, both in North America and Europe. It is another member of the Bichon group, as reflected partly by its white coat.

BREED ORIGINS

Almost certainly, the ancestors of this breed were brought from Europe to the Madagascan port of Tuléar, as commemorated by its name. This probably occurred as early as the 1600s, and these small dogs soon became status symbols for wealthy people living on this island, which lies off the east coast of Africa. Being bred here in isolation over the course of hundreds of generations, these dogs gradually diverged somewhat in appearance from their ancestors. It was prohibited for all but the nobility to own them, and they remained unknown elsewhere, right up until the 1950s. A small number were then permitted to leave the island and taken to Europe, while in America, they were not seen until the mid-1970s.

WET DOG! Although traditionally the coat falls forward over the face, the wet coat reveals the unmistakable Bichon profile. A similar but now extinct breed existed on the island of Réunion.

COAT The rather fluffy, cottony texture of the Coton de Tuléar's coat is a distinctive feature of these dogs. Although white is the traditional colour for the breed, individuals with cream or black patches occasionally occur.

French Bulldog

ORIGIN France

HEIGHT 28–30 cm (11–12 in)

WEIGHT 9.1–12.7 kg (20–28 lb)

EXERCISE LEVEL

COAT CARE

REGISTERED KC, FCI, AKCs

COLOURS Cream, gold, liver, black and white, black brindle

The bat-like ears and stocky build of the French Bulldog are very distinctive. Its short coat means that grooming is minimal, but it can be prone to snoring, because of its compact facial shape.

 CREAM

 GOLD

 GOLD AND WHITE

 BLACK AND WHITE

 BLACK BRINDLE

BREED ORIGINS

There used to be a Toy Bulldog breed which was widely kept by lacemakers in the English city of Nottingham. Forced out by increased mechanization, during the 1850s many of these skilled craftspeople emigrated to northern France. Not surprisingly, they took their pets with them, and some crossbreeding with local dogs occurred. Crosses with terriers may have resulted in the raised ears that are so characteristic

BLACK AND WHITE The markings may be very variable, as can be seen by comparing this example with the dog on the right.

of the breed today. Word of these bulldogs spread to the city of Paris, and soon they became fashionable pets in the capital. They became popular too in other parts of Europe and especially the United States, but in Britain, the breed proved controversial when it was first introduced during the 1890s.

GOOD COMPANION
The French Bulldog is a lively, friendly breed with relatively modest exercise needs.

BRINDLE Mixing of light and dark hairs in the coat is not uncommon in French Bulldogs, as is a white patch on the chest.

German Spitz

ORIGIN Germany

HEIGHT 20–41 cm (8–16 in)

WEIGHT 3.2–18.0 kg (7–40 lb)

EXERCISE LEVEL

COAT CARE

REGISTERED KC, FCI, AKCs

COLOURS Range of solid colours; bi-colours allowed in Miniature and Toy

The family of German Spitz breeds can be separated by size, with the Giant being the largest. There is also a Standard variety, as well as Miniature and Toy forms. They are all similar in temperament.

 BLACK
 CREAM
 GREY
 GOLD
 DARK BROWN

BREED ORIGINS

The origins of the German Spitz date back at least to 1450, and since then, as in the case of other breeds, there has been a tendency to scale these dogs down in size, creating companion breeds. There is also frequently confusion between the German Toy Spitz and the Pomeranian, because they share a common ancestry and are very similar in appearance. The German breed was created first, with the Pomeranian subsequently being

FULL COAT The ruff of fur around the neck is more pronounced in the winter, when the coat is at its most profuse. This contrasts with the short hair on the lower part of the legs.

developed on separate lines in the United Kingdom, from imported German stock, to the extent that they have now existed as separate bloodlines for over a century. There are some differences in the recognition of the different Spitz breeds as far as coloration is concerned. The Giant variety exists in solid colours only, while bi-colours are also seen in the case of the Miniature and Toy variants of the breed.

FACIAL APPEARANCE The German Spitz breeds are described as being vulpine, or fox-like, as a result of their facial appearance. A white blaze between the eyes is often a feature of bi-colours.

Havanese

ORIGIN Cuba
HEIGHT 20–36 cm (8–14 in)
WEIGHT 3.2–5.9 kg (7–13 lb)
EXERCISE LEVEL
COAT CARE
REGISTERED FCI
COLOURS Black, white, blue, gold, dark brown

Lively by nature but easy to train, the Havanese has established a following that extends far beyond Cuba where it developed. They are versatile companions, watchdogs, and even poultry herders.

BLACK   CREAM   BLUE   GOLD   DARK BROWN

BREED ORIGINS

The Havanese is of Bichon stock, with its ancestors probably having been introduced to Cuba quite early during the settlement of the New World, when the island was a significant stopping-off point for ships from Europe. The breed is named after Havana, Cuba's capital city. They thrived on the island for centuries, but became much rarer after the Communist take-over in 1959. Many of those who fled to the United States took their Havanese with them, and this actually boosted the breed's popularity in North America. Today, they are seen at shows around the world.

COAT The Havanese's coat has a soft texture and, as with other Bichons, tends to be white in colour. The muzzle of these dogs is long and tapered.

STYLING The longer hair on the head reflects the breed's origins in a hot climate, protecting the eyes from the sun. It is traditionally tied up into a topknot.

King Charles Spaniel

ORIGIN United Kingdom
HEIGHT 25–28 cm (10–11 in)
WEIGHT 3.5–6.3 kg (8–14 lb)
EXERCISE LEVEL
COAT CARE
REGISTERED KC, FCI, AKCs
COLOURS Solid tan, black and tan, Blenheim (white and tan), tri-colour

Despite its spaniel name, this has never been a gundog, but was a royal toy. Diarist Samuel Pepys noted of King Charles 'the silliness of the King, playing with his dog all the while'.

RED/TAN

BLACK, WHITE, AND TAN

BREED ORIGINS
When spaniels were first developed, larger pups were chosen for working dogs, but smaller ones eventually became toy companion breeds. Early examples had a longer muzzle, like the Cavalier King Charles today, but crossing with snub-nosed oriental breeds in the 18th century gave it a new look.

An affectionate dog that fits well into urban life, the King Charles

Spaniel's drawback is that it is prone to health problems and shorter-lived than many small dogs.

ROYAL COLOURS Some of this breed's colours have regal names. Tan is called ruby and tan and white Blenheim, and in the United States tri-colour is Prince Charles and black and tan is King Charles.

Lhasa Apso

ORIGIN Tibet
HEIGHT 25–28 cm (10–11 in)
WEIGHT 5.9–6.8 kg (13–15 lb)
EXERCISE LEVEL
COAT CARE
REGISTERED KC, FCI, AKCs
COLOURS Range of colours from black to cream; black and white

The long, flowing coat of the Lhasa Apso is very elegant, but its condition can only be maintained with daily grooming sessions. Occasionally, a smooth-coated individual crops up in a litter.

BLACK

CREAM

GREY

GOLD

BLACK AND WHITE

BREED ORIGINS
These small dogs were considered sacred by the Tibetan monks who kept them in their monasteries. They were believed to be a repository for the souls of dead monks. Unsurprisingly, therefore, Lhasa Apsos were not sold to outsiders. Occasionally, however, the Dalai Lama who ruled Tibet would give a pair as a gift to the Chinese Emperor. It was probably

not until the late 19th or early 20th century that the breed first reached the West, and it was not until after World War I that it started to become established in Britain. This proved to be a protracted process, with these striking dogs not becoming well known until the 1960s.

COAT The Lhasa's hair is very dense, and offers excellent protection against the elements.

Löwchen

ORIGIN France
HEIGHT 25–33 cm (10–13 in)
WEIGHT 4.5–8.1 kg (10–18 lb)
EXERCISE LEVEL
COAT CARE
REGISTERED KC, FCI
COLOURS No restrictions on colour or patterning

When its coat is trimmed, the Löwchen looks rather like a lion, justifying its alternative name of Little Lion Dog. Löwchen is pronounced as 'lerv-chun', and this is a very ancient breed.

BLACK   CREAM   RED/TAN   DARK BROWN   TAN AND WHITE

BREED ORIGINS

It is believed that the breed was widely known across Europe as long ago as the 1500s and, in spite of its Germanic name, the Löwchen's origins are believed to lie in France. The coat was trimmed into the lion-cut, which removes hair from the lower body and upper legs, so that they could act as bed-warmers for the nobility, while the resulting leonine appearance was believed

to convey strength. In 1973, numbers of the breed had plummeted to the extent that it was estimated that there were fewer than 70 still alive in the world. Thanks to publicity surrounding their plight, breeders have successfully taken up the challenge of preserving this breed.

UNTRIMMED In the Löwchen's untrimmed state, its Bichon family resemblance is clear.

Maltese

ORIGIN Malta
HEIGHT 23–25 cm (9–10 in)
WEIGHT 1.8–5.9 kg (4–13 lb)
EXERCISE LEVEL
COAT CARE
REGISTERED KC, FCI, AKCs
COLOURS White

Although it was once called the Maltese Terrier, there has never been anything of the terrier about this breed; it has also been called, more understandably, the Bichon Maltais. It is an engaging little dog, seemingly without fear or awareness of its diminutive size.

BREED ORIGINS

This breed has been kept as a companion since Phoenicians brought the ancient Melita breed to Malta 2000 years ago. A pure line of descent from that dog is unlikely, and today's Maltese probably has both miniature spaniels and the Miniature Poodle in its heritage. It is active and playful, but with maturity adapts to a more sedentary lifestyle and city life. It is good with children or other dogs.

PERFECTLY COIFFED The long silky coat lacks an undercoat and mats easily. The demands of daily grooming are the biggest commitment with this breed.

Papillon

ORIGIN France

HEIGHT 20–28 cm (8–11 in)

WEIGHT 4.0–4.5 kg (9–10 lb)

EXERCISE LEVEL

COAT CARE

REGISTERED KC, FCI, AKCs

COLOURS White with a range of colours

It may look like a stuffed toy, have a name meaning butterfly in French, and have been a favourite prop for romantic portraits, but this breed is no brainless lapdog: the fluff is all on the outside.

GOLD AND WHITE   BLACK AND WHITE   TAN AND WHITE   BLACK, WHITE, AND TAN

BREED ORIGINS

These small companions date back to the Renaissance under the name Continental Spaniel, and are still called Continental Toy Spaniels. They may be descended from the Spanish Dwarf Spaniel of the 16th century, crossed with northern spitz types for a more delicate face. While its history is not well recorded in writing, it was a favourite in works of art, depicted in frescoes and oil paintings from Titian's *Venus of Urbino* to Largillière's portrait of Louis XIV and his family. In many of these, the structure of the dogs' ears is unclear, and it seems that

DOGS WITH WINGS At first, calling a dog 'butterfly' might not seem descriptive, but a glance at the ears and facial markings makes it clear how apt the name is.

the Papillon appeared in the 16th century, with the original drop-eared type being given the name of Phalène sometime later in order to distinguish them.

BREED QUALITIES

With their fine, silky coat, plumed tail, and extraordinary ears, it is not hard to see why this breed became popular. The coat, which lacks an undercoat, needs less attention than might be expected to keep it looking picture-perfect. Papillons can be possessive of their owners and territory, but given an outlet for their energy make engaging companions.

QUICK LEARNER The Papillon loves outdoor exercise, and given a little training, its playful nature and surprising speed and athleticism make it adept at obedience trials, performing tricks, and agility classes for small dogs.

Pekingese

ORIGIN China
HEIGHT 15–23 cm (6–9 in)
WEIGHT 3.0–5.5 kg (7–12 lb)
EXERCISE LEVEL
COAT CARE
REGISTERED KC, FCI, AKCs
COLOURS Any colour

According to legend, this breed is the result of a mating between a lion and a monkey. The tale does an equally good job of explaining its appearance or describing its personality.

BLACK

RED/TAN

GOLD

TAN AND WHITE

BREED ORIGINS

The origins of the Peke are far too distant to be known: it was recently confirmed as one of the world's most ancient breeds by DNA analysis, showing just how long-standing the desire to keep dogs as companions is. It was kept at the Chinese imperial court in the Forbidden City, and brought back to the United Kingdom in the 1860s, having been taken from the court in the Opium Wars. Today, it is a parent of many crossbreeds with names like 'Peke-a-Pom'.

BREED QUALITIES

This breed behaves as if it is well aware of its royal past. They can be very obstinate, and it is surprising just how heavy such a small dog is when it does not wish to go somewhere. Pekingese tend to be loyal to their owners, wary of strangers, and inclined to bark like little watchdogs.

ROYAL RULES This breed is still true to the standard written by Dowager Empress Tzu Hsi, with hairy paws for silence, a colour to match every robe, a ruff for dignity, and bow legs to prevent it wandering.

Pomeranian

ORIGIN Germany

HEIGHT 20–28 cm (8–11 in)

WEIGHT 1.8–3.2 kg (4–7 lb)

EXERCISE LEVEL

COAT CARE

REGISTERED KC, FCI, AKCs

COLOURS White, cream, grey, blue, red, brown, black

It resembles nothing so much as an animated powder puff, but this dog believes it is still as big as its ancestors. The Pomeranian is also called the Zwergspitz or Dwarf Spitz and the Loulou.

 BLACK CREAM RED/TAN GOLD

BREED ORIGINS

The Pomeranian takes its name from a region along the Baltic coast that has been part of many countries over the centuries: once German, it is now in Poland. The German Spitz family was first brought to the United Kingdom by Queen Charlotte at the start of the 19th century, and British breeders succeeded in diminishing its size through the century. This may have been helped by a Volpino

BEST BRUSHED The long, straight coat has a dense undercoat and needs frequent attention with a damp brush to prevent tangles forming.

brought back from Italy by Queen Victoria; her patronage ensured the popularity of the fledgling type.

BREED QUALITIES

Smart and energetic, this is a good family companion and suits city life. It is protective of its territory and will bark noisily, so makes an effective watchdog, although unable to do much physical damage to an intruder. It will also challenge larger dogs, seemingly unaware of its size. These are long-lived dogs, although they do suffer from several health problems including slipping kneecaps and eye problems.

COLOUR INFLUENCES SIZE The earliest Poms tended to be both white and larger, but as an ever smaller size has been pursued, red and sable tones have become most common.

Poodle (Miniature and Toy)

ORIGIN France
HEIGHT 23–38 cm (9–15 in)
WEIGHT 1.8–5.5 kg (4–18 lb)
EXERCISE LEVEL
COAT CARE
REGISTERED KC, FCI, AKCs
COLOURS Any solid colour

The full-sized or Standard Poodle can still be seen as a working breed, but these smaller types were created purely for the pleasure of their company.

 BLACK
 CREAM
 BLUE
 GOLD
 DARK BROWN

BREED ORIGINS

Wherever the full-sized Poodle originated, there is no doubt that the smaller versions of the breed were developed in France. These dogs were never intended to be gundogs, although they will point and show all the instinctive drives of their larger ancestors. They have been, and still are, popular as circus dogs, at least in part for their great intelligence. Since the 18th century they have danced, acted out comedies, tragedies, and battles, reportedly walked tightropes, and even played cards and performed magic tricks, responding to the slightest signals from their trainers.

BREED QUALITIES

If they are allowed, these small poodles will make responsive and entertaining companions. Treated as fashion accessories, they can become bored and destructive. Grooming depends on the clip; some health problems – such as ear infections – can be more troublesome.

KEEPING IT SIMPLE Puppies may be shown in a plain, all-over clip. For adults, show rules are stricter, but there is nothing to stop an owner keeping this easy-care look.

TOY POODLE The very smallest of the sizes, this is the ultimate choice for bijou urban homes. The smallest are the longest lived, lasting around 14 years.

MINIATURE POODLE This size was highly popular in the circus ring, and was a must-have pet in the mid-20th century. Overbreeding meant that it slipped from pole position, but this has been a good thing for the quality of the breed.

Pug

ORIGIN China
HEIGHT 25–28 cm (10–11 in)
WEIGHT 6.4–8.2 kg (14–18 lb)
EXERCISE LEVEL
COAT CARE
REGISTERED KC, FCI, AKCs
COLOURS Silver, apricot, fawn, black

They look frowning, but these mini-mastiffs are full of energy and cheer. The name may come from an old English word for a mischievous devil; some European countries call them Mops.

BLACK   GREY   GOLD

BREED ORIGINS
This breed was miniaturized at least 2,000 years ago in China, where it was known as the Lo-Chiang-Sze or Foo, and kept by nobles and monks. In the 16th century it reached Europe on ships of the Dutch East Indies Trading Company, and is said to have saved the life of William of Orange by barking at an assassin. It arrived in the United Kingdom when Dutch royalty took the throne in the 17th century, and remained a royal pet, owned by Queen Victoria.

BREED QUALITIES
The word pugnacious might have been taken from this breed: they are intelligent and can be quite obstinate. Their stare looks defiant and stern, but it masks a playful personality, and a pug can be an enlivening and enchanting companion.

ANCIENT LIKENESS This breed still bears some resemblance to the foo dog or lion dog statues that are seen defensively flanking the doors of palaces and temples in China.

CHANGING FASHIONS The original Pug face, seen in paintings such as Hogarth's self portrait with his Pug, Trump, was longer. The flat profile of today's dog leads to breathing and eye problems.

CHIC COLOURS Pale-coloured Pugs were the most fashionable until the 19th century, when traveller and author Lady Brassey is thought to have brought new black dogs back from the East.

Shih Tzu

ORIGIN Tibet/China

HEIGHT 20–28 cm (8–11 in)

WEIGHT 4.1–7.3 kg (9–16 lb)

EXERCISE LEVEL

COAT CARE

REGISTERED KC, FCI, AKCs

COLOURS Any colour

While the pronunciation of the name is a matter of some dispute and not a little humour, the translation is 'lion dog'. This breed lives up to it, being courageous and sometimes a little haughty.

BLACK   BLUE   GOLD   BLACK AND WHITE   TAN AND WHITE

BREED ORIGINS

It was thought that this breed was a cross between the Pekingese and the Lhasa Apso, which is what it looks like, but recent DNA analysis showed it to be one of the most ancient breeds in its own right. It seems to have come from Tibet to China, where it became a favourite in the court, and spread from there, which is why it is generally regarded as a Chinese, rather than Tibetan breed. They

FLOWER-LIKE FACE The long hair on the brow, which gives the nickname Chrysanthemum Dog, can be tied up in a topknot; some owners trim it, but this is not allowed for showing.

PERFECT SYMMETRY Bi-coloured Shih Tzus are commonly seen, and in this coat a white blaze extending from the nose over the face and head and a white tip to the tail are highly desirable.

arrived in Europe in the early 20th century, and have become well loved and established across the world.

BREED QUALITIES

The abundant coat has a long topcoat and a woolly undercoat, so needs regular and thorough grooming. This is a good-natured family dog, relaxed around other dogs and well-behaved children, although it is occasionally stubborn. It also makes an alert watchdog, and although it is usually quiet indoors it will bark vociferously at anything it feels is wrong.

BLACK-AND-WHITE ADULT The fine undercoat of the Shih Tzu can become easily matted, so this is definitely not a breed for owners averse to grooming.

Airedale Terrier

ORIGIN United Kingdom
HEIGHT 58 cm (23 in)
WEIGHT 20.0 kg (44 lb)
EXERCISE LEVEL
COAT CARE
REGISTERED KC, FCI, AKCs
COLOURS Black and tan

Too large to fit the description of an 'earth dog', the Airedale is sometimes called the 'King of Terriers'. Older names include the Bingley Terrier, pinpointing its earliest roots in Yorkshire, and the Waterside Terrier, because of its otter-hunting past.

BEST MATE Airedale owners report them to be loyal, brave, and energetic friends.

BREED ORIGINS
The Airedale is a typical terrier in every respect other than size. A cross of the now-vanished Old English Broken-haired Terrier and the Otterhound, it was bred to pursue prey in the water. It has also been a messenger and police dog, but its notorious stubbornness limits its usefulness.

STREET FIGHTER Although this breed is quiet indoors and makes a good urban companion, it has a tendency to pick fights with other dogs.

American Pit Bull Terrier

ORIGIN United States
HEIGHT 46–56 cm (18–22 in)
WEIGHT 22.7–36.4 kg (50–80 lb)
EXERCISE LEVEL
COAT CARE
REGISTERED AKCs
COLOURS Any colour

This is the love-it-or-hate-it poster child of the fighting breeds and bull terriers class. It is muzzled, microchipped, and barred from housing complexes, parks, cities, and whole countries.

RED/TAN   GOLD AND WHITE   BLACK AND WHITE   TAN AND WHITE   BLACK BRINDLE

BREED ORIGINS
The history of the Pit Bull is that of the American Staffordshire until the mid-20th century, when the two split. The Pit Bull has come off badly: limited recognition means no strong common breeding policy, while leash laws preclude them from trials in which they used to excel. They are dog-aggressive, but human-aggressive individuals would have been culled in the breed's past, and in the right hands this loyal dog should be less human-aggressive than a mastiff: however, no powerful dog should be left alone with children.

IMAGE PROBLEM Pit Bulls are too often bought as a macho accessory by owners who encourage aggression, and suffer from the inevitable results. Cropped ears add to the desired 'hard' look.

American Staffordshire Terrier

ORIGIN United States
HEIGHT 43–48 cm (17–19 in)
WEIGHT 18.2–22.7 kg (40–50 lb)
EXERCISE LEVEL
COAT CARE
REGISTERED FCI, AKCs
COLOURS Any colour, with or without white

Not identical to the original Staffordshire Terrier in the United Kingdom, this heftier breed is closer to the American Pit Bull. This fighter is gentle around people, but remorseless with other dogs.

BLACK   DARK BROWN   BLACK AND WHITE   TAN AND WHITE   BLACK AND TAN

BREED ORIGINS

Bull terriers, including the Staffordshire, were brought to the United States in the 19th century and kept as fight and farm dogs. In the 20th century, with fighting outlawed, some turned respectable as Staffies – with 'American' added later to avoid confusion with the British breed – while others are known as Pit Bulls. It is still possible for dogs to be registered as one breed in one association and the other elsewhere. Fighting dogs were once renowned for their gentleness around humans, but their owners were experienced handlers who spent much time socializing them as pups; with the same care today, this powerful little dog is an affectionate companion.

SMALL BUT STRONG Although the mastiff guard breeds are bigger, the strong jaws and tenacious grip of these smaller dogs can do as much damage.

Belgian Griffons

ORIGIN Belgium
HEIGHT 18–20 cm (7–8 in)
WEIGHT 3.2–6.8 kg (7–15 lb)
EXERCISE LEVEL
COAT CARE
REGISTERED KC, FCI, AKCs
COLOURS Black, red, black and tan

Depending on the registry, these can be one or three breeds. One or all, they are tolerant and amiable companions, gentler than many terriers. Ravaged by two world wars, they remain rare.

BLACK   RED/TAN   BLACK AND TAN

BREED ORIGINS

In Europe, the wirehaired dogs are either Griffon Bruxellois or Griffon Belge according to colour, and all the smooth-coated dogs are called Petit Brabançon. Elsewhere, the smooth-coated dogs are a variety within a breed called Brussels Griffon or Griffon Bruxellois. All are descended from the Griffon d'Écurie or Stable Griffon, with probable input from the Affenpinscher, the Dutch Smoushond, the Yorkshire Terrier, toy spaniels from the United Kingdom, and Pugs.

COLOUR DISTINCTION (right) The rough, reddish coat makes this a Griffon Bruxellois in Europe; the Griffon Belge is black or black and tan.

LITTLE SMOOTHIES (left) Because 'griffon' indicates a rough coat, in Europe these dogs are called Petit Brabançon, after a Belgian province.

Border Terrier

ORIGIN United Kingdom
HEIGHT 25 cm (10 in)
WEIGHT 5.0–6.8 kg (11–15 lb)
EXERCISE LEVEL
COAT CARE
REGISTERED KC, FCI, AKCs
COLOURS Grey, wheaten, tan or red, blue and tan

Although it has become a popular family companion, this dog still shows itself to be a true hunting type. It has a compact build, persistent but amenable temperament, and hardy constitution.

GREY

RED/TAN

GOLD

BREED ORIGINS
Like so many working dogs, this breed comes from undocumented origins. Dogs like these were working in the English-Scottish border area in the late 18th century, killing rats and foxes, and possibly otters and badgers. Their descendants include not only the Border Terrier, but also the less widely recognized Fell and Patterdale Terriers, kept as working dogs. The name Border Terrier was in use for this type by the end of the 19th century, and the breed was recognized in the early 20th century.

BREED QUALITIES
This terrier is popular in the United Kingdom, and is in the top ten breeds. This has happened only recently, and it is less popular elsewhere, so it has not been overbred, and remains true to its original type. It has a more tolerant, less snappy personality than many terriers, and is more trainable and a fine family dog – albeit still terrier enough to need active owners.

PERFECT SIZE The Border is an ideal vermin hunter, leggy enough to run good distances, but small enough to fit down a fox's earth.

COAT CARE The hard coat is weatherproof and easy to maintain, shedding dirt with a quick brush. A sleeker look is achieved by hand-stripping the dead hair twice a year.

Boston Terrier

ORIGIN United States
HEIGHT 38–43 cm (15–17 in)
WEIGHT 6.8–11.4 kg (15–25 lb)
EXERCISE LEVEL
COAT CARE
REGISTERED KC, FCI, AKCs
COLOURS Brindle, seal, or black with white markings

With a heritage of mastiffs and fighting dogs, one might expect this to be a bullish breed, but it is one of the most relaxed breeds to carry the 'terrier' label, even something of a layabout.

BLACK AND WHITE
BLACK BRINDLE

BREED ORIGINS
The Boston dates back to the late 19th century and is a blend of old English and French Bulldogs and the now-extinct White Terrier, with constant selection for smaller size. The breed was an immediate success, the first American breed to gain recognition, and has remained a favourite with the public ever since due to its engaging, compliant personality.

TRIM LOOKS The ears are naturally erect and batlike, but are sometimes cropped to 'improve' the line. The tail is naturally short, and not now docked.

Bull Terrier

ORIGIN United Kingdom
HEIGHT 53–56 cm (21–22 in)
WEIGHT 23.6–28.2 kg (52–62 lb)
EXERCISE LEVEL
COAT CARE
REGISTERED KC, FCI, AKCs
COLOURS Any colour except blue or liver

Instantly recognizable for its convex Roman nose, this dog was first developed as a fighting breed. It is usually a trustworthy and stable breed, but no powerful dog is ideal for a novice owner.

 BLACK AND WHITE
 TAN AND WHITE
 BLACK, WHITE, AND TAN
 BLACK BRINDLE

BREED ORIGINS
This breed was developed by John Hinks early in the 19th century. He crossed the White English Terrier, now extinct, with the Bulldog, and the result was instantly successful as a fighter and as a companion. Active and highly intelligent, Bull Terriers should be kept busy. They are tolerant, and do not bite readily, but also do not let go easily, and young dogs may play too roughly for children.

ORIGINAL COLOUR Hinks preferred white, still the only colour allowed in some registries, but it carries an increased risk of deafness and health problems. Head markings are not penalized.

Cairn Terrier

ORIGIN United Kingdom
HEIGHT 23–25 cm (9–10 in)
WEIGHT 5.9–6.4 kg (13–14 lb)
EXERCISE LEVEL
COAT CARE
REGISTERED KC, FCI, AKCs
COLOURS Cream, wheaten, red, sandy, grey, brindled

This typically compact, shaggy little terrier from Scotland has long been a popular breed. It has a robust constitution and an equally robust temperament.

CREAM   GREY   BLACK BRINDLE

BREED ORIGINS

The exact origins of the Cairn are uncertain, but are almost certainly linked to those of other breeds such as the Scottish, Skye, and West Highland White Terriers. Its name comes from marker cairns built of stones, and its use in hunting out vermin that took refuge in them. Today, it still loves to chase and dig, and may not be for those who love their lawn. It makes a good watchdog and city companion, with a more obedient character than some other terriers. It is cheerful and entertaining, as long as it is entertained in turn.

COAT CARE The hard, wiry top coat of the Cairn can be trimmed around the eyes, but is best 'stripped' by hand, or plucked out to reveal the soft undercoat, in summer.

Irish Terrier

ORIGIN Ireland
HEIGHT 46 cm (18 in)
WEIGHT 11.4–12.3 kg (25–27 lb)
EXERCISE LEVEL
COAT CARE
REGISTERED KC, FCI, AKCs
COLOURS Yellow, wheaten, red

These are also called Irish Red Terriers, or by their fans, Daredevils. Even the breed standards mention the breed's 'heedless, reckless pluck'. They are animated hunters and loyal defenders of the home.

RED/TAN   GOLD

BREED ORIGINS

These dogs emerged from the general stock of guards and vermin-hunters through selective breeding in the 19th century, and by the end of the century they had become the first Irish breed recognized by the Kennel Club and been exported to the United States. Still used for hunting in Ireland, they are more often seen as household and family companions. Provided that they are given enough exercise to use up some of their boundless energy, they can be very civilized indoors: they are tractable with people, but unreliable around dogs or other small pets.

IRISH LOOKS Deeper red coats predominate because they tend to be harder in texture than pale coats. The tail was customarily docked: left natural, it should be held high but not curled over.

Jack Russell Terrier

ORIGIN United Kingdom
HEIGHT 25–30 cm (10–12 in)
WEIGHT 4–7 kg (9–15 lb)
EXERCISE LEVEL
COAT CARE
REGISTERED FCI
COLOURS Bi-coloured or tri-coloured

These terriers are full of character, and have an adventurous side to their natures, which can occasionally lead them into trouble, as they have little fear.

BLACK AND WHITE

BLACK AND TAN

BLACK, WHITE, AND TAN

WELL TRAVELLED The first man to walk to both Poles, Ranulph Fiennes, was accompanied by his Jack Russell, Bothie – an extraordinary feat for a British rural hunting breed.

BREED ORIGINS
The Jack Russell Terrier is named after its creator, who obtained a distinctive terrier bitch in May 1819, while studying at Oxford University. He developed a terrier that was bold enough to venture underground to drive out a fox from its earth, and yet could also run well. They were later crossed with a range of other dogs, which helps explain their variable appearance.

BREED QUALITIES
Jack Russell Terriers remain popular, both as companions and working dogs, often being seen on farms. They also prove to be alert watchdogs, with a surprisingly loud bark for their diminutive stature.

PERFECT SIZE To chase foxes into earths, working dogs must never be more than 35 cm (14 in) around the chest.

Kerry Blue Terrier

ORIGIN Ireland
HEIGHT 43–48 cm (17–19 in)
WEIGHT 15.0–18.2 kg (33–40 lb)
EXERCISE LEVEL
COAT CARE
REGISTERED KC, FCI, AKCs
COLOURS Blue

Also known as the Irish Blue Terrier, this breed was first noted in Kerry in the southwest, but never restricted to that corner of Ireland. It is traditionally the national dog of Ireland, but surprisingly rare for a breed with such status.

BREED ORIGINS

The origins of this breed are uncertain, and ancestors may include the Soft-coated Wheaten Terrier crossed with the Bedlington Terrier, the Irish Terrier, and even the Irish Wolfhound. The blue, curly coat has attracted the legend that such a dog swam ashore and was considered so fine that he was mated to all the local wheaten-coloured terriers; it is not impossible that there is some genetic influence from a Portuguese Water Dog on a visiting boat. The breed was a farm favourite, used for hunting vermin and otters, but only officially recognized in the late 19th century.

BREED QUALITIES

Today the breed is most likely to be found as a household dog, although it is still sometimes used for hunting. They can be time-consuming to groom, especially if the beard is left full, but make energetic, spirited companions.

YOUTHFUL COLOUR Kerry Blues are born black and their coats gradually lighten as they mature. They can stay dark in colour until they are fully grown, turning blue as late as two years old.

COAT CARE The wavy coat is soft and silky. Once it would have been allowed to form weatherproof cords, but it is now usually brushed every day or two and trimmed every six to ten weeks.

Manchester Terrier

ORIGIN United Kingdom
HEIGHT 38–41 cm (15–16 in)
WEIGHT 5.5–10.0 kg (12–22 lb)
EXERCISE LEVEL
COAT CARE
REGISTERED KC, FCI, AKCs
COLOURS Black and tan

This breed name means something different on each side of the Atlantic. In the United Kingdom, it has one size, but in the United States there is a Toy version, similar to the English Toy Terrier.

BREED ORIGINS

Many of the British terrier breeds are descended from old black-and-tan types traceable back to the Middle Ages. The Manchester Terrier was created from this stock in the 19th century, and was the work of John Hulme. He crossed the terriers with Whippets for speed, and the resulting breed, excellent for ratting and rabbiting, was known for a time as 'The Gentleman's Terrier'. It is still a good outdoor companion, but is inclined to challenge other dogs and too independent-minded to be a popular household dog.

EAR TYPES British dogs are shown with natural ears, but American dogs may still have them cropped. The end of cropping dented the breed's popularity in the United Kingdom.

Miniature Pinscher

ORIGIN Germany
HEIGHT 38–41 cm (15–16 in)
WEIGHT 5.5–10.0 kg (12–22 lb)
EXERCISE LEVEL
COAT CARE
REGISTERED KC, FCI, AKCs
COLOURS Tan, black and tan; some allow blue or chocolate and tan

Also called the Zwergpinscher, this might look like a recent miniaturization of a working breed to make a toy companion, but in fact it has long been a compact working ratter.

RED/TAN   BLACK AND TAN

BREED ORIGINS

This breed was developed from larger German Pinschers at least 500 years ago, but early dogs were tough ratters, since refined into a dog similar to the English Toy Terrier. It will pursue with relish, dig enthusiastically, and challenge dogs far larger than itself. It makes an effective watchdog and lively companion.

CHANGING FASHIONS American standards may still call for a docked tail and cropped ears, but European dogs are now shown undocked with either erect or dropped ears.

Parson Russell Terrier

ORIGIN United Kingdom
HEIGHT 28–38 cm (11–15 in)
WEIGHT 5–8 kg (11–18 lb)
EXERCISE LEVEL
COAT CARE
REGISTERED KC, FCI, AKCs
COLOURS White and black or brown, tri-colour

This breed is less popular in rural pursuits but has won wider recognition in show registries than the Jack Russell Terrier. The longer legs allowed dogs to keep up with mounted hunters.

 BLACK AND WHITE

 TAN AND WHITE

 BLACK, WHITE AND TAN

BREED ORIGINS

This and its short-legged near-namesake were developed from white terriers used to pursue foxes underground. These went on to be recognized as Fox Terriers, but moved away from the working type, becoming too large to fit down earths. Reverend John 'Jack' Russell developed his own fast and furious dogs from the same stock, and they remain closer to their roots. For a long time both the types were classed together, but after much dispute, this breed is now recognized separately.

CHOICE OF COATS This breed has two versions, the wirehaired or broken coat seen here and preferred by Russell himself, and a sleeker smooth-haired type. Both are easy to care for and equally popular.

Scottish Terrier

ORIGIN United Kingdom
HEIGHT 25–28 cm (10–11 in)
WEIGHT 8.6–10.5 kg (19–23 lb)
EXERCISE LEVEL
COAT CARE
REGISTERED KC, FCI, AKCs
COLOURS Black, wheaten, black brindle, red brindle

Once called the Aberdeen Terrier, and also generically called a Skye Terrier, the Scottie was nicknamed Diehard by the 19th-century Earl of Dumbarton, who had a famous pack of terriers.

 BLACK

 GOLD

 BLACK BRINDLE

BREED ORIGINS

This breed is descended from terriers of the Scottish Western Isles, known as a type since the 16th century. It was developed in the 19th century, with all Scotties traceable back to one bitch, Splinter. They became hugely fashionable in the United States in the 1930s, possibly helped by President Roosevelt's pet, Fala;

George W Bush's two Scotties have not worked similar magic. More companions than true terriers, they are loyal, stubborn, and spirited.

SCOTTIE LOOKS Instantly recognizable for its extravagant beard, the Scottie has an insulating double coat and may appreciate clipping or stripping in warmer climates. The ears are naturally pricked and quite narrow.

Skye Terrier

ORIGIN United Kingdom
HEIGHT 25 cm (10 in)
WEIGHT 8.6–11.4 kg (19–25 lb)
EXERCISE LEVEL
COAT CARE
REGISTERED KC, FCI, AKCs
COLOURS Black, grey, fawn, cream

This breed is immortalized in Greyfriars Bobby, who is said to have spent 14 years sitting on the grave of his master in Greyfriars cemetery in Edinburgh until his own death.

 BLACK
 CREAM
 GREY
 GOLD

BREED ORIGINS

Terriers on the Isle of Skye with hair covering their faces were described in the 16th century, but those could have resembled either this terrier or the Scottish Terrier, which was drawn from island stock. Their dwarf stature may have come from the same roots as the Swedish Vallhund or Welsh Corgis; there are also tales of a Spanish shipwreck and Maltese dogs coming ashore. The long coat, covering a graceful build, made it popular as a pet, but numbers have declined recently.

COAT CARE The long coat that is part of this breed's appeal is not very prone to matting, but it was kept clipped on working dogs.

UP OR DOWN? The ears of a Skye can be either pricked or dropped. Pricked ears are most common.

Smooth Fox Terrier

ORIGIN United Kingdom
HEIGHT 25–28 cm (10–11 in)
WEIGHT 6.8–10.0 kg (15–22 lb)
EXERCISE LEVEL
COAT CARE
REGISTERED KC, FCI, AKCs
COLOURS White, white and tan, white and black, tri-colour

The Smooth Fox Terrier is drawn from the same stock as the Jack and Parson Russell. This breed is now kept almost entirely as a companion, though not entirely well suited to city life.

 BLACK AND WHITE
 TAN AND WHITE
BLACK, WHITE AND TAN

BREED ORIGINS

A fox terrier was any dog that would drive foxes from their earths. This type was shown in the 1860s, and ancestors may include Beagles and even Bull Terriers. Although no longer a working dog, it is energetic and stubborn; it can be snappish, especially with younger children. A wire-coated variant was originally recognized alongside the smooth-coated version in many registries under the generic term 'fox terrier', but the Wire Fox Terrier is now regarded as a separate breed.

SMOOTH FOX TERRIER
The back is strong and the chest is deep. The coat is straight and smooth.

Staffordshire Bull Terrier

ORIGIN United Kingdom

HEIGHT 36–41 cm (14–16 in)

WEIGHT 10.9–17.3 kg (24–38 lb)

EXERCISE LEVEL

COAT CARE

REGISTERED KC, FCI, AKCs

COLOURS Any colour except liver; solid or with white

The Staffie, although similar to some banned breeds, has so far not been subject to legislation in its homeland and most of Europe. It may look and walk like a thug, but it can be a pushover.

BLACK

RED/TAN

GOLD AND WHITE

BLACK AND WHITE

BLACK BRINDLE

BREED ORIGINS

This breed has its roots in dogfighting, but the Staffie became a respectable recognized breed in the early 20th century. It is sweet-natured with humans but a ruthless fighter of any other dog. They are not recommended as solitary guards, because they should be well socialized; exercising them anywhere near other dogs is tricky.

FIGHTING FACE For dog fights, relatively long muzzles were needed, so short-faced bull-baiters were crossed with terriers to produce the breed.

West Highland White Terrier

ORIGIN United Kingdom

HEIGHT 25–28 cm (10–11 in)

WEIGHT 6.8–10.0 kg (15–22 lb)

EXERCISE LEVEL

COAT CARE

REGISTERED KC, FCI, AKCs

COLOURS White

A perennially popular breed, the Westie has been used as the face of dog food and, along with a black Scottish Terrier, Scotch whisky. This dog is a bundle of fun that was created for a very sober reason.

BREED ORIGINS

The Westie is derived from white pups in wheaten Cairn Terrier litters. In the 19th century, these dogs flushed out game for guns, and were occasionally mistaken for prey and shot. So a white terrier that was easily distinguished from the quarry at any distance was developed; some credit the breed to Colonel ED Malcolm, others to the 8th Duke of Argyll. Friendly, they are entertaining companions.

ITCHY COAT Although the white coat saved the lives of working dogs, it had a price. White dogs are more susceptible than others to skin problems, and the Westie is particularly prone to allergies due to environmental factors or foods.

Yorkshire Terrier

ORIGIN United Kingdom
HEIGHT 23 cm (9 in)
WEIGHT 3.2 kg (7 lb)
EXERCISE LEVEL
COAT CARE
REGISTERED KC, FCI, AKCs
COLOURS Steel-blue and tan

Although most registries now place the diminutive Yorkie in the toy or companion category, it was created as a ratter by miners and mill workers who never envisaged a bow in its hair. It remains a terrier at heart, and will challenge anything.

BREED ORIGINS

In the mid-19th century, Yorkshire was at the heart of the United Kingdom's industrial revolution. Many workers migrated to the area from Scotland, bringing their dogs with them. Clydesdale, Paisley, Skye, and Waterside and English Black-and-Tan Terriers may have been involved in its ancestry. From this mix came a dog with an excess of spirit, valued for killing vermin. Today the breed is right at the top of the popularity stakes in the United States, but its size and spirit may be suffering from overexposure. Selective breeding for small size has led to slipped kneecaps and breathing problems in some lines.

EVERYDAY COAT The long, luxuriant, silvered coat takes time to develop. Pet owners usually find it easier to trim dogs back to a shorter length.

MINI-DOGS Even the smallest Yorkies still produce the occasional pup larger than themselves. This is no bad thing: breeding for ever-smaller dogs can lead to health problems.

Afghan Hound

ORIGIN Afghanistan
HEIGHT 64–74 cm (25–29 in)
WEIGHT 22.5–27.5 kg (50–60 lb)
EXERCISE LEVEL
COAT CARE
REGISTERED KC, FCI, AKCs
COLOURS Any colour, solid or shaded

The Afghan is perhaps the best known of the sighthounds. Originally at home in the harsh terrain and climate of the Afghan mountain ranges, it became a fashionable companion breed.

 BLACK CREAM GREY GOLD DARK BROWN

BREED ORIGINS

The Afghan is among the most ancient of all breeds. What is not clear is how thousands of years ago it came to the mountains of Afghanistan, far from the Arabian peninsula where dogs of this type originated. In its homeland, where it is still used for hunting, it is known as the Tazi, and a shorter-haired version exists; it is also called the Baluchi Hound. In the west, the longhaired version is an established companion breed, prized for its aristocratic appearance and luxurious coat. These dogs lose their poised reserve when exercising and show their ancestors' speed and independence; sound obedience training is required if you want them to return to you. They are long-lived for large dogs, reaching 12 to 14 years.

ANY COLOUR YOU LIKE Although the golden coat is popular and seen as the 'classic' Afghan look, any solid shade or combination is possible and allowed.

American Foxhound

ORIGIN United States
HEIGHT 53–64 cm (21–25 in)
WEIGHT 29.4–34.0 kg (65–75 lb)
EXERCISE LEVEL
COAT CARE
REGISTERED FCI, AKCs
COLOURS Any colour

Leaner and lighter than its European counterpart, the American Foxhound will act as an individual hunter or as a pack member, making it adaptable to a wider range of hunting styles.

 GOLD AND WHITE BLACK AND WHITE TAN AND WHITE BLACK AND TAN BLACK, WHITE AND TAN

BREED ORIGINS

These dogs are descended from English hunting dogs brought to the United States in the 1860s. Irish and French hounds were added to the mix, taking the breed in a slightly different direction. Today, show lines also find a place as good-natured companions. They are loyal to their family and good with children, but like all hunting dogs are not trustworthy around other non-canine pets. They are a fairly healthy breed, usually living over a decade.

WORKING DOGS When seeking a family companion, choose show bloodlines. Dogs that are bred for working do not make good pets.

Basenji

ORIGIN Zaire

HEIGHT 41–43 cm (16–17 in)

WEIGHT 9.5–11.0 kg (21–24 lb)

EXERCISE LEVEL

COAT CARE

REGISTERED KC, FCI, AKCs

COLOURS Black and white, tan and white, black, or brindle

This dog resembles those depicted in tomb paintings from ancient Egypt, and has primitive characteristics, such as a tendency to howl rather than bark, that seem to show it is an ancient breed.

 BLACK

 BLACK AND WHITE

 TAN AND WHITE

BREED ORIGINS
The story of the Basenji breed today begins in the 1930s with dogs brought from Africa to Europe and originally called Congo Dogs. They are not easily trained, but are reliable with children. Although long-lived, they are prone to an inheritable disorder of the kidneys.

PRIMITIVE LOOKS These small dogs are muscular and powerful. The tail is typically carried in a curl over the rump.

NO WORRIES A wrinkled face gives this affectionate, intelligent, and energetic breed a misleadingly anxious look.

Basset Hound

ORIGIN United Kingdom

HEIGHT 33–36 cm (13–14 in)

WEIGHT 18.1–27.2 kg (40–60 lb)

EXERCISE LEVEL

COAT CARE

REGISTERED KC, FCI, AKCs

COLOURS Any hound colour

The best known of all the bassets, this breed has lost any geographical qualification of its name. The exact location of its origin is hazy, but it is regarded as a classically British breed.

  GOLD AND WHITE

 TAN AND WHITE

 BLACK, WHITE, AND TAN

BREED ORIGINS
The Basset is descended from dwarfed bloodhounds, and dates back to at least the 1500s. The first breed description may be Theseus's account of his hounds in Shakespeare's *A Midsummer Night's Dream*: 'With ears that sweep away the morning dew/Crook-kneed, and dewlapped like Thessalian bulls/Slow in pursuit, but matched in mouth like bells'.

Today the Basset is more often a household dog than a hunting companion. This is an affectionate, amenable breed, good with children. It can be easily distracted, so needs consistent, patient training.

BULKY BUILD The short, crooked legs make the Basset slow, but it should never be clumsy. Lighter types are still used in hunting work, more in the United States than in Europe.

Beagle

ORIGIN United Kingdom

HEIGHT 33–39 cm (13–15 in)

WEIGHT 8.2–13.6 kg (18–30 lb)

EXERCISE LEVEL

COAT CARE

REGISTERED All

COLOURS Any hound colour

GOLD AND WHITE

BLACK, WHITE, AND TAN

The Beagle is most often described in breed standards as a 'merry' hound. It has a bell-like baying voice and a lively, curious personality, and can make an excellent family dog.

BREED ORIGINS

The Beagle probably derives from the larger Harrier breed, and has been used for hunting in Britain since the Middle Ages. These small dogs could even be carried by mounted hunters in saddlebags, and were bred to pursue rabbits and birds, either in packs or solo. Today, the breed varies in size from place to place, but has a distinct personality.

ENDEARING LOOKS
The affectionate nature of the Beagle is advertised in its typically appealing expression, but with the exception of Snoopy they are not to be trusted around small animals such as birds.

BEAGLE BODY The Beagle resembles a small Foxhound. It has a sturdy build, with a tail carried high or 'gaily', and a short, sleek coat that is easy to care for.

BREED QUALITIES

Beagles are highly sociable, and crave company, either human or canine. If they are to be left alone at all, keep at least two. They may pine alone, and a howling Beagle will make no friends among neighbours.

In the right home, Beagles can be a delight: cheerful, affectionate dogs that are not aggressive, they are good with children and friendly with other dogs. They are not the easiest to train, however, and tend to follow their own noses when out and about.

Black-and-Tan Coonhound

ORIGIN United States
HEIGHT 58–69 cm (23–27 in)
WEIGHT 24.9–34.0 kg (55–75 lb)
EXERCISE LEVEL
COAT CARE
REGISTERED FCI, AKCs
COLOURS Black and tan

Coonhounds are a specialized group of hunting dogs, bred to track and 'tree' the raccoon or oppossum and then await the hunter's arrival. They hunt by scent, and have a distinctive baying call.

POWER HOUND This large hound has a strong, well-proportioned build, with a deep chest and a strong tail. Long legs and a rhythmic stride give it speed.

BREED ORIGINS

The Black-and-Tan Coonhound was developed in the 18th century in the United States, although it was not officially recognized until 1945. It was created by crossing Bloodhounds and Foxhounds, and the Kerry Beagle may also have contributed to its development. The Coonhound howls as it works, and the following hunter can tell from the sound when the quarry has been treed.

Although intended for hunting raccoons, the breed is a versatile and capable hunter and has also been used very successfully to hunt larger game such as deer and even mountain lion and bears. This is the best known of all the coonhound breeds, and popular for its trainable temperament. It can make a good watchdog, and is an asset to homes that can provide plenty of exercise and interest.

COONHOUND HEAD The head is finely modelled, with no folds in the skin. The ears are set low and well back, hanging in graceful folds; they should reach past the end of the nose.

PRACTICAL COAT The short, sleek coat is largely coal black with rich tan markings confined to the muzzle, limbs, and chest. The insulating coat withstands extremes of both heat and cold well.

Bloodhound

ORIGIN Belgium

HEIGHT 58–69 cm (23–27 in)

WEIGHT 30.0–50.0 kg (66–110 lb)

EXERCISE LEVEL

COAT CARE

REGISTERED KC, FCI, AKCs

COLOURS Black and tan, liver/red and tan, red

Developed in Belgium as the Chien de St Hubert and in England as the Bloodhound, this massive scenthound is synonymous with tracking, and has been used to trace criminals and runaway slaves.

RED/TAN

BLACK AND TAN

BREED ORIGINS

This droopy breed is said to be directly descended from the packs of hounds belonging to St Hubert, patron saint of hunters, in the 7th century. These dogs were maintained for centuries by Benedictine monks at the Abbaye de Saint-Hubert in the Ardennes, and by tradition six dogs were sent every year to the king of France for the royal packs. Taken to Britain by the Normans, the same lines became known as the Bloodhound, referring not to an ability to scent blood, but to a dog of 'pure' blood, belonging to the nobility.

BREED QUALITIES

A gentle, affectionate breed, the Bloodhound needs to be watched around children only because it may bowl them over. It is too easily distracted by interesting scents to be highly trainable, and knows how to use those mournful eyes. Sadly, it can be short-lived and is one of the breeds most prone to bloat; joint problems and cancers are also issues, as in most large breeds.

CLASSIC LOOKS Although Bloodhounds now come in a limited range of shades, there was once a wider selection. It included a white strain, known as the Talbot Hound, which had died out by the 17th century.

Borzoi

ORIGIN Russia
HEIGHT 69–79 cm (27–31 in)
WEIGHT 34.0–47.6 kg (75–105 lb)
EXERCISE LEVEL
COAT CARE
REGISTERED KC, FCI, AKCs
COLOURS White, golden, tan, or grey with black markings, either solid or mixed

This elegant and reserved dog comes from a heritage of hunting wolves in Russia, and has also been called the Russian Wolfhound. In the last century, it has moved successfully from hunt to home.

 CREAM
 GOLD
 GOLD AND WHITE
 BLACK AND WHITE
 TAN AND WHITE

BREED ORIGINS

Sighthounds had arrived in Russia from their original home in southwestern Asia by the Middle Ages. Here, they developed into the Borzoi, a Russian term for all sighthounds, including some rarities virtually unknown in the West, such as the Taigan and Chortaj. The Borzoi had spread westwards into Europe by the 19th century, where it became favoured as a high-status pet and an aristocratic household dog, and was bred for companionship rather than hunting.

Today it is widely known as a household pet, but it has retained all its ancestors' athleticism and free spirit. It remains a hunter at heart, and cannot be trusted to resist the urge to hunt any small animal, so will not live peacefully with non-canine pets. Although this breed needs plenty of exercise, it quickly wearies of very young children's rough and tumble play, and prefers an ordered life.

NOBLE NOSE The head is distinctively long and narrow, with a slightly arched muzzle and ears that lie back on the neck when relaxed.

COAT CARE The silky coat presents a challenge when shed for the summer, but is otherwise not that hard to care for. Brush regularly and clip hair between the toes.

FAST MOVER Like all sighthounds, the Borzoi is capable of amazing feats of speed, and is easily distracted while out and about. Constant vigilance is needed when exercising these dogs.

Dachshunds

ORIGIN Germany

HEIGHT 18–23 cm (7–9 in)

WEIGHT 6.8–11.3 kg (15–25 lb)

EXERCISE LEVEL

COAT CARE

REGISTERED KC, FCI, AKCs

COLOURS One colour, bi-colour, or dappled or striped; no white

This breed group has a complex set of categories according to both size and coat type, which differ from country to country. Dogs bred for working differ from those that are bred for showing.

CREAM   BLUE   RED/TAN   GOLD   BLACK AND TAN

BREED ORIGINS

Dwarfed or short-legged dogs have been known for thousands of years, and the Dachshund, also called the Dackel or Teckel in Europe, has been known as a type since the Middle Ages. Bred from the hunting dogs known as Bracken, they were selected because their short stature made them suitable for working underground, hence their name, which means 'badger dog'.

Today, these dogs are kept both as hunting companions and household pets. Those bred for working have shorter spines and longer legs than those bred for showing; the latter are more prone to spine problems, always a risk with this build.

FULL OF POTENTIAL The different sizes of Dachshunds are not distinct breeds, so what a puppy may be is always open to chance, although lines tend to produce certain sizes consistently.

WIREHAIRED DACHSHUND This type of Dachshund is reputed to be the best balanced of the three coats, less feisty than the smooth-coated original but bolder than the longhairs.

BREED DIFFERENCES

As well as the various sizes of Dachshunds (*see* box), there are three different coats: the Smooth-haired, the Wirehaired, and the Longhaired. The Smooth-haired is the oldest, the original hunting dog. The Wirehaired was created by crossing with rough-haired Pinschers, and using the Dandie Dinmont Terrier to improve the head type. The Longhaired is thought to come from crosses with short-legged spaniels, with further work to miniaturize the resulting dogs. The differences are more than cosmetic: all of these crosses also affected the temperament.

BREED QUALITIES

Although it is a small dog that can adapt to urban life, needing little space for exercise, some caution is needed when choosing this popular breed. They are variable in temper, and some seem to have the will of a much larger dog in concentrated form. Be prepared to give firm and

SMOOTH-HAIRED DACHSHUND The original coat, this shorthaired type is the most excitable. They can be fearful and snappish.

consistent training when they are young or face a lifetime of challenge – and these robust small dogs often live on into their mid- to late teens.

Sizes of Dachshund

British and American clubs tend to recognize two sizes of Dachshund, the Standard and the Miniature, with the dividing line between the two set at 5 kg (11 lb). Continental European clubs classify by chest circumference – a vital statistic for an earth dog. Dachshunds have a chest of 35 cm (14 in), Miniatures 30–35 cm (12–14 in), and Rabbit Dachshunds or Kaninchen Teckel below 30 cm (12 in).

LONGHAIRED DACHSHUND Spaniel heritage has given this breed not only a silky coat but a tendency to be much less tenacious than their Smooth-haired cousins, and even rather shy.

Deerhound

ORIGIN United Kingdom

HEIGHT 71–76 cm (28–30 in)

WEIGHT 36.3–45.4 kg (80–100 lb)

EXERCISE LEVEL

COAT CARE

REGISTERED KC, FCI, AKCs

COLOURS Grey, brindle, yellow, sandy-red, or red fawn with black points; some white allowed

Historically Scottish, this is also called the Scottish Deerhound. Its original purpose was hunting deer, but it is now most often a gentle, friendly, and undeniably impressive companion.

 GREY RED/TAN GOLD BLACK BRINDLE

BREED ORIGINS

Rough-coated hounds have been recorded for over 500 years, probably descended from ancient imported short-coated sighthounds crossed with longer-coated dogs suited to the Scottish Highlands' climate. Packs hunted deer, but with the demise of the clan system and the shift to hunting with guns, the breed declined by the 18th century. It was revived in the 19th century, but remains rare.

This is an intelligent and trainable hound, sociable with both children and other dogs. It does not need a large home, as adults are layabouts indoors, but a good-sized outdoor space and thorough daily exercise are vital.

DEERHOUND LOOKS Everything from the head to the tail has a long, strong, tapering line. The coat is shaggy, never woolly, and much softer on the head, chest, and stomach than elsewhere.

Drever

ORIGIN Sweden

HEIGHT 30–41 cm (12–16 in)

WEIGHT 13.6–15.0 kg (30–33 lb)

EXERCISE LEVEL

COAT CARE

REGISTERED FCI

COLOURS Fawn and white, black and white, tri-colour

Also called the Swedish Dachsbracke, this accomplished scenthound is among the most popular hunting dogs in its homeland. It is used to track and drive quarry towards the hunters.

 GOLD AND WHITE BLACK AND WHITE BLACK, WHITE, AND TAN

SLOW BUT STEADY Short legs mean this is not the fastest of hounds, but it has incredible stamina and a tenacious desire to hunt.

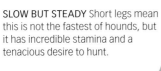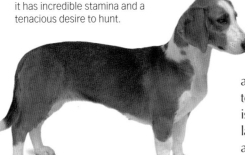

BREED ORIGINS

This is a recreation of a historic type, bred from the Westphalian Dachsbracke crossed with local hounds. Its compact size makes it suited to slowly driving flighty deer towards guns, and this hardy, robust breed is a tenacious hunter. When hunting is not available, these dogs make laid-back, amenable companions, although they are self-contained and not the ideal family dog.

TIDY FACE The Drever head is large, but well proportioned. Unlike some other hounds, it has close-fitting eyelids and lips, rather than droopy folds.

English Coonhound

ORIGIN United States
HEIGHT 53–69 cm (21–27 in)
WEIGHT 18.1–29.5 kg (40–65 lb)
EXERCISE LEVEL
COAT CARE
REGISTERED AKCs
COLOURS Any hound colour; most often red tick

Despite its misleading name, this robust scenthound is an entirely American breed. It was first bred for hunting raccoons and similar quarry, a role that it still fulfils today, mostly in the southern states.

 BLUE
 RED/TAN
 BLACK AND WHITE
 TAN AND WHITE
 BLACK, WHITE AND TAN

BUILD AND COAT This is a relatively small coonhound, but powerful and strong-boned. It slopes from the shoulders to the rump, but the long ears and drooping lips are typical of the type.

BREED ORIGINS

This breed is also sometimes called the Redtick Coonhound, a name perhaps more suitable, since its ancestors included not only English but French dogs, bred in the early 19th century.

This is first and foremost a hunting dog, robust and active with high energy levels. It does make a good-tempered household and family companion, as long as there are no small, non-canine pets to consider.

Finnish Hound

ORIGIN Finland
HEIGHT 56–63 cm (22–25 in)
WEIGHT 20.0–25.0 kg (44–55 lb)
EXERCISE LEVEL
COAT CARE
REGISTERED FCI, AKCs
COLOURS Tri-colour

The Suomenjokoira or Finsk Stovåre is a versatile tracker used for tracking hare and fox by scent. A medium-sized breed with a resonant voice, it is the most popular of Finland's working dogs.

BREED ORIGINS

Some accounts say this Harrier-like breed dates from the 18th century and was created by a goldsmith named Tammelin using Swedish, German, and French hounds. The official standard, however, dates its origins not further back than the 1890s, after the creation of the Finnish Kennel Club, and merely mentions Finnish dogs that resembled European breeds. However it began, it is an enthusiastic hunter that brings prey to bay for the hunter; it will also find shot birds, but does not retrieve.

KEEN NOSE This tireless hound will relish hunting in all conditions. It works independently, tracking the quarry and bringing it to bay.

Greyhound

ORIGIN United Kingdom
HEIGHT 69–76 cm (27–30 in)
WEIGHT 27.2–31.7 kg (60–70 lb)
EXERCISE LEVEL
COAT CARE
REGISTERED KC, FCI, AKCs
COLOURS Black, white, red, blue, fawn, fallow, or brindle, with or without white

There are Italian, Hungarian, Russian, and other Greyhounds, and this member of the group is also known as the English Greyhound. Closely resembling dogs in ancient art, it is renowned for its speed.

 BLACK
 BLUE
 RED/TAN
 GOLD
 BLACK AND WHITE

BREED ORIGINS

Ancient Egyptian art shows dogs similar to the modern Greyhound, and is seized upon as evidence of the breed's antiquity. However, DNA analysis in 2004 put it surprisingly close to herding dogs, implying that while this deep-chested, narrow-waisted, finely tapered type of dog has been around for millennia, the modern breed sprang from a wider genetic base more recently.

The 'grey' does not refer to colour, but comes from Old English, and is thought to mean 'fine'. Greyhounds were used in hunting large and small game, and today are principally used in racing.

BREED QUALITIES

Despite their speed in pursuit, the Greyhound at home can be a relaxed and relaxing companion, although not ideal for city life and families with young children. It tends to forget its training when it sights potential prey, but is otherwise tractable.

BUILT FOR SPEED Greyhounds can reach speeds of 69 kph (43 mph); retired racing dogs can find it hard to break the habits of a lifetime when they see small animals.

LIVE FAST, RETIRE YOUNG Racing dogs have a short working life, and rescue organizations often have adult dogs to home. Away from the track, the Greyhound is typically quiet and gentle.

Irish Wolfhound

ORIGIN Ireland
HEIGHT 81–86 cm (32–34 in)
WEIGHT 47.6–54.4 kg (105–120 lb)
EXERCISE LEVEL
COAT CARE
REGISTERED KC, FCI, AKCs
COLOURS Grey, steel-grey, brindle, red, black, pure white, fawn, wheaten

This massive breed makes it easy to imagine the fearsome Celtic hounds known as Cú Faoil used for hunting wolves, elk, and boar, and partly responsible for the local extinction of all three.

GREY   RED/TAN

SHAGGY DOG The coarse, wiry top coat is best stripped out by plucking in summer, leaving a sleek, soft undercoat for the warmer months.

THE EYES HAVE IT For all its size and power, this is the original gentle giant, most likely to lick you to death.

BREED ORIGINS

The ancestors of this hound probably came to Ireland via the Roman Empire, and large, shaggy hounds are prominent in ancient Irish writing. By the 19th century numbers were seriously depleted; this is not a dog suited to hunting with a gun.

The breed was saved by a Captain Graham, who used Deerhound, Great Dane, and Borzoi lines to inject new blood.

Today, the breed is a mellow household companion, good with children and other dogs and perhaps less inclined to chase than some other sighthounds. Sadly, it is not long-lived, and is prone to bone cancer and gastric torsion, like other giant and deep-chested breeds.

Saluki

ORIGIN Iran
HEIGHT 51–71 cm (20–28 in)
WEIGHT 20.0–29.9 kg (44–66 lb)
EXERCISE LEVEL
COAT CARE
REGISTERED KC, FCI, AKCs
COLOURS Any colour or colours except brindle

Also called the Arabian Greyhound, Persian Greyhound, or Gazelle Hound, this swift and elegant sighthound has been known in the Middle East and used in the hunt for millennia.

 BLACK   GOLD   GOLD AND WHITE

BREED ORIGINS

The Saluki closely resembles ancient images of hunting dogs, and recent DNA analysis confirmed that it is not a modern recreation but a truly ancient breed. It predates Islam, and while dogs are generally regarded as unclean in the religion, the Saluki was always an exception; the white spot often found on its chest is known as 'the kiss of Allah' by the Bedouin. It was first brought to the United Kingdom in the 1840s, but only became popular at the start of the 20th century. Today it is established across the world as a graceful companion, at ease in family and city homes.

NATURAL VARIATION Because the breed was historically scattered across a wide area, a range of geographically isolated local types emerged. The coat varies in colour between places, and both smooth and feathered types exist.

Sloughi

ORIGIN Morocco
HEIGHT 60–70 cm (24–28 in)
WEIGHT 20.0–27.0 kg (44–59 lb)
EXERCISE LEVEL
COAT CARE
REGISTERED KC, FCI, AKCs
COLOURS Sand to fawn, may have black shading or white markings

Although it is sometimes called the Arabian Greyhound and classed with the Saluki, recent DNA analysis has shown the Sloughi to be a distinctively African breed.

 GOLD   GOLD AND WHITE

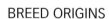

BREED ORIGINS

When looking at the relationships between animals, a mixture of archaeology, written records, and the looks of the breed have in the past been the only tools available. Beyond a certain distance, these can give no great certainty. The advent of genetic studies has shone a new light on the history of dog breeds, and revealed some surprises. Although it looks close to the other breeds sometimes called greyhounds, the Sloughi appears to have spent all of its genetic history in Africa, almost entirely untouched by any new input. It has needed none: a slender, sand-coloured dog, it is in many ways the perfect hound for its home. A slightly high-strung breed and suspicious of strangers, it is content as the companion of a consistent, quiet owner but not a choice for a rowdy household with children.

HAPPY MEDIUM The Berbers kept two lines of Sloughis: the small, fine desert Sloughi, and a larger mountain Sloughi. Elsewhere, the breed has developed as a blend of the two.

Swedish Elkhound

ORIGIN Sweden
HEIGHT 58–64 cm (23–25 in)
WEIGHT 29.9 kg (66 lb)
EXERCISE LEVEL
COAT CARE
REGISTERED FCI
COLOURS Shades of grey with cream to white markings

The official national breed of Sweden, this dog is also known by the name of Jämthund. Once there were many more regional elkhounds, and this one originated in Jämtland in northern Sweden.

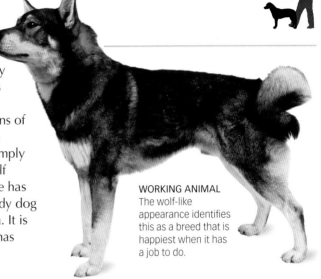

BREED ORIGINS

This dog dates back many centuries, and was traditionally used for hunting not only elk but bears, wolves, and even the agile Scandinavian lynx, driving the quarry until it was trapped and then awaiting the hunters' arrival. It was only recognized in the latter part of the 20th century; until then it was judged as part of the Norwegian Elkhound breed, a politically unpopular union. In truth, many physically isolated communities developed their own slightly different strains of hunting dog over the centuries; this one simply survived and got itself noticed. This heritage has created a strong, hardy dog of enormous stamina. It is also intelligent, and has proved adaptable.

WORKING ANIMAL
The wolf-like appearance identifies this as a breed that is happiest when it has a job to do.

Whippet

ORIGIN United Kingdom
HEIGHT 43–51 cm (17–20 in)
WEIGHT 12.7 kg (28 lb)
EXERCISE LEVEL
COAT CARE
REGISTERED KC, FCI, AKCs
COLOURS Any colour

This Greyhound in miniature is one of the fastest sighthounds in existence. Both its official name and the nickname 'snap dog' are said to refer to it moving as fast as a snapped or cracked whip.

BLACK

CREAM

BLUE

RED/TAN

BREED ORIGINS

The Whippet was created in the north of England in the 19th century. Hare coursing was a popular sport, and crossing Fox Terriers with the Greyhound – which was too large for the sport – created the Whippet. Despite its graceful, slight appearance, this is a hardy hunter, with all the tenacity of its terrier antecedents when on a scent. At home, it is a gentle, affectionate breed, relaxed around children and other dogs and even something of a couch potato, especially in winter.

TAKE COVER Thin skin and a fine, close coat provide little protection or insulation. A jacket in cold weather is practical, not a fashion statement.

American Cocker Spaniel

ORIGIN United States

HEIGHT 36–38 cm (14–15 in)

WEIGHT 10.9–12.7 kg (24–28 lb)

EXERCISE LEVEL 🐕

COAT CARE ✂️

REGISTERED KC, FCI, AKCs

COLOURS Black, cream, red, brown; solid or with white; tan points

In the United States this breed is simply the Cocker Spaniel, and the original type is known as the English Cocker Spaniel, but international registries give each their national identity.

 BLACK

 RED/TAN

 GOLD

 GOLD AND WHITE

 BLACK AND WHITE

BREED ORIGINS

This breed has the same early history as the English Cocker, but American breeders pursued a prettier dog, with longer, silkier hair, rather than working qualities. In 1936 a group broke away and formed an 'English Cocker Spaniel' club. Some solid

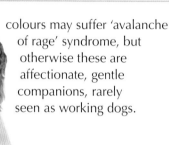

colours may suffer 'avalanche of rage' syndrome, but otherwise these are affectionate, gentle companions, rarely seen as working dogs.

BEAUTY REGIME The dense coat is prone to dry or oily seborrhea, and hair on the ears must be trimmed to let air reach the ear canals, minimizing infections. The hairy feet are magnets for debris.

Brittany

ORIGIN France

HEIGHT 48–51 cm (19–20 in)

WEIGHT 15.9–18.1 kg (35–40 lb)

EXERCISE LEVEL 🐕

COAT CARE 🖌

REGISTERED KC, FCI, AKCs

COLOURS Black and white, orange and white, liver and white, tri-colour

A favourite gundog in France, this breed is also popular abroad. Although it is known as the Epagneul Breton in its homeland, elsewhere the 'spaniel' is usually omitted; it is more of a setter.

 BLACK AND WHITE

 TAN AND WHITE

BLACK, WHITE, AND TAN

BREED ORIGINS

One of the oldest breeds of this type in France, this was almost extinct at the start of the 20th century, when it was revived by breeder Arthur Enaud through outcrossing and renewed selections. Its popularity is as much due to its relaxed tolerance of children and other dogs as its working abilities, and this is an obedient, affectionate companion for anyone who can provide sufficient activity.

TRUE COLOURS In the United States, only brown and red shades, seen as 'classic' French colours, are allowed. In Europe, black is also allowed, as it was in the original French breed standard that was drawn up in 1907.

English Cocker Spaniel

ORIGIN United Kingdom
HEIGHT 38–43 cm (15–17 in)
WEIGHT 11.8–15.4 kg (26–34 lb)
EXERCISE LEVEL
COAT CARE
REGISTERED KC, FCI, AKCs
COLOURS Black, cream, red, brown, solid or with white, tan points

In the United Kingdom, this breed is simply the Cocker Spaniel, but elsewhere its nationality is added to distinguish it from the American Cocker Spaniel. Side by side, nobody could mistake the two today.

 BLACK
 RED/TAN
 GOLD
 GOLD AND WHITE
 BLACK AND WHITE

BREED ORIGINS

Spaniels were used to flush game into nets as early as the 16th century. Cockers, specializing in woodcock, were described in the 19th century. These dogs are now the second most popular breed in their homeland, and show and working lines have diverged. Working dogs are smaller, with shorter coats, and boundless energy, while show dogs need more coat care but less mental and physical stimulation.

COLOUR AND TEMPERAMENT A rare condition called 'avalanche of rage' syndrome can affect solid-coloured, but not bi-coloured, dogs.

English Pointer

ORIGIN United Kingdom
HEIGHT 53–61 cm (21–24 in)
WEIGHT 20.0–29.9 kg (44–66 lb)
EXERCISE LEVEL
COAT CARE
REGISTERED KC, FCI, AKCs
COLOURS White and black, liver, lemon, or orange

Many registries officially list this aristocratic-looking dog simply as the Pointer, but given the number of pointing breeds in the world, it is widely given its national identity for the sake of clarity.

 GOLD AND WHITE
 BLACK AND WHITE
 TAN AND WHITE

BREED ORIGINS

It is thought that Greyhounds, Bloodhounds, setters, foxhounds, and even bulldogs contributed to their development of pointers. Pointers are recorded in England as far back as 1650, but continental breeds such as the Spanish Pointer were involved in their creation. By the 18th century these were perhaps the most popular hunting dog, and became popular in the United States by the 1900s.

A fast and reliable scenter that can quickly cover a wide area, the English Pointer is especially adept at finding feathered game, and is used for hunting and in competitive trials, in which they excel. As companions, they are serious and sensitive, but they are also biddable and gentle.

English Setter

ORIGIN United Kingdom
HEIGHT 61–64 cm (24–25 in)
WEIGHT 18.1–31.8 kg (40–70 lb)
EXERCISE LEVEL
COAT CARE
REGISTERED KC, FCI, AKCs
COLOURS White and black, orange, lemon, or liver, tri-colour

This elegant breed combines old-fashioned looks with old-fashioned manners. It is a proficient tracker, setter, and retriever of birds, but just as happy as an active family dog, and a peaceful companion.

GOLD AND WHITE

BLACK AND WHITE

TAN AND WHITE

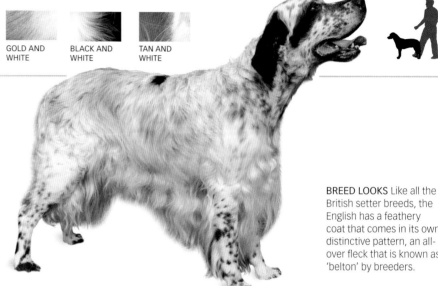

BREED ORIGINS

The first setters were developed in France from Spanish and French spaniels, and were in England by the 16th century, but the modern breed was developed by Sir Edward Laverack in the 19th century. It is now split into the show lines and the often lighter-built working or field lines, which include the strain known as Llewellin Setters.

BREED LOOKS Like all the British setter breeds, the English has a feathery coat that comes in its own distinctive pattern, an all-over fleck that is known as 'belton' by breeders.

English Springer Spaniel

ORIGIN United Kingdom
HEIGHT 48–51 cm (19–20 in)
WEIGHT 22.2–24.9 kg (49–55 lb)
EXERCISE LEVEL
COAT CARE
REGISTERED KC, FCI, AKCs
COLOURS Liver and white, black and white, tri-colour

One of the oldest surviving spaniel breeds, this is still a popular working dog and household companion in the United Kingdom, and also among the top breeds registered in showing circles.

BLACK AND WHITE

BLACK, WHITE, AND TAN

BREED ORIGINS

Dogs of this type can be seen in paintings from the 17th century, but were then simply spaniels, not springers, used on furred game, and cockers, used for birds. In fact, this breed has been shown by American hunters to be a proficient bird dog. It is strongly split into working and show lines, but show lines still need exercise and stimulation, or for all their gentleness they may become destructive.

SHOW AND FIELD
This is a show type dog, with pendulous ears and lips, and a long coat that is mainly coloured. Field types are lighter and more wiry with a fairly short, feathery coat, predominantly white for visibility.

French Spaniel

ORIGIN France

HEIGHT 55–61 cm (22–24 in)

WEIGHT 20.0–25.0 kg (44–55 lb)

EXERCISE LEVEL

COAT CARE

REGISTERED FCI, AKCs

COLOURS White and brown, from cinnamon to dark liver

This breed is known as the Epagneul Français in its homeland, where it is also patriotically claimed by its admirers to be the origin of all the diverse varieties of hunting spaniels.

FRENCH COAT The coat is generally flat and silky, softened by longer feathering on the ears, legs and tail, usually seen with medium brown spotting.

As with other French breeds, it lost out in favour of British breeds in the 19th century and was on the verge of extinction, but it was rescued by a priest, Father Fournier. The breed remained almost unknown outside France until the 1970s, when it was introduced to Canada, where it has become a popular bird dog with hunters.

BREED QUALITIES

Rustic in looks, this is an ideal country dog that will encourage long walks, but it is calm indoors and rarely barks, so can adapt to city life too. It is gentle and obedient, and like most of the French gundogs has a sensitive temperament that craves affection and needs soft words to give its best.

BREED ORIGINS

Despite its name, this old breed, which dates back to the 17th century, is more of a pointer or setter than a spaniel. Early dogs of this type would set or point very low, so a hunter behind them could throw a net over them onto the game ahead. As hunting methods changed, the higher pointing style was developed, and this breed is still a fine pointer and retriever. It is also good for flushing game in water and over wild, rugged terrain, although it is not the fastest of spaniels.

SIMILAR FEATURES This breed is thought to be related to the Small Munsterlander and the Dutch Partridge Dog. While conventional thought has it that this type of dog spread from Spain to France and beyond, some believe that it is fundamentally Danish.

German Pointers

ORIGIN Germany

HEIGHT 59–66 cm (23–26 in)

WEIGHT 24.9–31.8 kg (55–70 lb)

EXERCISE LEVEL

COAT CARE (sh) (lh)

REGISTERED KC, FCI, AKCs

COLOURS Black, brown; solid or with white in variable mixes of specks and patches

There are three types of this versatile hunting dog: the Kurzhaar (Shorthaired), Drahthaar (Wirehaired), and Stichelhaar (Longhaired). It will retrieve as well as point, and works in all kinds of terrain.

 BLACK

 DARK BROWN

 BLACK AND WHITE

  TAN AND WHITE

BREED ORIGINS

The ancestry of the German Pointer goes back to pointers that came to Germany from Spain and France. Once sophisticated shotguns were in use, bringing down distant birds in flight, these specialized dogs needed to expand their repertoire to include retrieving. Intensely focused breeding activity in Germany in the late 19th century saw British and French breeds mixed with the national stock to create a versatile and tireless hunting dog. The result of this was the range of German Pointers, of which the Shorthaired is the most successful. They are popular hunting dogs, with the intelligence to work independently.

SHORTHAIRED The coat may be patched, flecked, or both. Conformation and constitution are more important: a dog must be able to carry out any and all hunting activities.

BREED QUALITIES

Like most gundog breeds, these are loyal and affectionate dogs, gentle to handle and devoted to their family; German Pointers have always been household as well as hunting dogs. But they are powerful, with limitless energy, and need as much exercise as they can get. If neglected, they can be destructive or hyperactive, and they may become ardent escape artists.

SOFT MOUTH Because this breed retrieves as well as points, the muzzle must be long, broad, deep and strong so that the dog can carry game gently without damaging it.

GERMAN WIREHAIRED POINTER The wiry coat is quite water repellent making this the most weather resistant of the German pointers. The Longhaired is seen far less than the other two.

Golden Retriever

ORIGIN United Kingdom

HEIGHT 56–61 cm (22–24 in)

WEIGHT 27.2–34.0 kg (60–75 lb)

EXERCISE LEVEL

COAT CARE

REGISTERED KC, FCI, AKCs

COLOURS Gold

Having ruled the popularity stakes for years, the gregarious and genial Golden Retriever has begun to decline in numbers. It may be fashion, lifestyles making them harder to accommodate, or simply 'too much of a good thing' turning sour.

BREED ORIGINS

Developed in Scotland from the 1860s by Sir Dudley Majoribanks, Goldens started with Nous, a yellow puppy from a litter of black retrievers, and Belle, from the now-extinct Tweed Water Spaniel breed. The results were first shown in 1906 as 'any other colour' retrievers, and became a breed within a few years: recognition in North America came in the 1920s and 1930s. As with other highly popular dogs, overbreeding of this friendly, 'live-to-please' breed has led to health and temperament problems in some lines.

BIGGER AND BETTER
Improvements in guns in the 19th century meant a powerful retriever was needed to bring back birds downed over long distances, and the Golden fulfilled this role.

COLOUR COUNTS There are different lines of Goldens for field trials, working, assistance dogs, and showing. In the show lines, American dogs are darker than British dogs.

Gordon Setter

ORIGIN United Kingdom
HEIGHT 58–69 cm (23–27 in)
WEIGHT 20.4–36.2 kg (45–80 lb)
EXERCISE LEVEL
COAT CARE
REGISTERED KC, FCI, AKCs
COLOURS Black and tan

This black-and-tan setter is a tireless runner, bred to cover great tracts of the Scottish Highlands in pursuit of grouse, ptarmigan, and partridge. Less often seen as a working dog than in the past, it makes an ebullient companion.

CHANGING LOOKS Although black-and-tan setters were known in England and Scotland in the 16th century, this breed was originally a tri-colour; white is now limited to small markings.

BREED ORIGINS

Setters find birds that freeze to escape notice, and then similarly freeze: falcons or a thrown net accomplish the rest. This breed was developed by the Duke of Richmond and Gordon in Scotland in the early 19th century. Better guns and a decline in partridge in the 20th century made retrievers more useful, so this is usually a household companion today. Loyal and obedient, they can be bouncy.

Hungarian Vizsla

ORIGIN Hungary
HEIGHT 56–61 cm (22–24 in)
WEIGHT 22.2–28.1 kg (49–62 lb)
EXERCISE LEVEL
COAT CARE
REGISTERED KC, FCI, AKCs
COLOURS Chestnut-gold

This breed is called simply the Visla in the United States, and the Hungarian Shorthaired Pointer or Rövidszörü Magyar Vizsla in Europe. It is now popular both at home and abroad.

BREED ORIGINS

Pointers working with falcons were recorded in the 14th-century 'Vienna Chronicle' of Hungarian codes and laws. At first called the Yellow Pointer, it became the Hungarian Pointer, and by the 16th century the Vizsla, a name that may come from an old Hungarian word meaning 'search'. An influx of English and German pointers in the 19th century almost made the breed extinct, as did World War II, but today it is a popular breed at home and abroad, and has given rise to the Hungarian Wirehaired Vizsla.

LOOKS FAMILIAR The Vizsla was used in development of other breeds of similar lines, most notably the German Shorthaired Pointer and the Weimaraner; in turn, these same breeds may have been among the dogs used to re-establish the Vizsla after numbers fell in the 19th century.

Hungarian Wirehaired Vizsla

ORIGIN Hungary

HEIGHT 56–61 cm (22–24 in)

WEIGHT 22.2–28.1 kg (49–62 lb)

EXERCISE LEVEL

COAT CARE

REGISTERED KC, FCI, AKCs

COLOURS Gold

Also known in Europe as the Hungarian Wirehaired Pointer or Drotzörü Magyar Vizsla, this breed is less familiar than its shorthaired parent. However, its popularity is spreading in the United Kingdom, North America, and Australia.

BREED ORIGINS

The Hungarian Wirehaired Vizsla was developed in the early 20th century. Wanting a dog with a thicker coat and heavier frame, suitable for working in less favourable weather, breeders crossed the Vizsla with the German Wirehaired Pointer. Although it is not reliably recorded, it may be that griffon breeds, the Pudelpointer, and even the Red Setter were also used in the early stages. In all respects but the coat, the two Vizsla breeds are alike, sharing not only their looks but their deeply affectionate, gentle character and lively enthusiasm for games; they have always been part of the family.

GAINING GROUND The Wirehaired lacks an undercoat, so it is not a breed that can live outdoors. A medium-paced pointer that also retrieves well, this versatile breed is likely to spread as a hunting dog as much as a companion.

Irish Setter

ORIGIN Ireland

HEIGHT 64–69 cm (25–27 in)

WEIGHT 27.2–31.8 kg (60–70 lb)

EXERCISE LEVEL

COAT CARE

REGISTERED KC, FCI, AKCs

COLOURS Red-tan

In Irish, it is Modder rhu or Madra rua, the red dog, and although it is the most recent of the nine dog breeds native to the country, it is perhaps the best known.

BREED ORIGINS

This breed is sometimes called the Irish Red Setter, in deference to its Red-and-White antecedent. The solid coat existed by the 18th century, but only became fashionable in the 19th century. In the United States there are large Irish Setters, found in show halls, and smaller Red Setters, bred to be true to the working origins. Harder to train than other gundogs, they make good-natured, spirited companions.

GOOD LOOKS A silky, flowing coat has made this redhead a perenially popular companion.

Labrador Retriever

ORIGIN United Kingdom
HEIGHT 51–61 cm (22–24 in)
WEIGHT 24.9–34.0 kg (55–75 lb)
EXERCISE LEVEL
COAT CARE
REGISTERED KC, FCI, AKCs
COLOURS Yellow, chocolate, black

Anyone in search of a genial companion or family dog is likely to be advised 'if in doubt, get a Lab', and it seems most do. This is undoubtedly the most popular breed in the English-speaking world.

BLACK   GOLD   DARK BROWN

BREED ORIGINS

The ancestor of this breed was the St John's Dog, a precursor of the Newfoundland. Brought to the United Kingdom by fishermen, it was the start of the Curly-coated, Flat-coated, and Labrador Retrievers, its proven ability in pulling nets ashore by their floats now applied to safely retrieving game. Labradors were named by the early 19th century and became common by the end of the century, appearing in the United States early in the 20th century.

BREED QUALITIES

The trainable, obedient nature of this breed has made it the world's favourite assistance dog, and individuals have learned to do everything from negotiating traffic to putting their owner's cash cards into machines for them. They make wonderfully happy, exuberant family dogs, but have boundless energy and a boundless appetite.

COLOUR TRENDS
Chocolate and yellow pups occurred from the start and were eventually recognized. The yellows have become ever paler, until almost all are pale cream today, although shades down to 'red fox' are allowed.

ORIGINAL COLOUR Labs were at first strongly preferred in black, as shown by the first painting of one, *Cora, a Labrador Bitch* by Edwin Landseer.

IT'S NOT WORK As in many other gundog breeds, there are distinct show lines and separate, usually more rangy, working dogs. Labs from working lines have even higher energy levels. Even a show Lab will retrieve anything with gusto.

Large Munsterlander

ORIGIN Germany
HEIGHT 58–65 cm (23–26 in)
WEIGHT 29.0–31.0 kg (64–68 lb)
EXERCISE LEVEL
COAT CARE
REGISTERED KC, FCI, AKCs
COLOURS Black and white

At home this is the Grosser Münsterländer, but it loses its accent abroad, and this spaniel-type German pointer has been quite a successful export. Although it is seen in modest numbers in show halls, it is appreciated as a versatile breed by hunters.

BREED ORIGINS
Ultimately these dogs are descended from medieval white or bi-coloured bird dogs, but the modern breed dates back to the 19th century breeding that produced the German Shorthaired, Wirehaired, and Longhaired Pointers. The last type of these is very rarely seen, but is the parent of this dog. Unwanted black-and-white puppies turned up in Longhaired Pointer litters, and in the 1920s they became a separate breed in Münster, named to distinguish them from the Small Munsterlander.

BREED QUALITIES
Field trials show this breed to be slow-maturing but worth the wait, as it works close to the hunter and is very responsive to training. It has always lived in the home, and is a calm, gentle character, reliable with children and other dogs.

BREED LOOKS The long, dense coat of this breed allows it to move through dense cover without problems, and also provides good insulation. The head should be solid black, but the rest of the coat is flecked and patched.

Small Munsterlander

ORIGIN Germany
HEIGHT 50–56 cm (20–22 in)
WEIGHT 14.0–16.0 kg (31–35 lb)
EXERCISE LEVEL
COAT CARE
REGISTERED KC, FCI, AKCs
COLOURS Brown and white

Although both come from the province of Münster, where this is called the Kleiner Münsterländer, this breed is not directly related to the Large Munsterlander. The two spring from different origins and differ in colour and size – although in North America this 'small' breed is becoming quite large.

BREED ORIGINS

The exact origins of the Small Munsterlander are unclear. Relaxed hunting laws and many new hunters in the 19th century brought an explosion in German breeding of pointers and retrievers. Adaptable hunting dogs called Wachtelhunds or German Spaniels were recorded in Münster; the breeders involved in turning these dogs into a breed included heath poet Hermann Löns, the Baron of Bevervörde-Lohburg, and a teacher named Heitmann. Still primarily a hunting companion, these make lively, affectionate pets for active households.

OLD-FASHIONED LOOKS Bred since the 1920s to a standard written by Friedrich Jungklaus, this dog has traits that were once common in all European hunting dogs.

IN DEMAND This breed is rare beyond Germany. Only a handful of dogs have been registered so far in the United Kingdom, while in the United States, hunters snap up available dogs quickly.

Weimaraner

ORIGIN Germany

HEIGHT 58–71 cm (23–28 in)

WEIGHT 31.8–38.6 kg (70–85 lb)

EXERCISE LEVEL

COAT CARE

REGISTERED KC, FCI, AKCs

COLOURS Grey

The word Vorstehhund, meaning pointer, is now usually dropped from this breed's name, and it is much more of an all-purpose dog, also competent in tracking and retrieving. They are sometimes nicknamed Grey Ghosts.

BREED ORIGINS

Some claim the Weimaraner is an ancient breed, discernable in a 17th-century painting by Van Dyck, but at this time it was still more a leash-hound, used to track and bring down large game. Its history only becomes certain at the start of the 19th century, when it was popular in the Weimar court of Karl August, Grand Duke of Saxe-Weimar-Eisenach, an enthusiastic huntsman. By this time, hunting of boar and stags was in decline, and a pointer for use against small game was much more useful. The older hound was crossed with Hühnerhund or bird-dog types to create the oldest of the German pointing breeds.

BREED QUALITIES

The Weimaraner is popular as a companion in many countries; overbreeding has led to temperament problems such as aggression and separation anxiety in some lines. The best Weimaraners are active, intelligent, cheerful companions, but they can be reserved with strangers.

BREED LOOKS Besides the more common shorthair, there is a longhair with a smooth or slightly wavy coat.

SPLIT PERSONALITY The Grey Ghost nickname comes not only from the breed's colour but its silent, stealthy action when working. In contrast, the off-duty Weimaraner is full of bounce and enthusiasm.

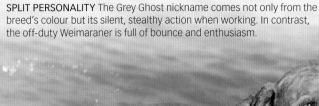

Belgian Shepherd Dog

ORIGIN Belgium

HEIGHT 56–66 cm (22–26 in)

WEIGHT 20.0–30.0 kg (44–66 lb)

EXERCISE LEVEL

COAT CARE

REGISTERED KC, FCI, AKCs

COLOURS Fawn with mask or traces of black overlay, black

Europe has four varieties of Chien de Berger Belge or Belgian Shepherd Dog: Groenendael, Malinois, Tervueren, and Lakenois. In North America, the first of these is called the Belgian Sheepdog.

 BLACK

 CREAM

 RED/TAN

 BLACK AND TAN

BREED ORIGINS

Across the world, herding dogs tend to have developed from local varieties without formal breeding, partly because they were the working dogs of the people, not high-status hunting dogs. At the end of the 19th century, breeders in Belgium set out to produce a small range of ideal types that could be recognized nationally: initial lists included as many as eight different types. In 1891 Professor Adolphe Reul of the Cureghem Veterinary Medical School organized a gathering of 117 representatives of the many diverse herding dogs from across the nation. The best were chosen, and the newly formed Belgian Shepherd Dog Club began some very close interbreeding involving a few stud dogs, working to a breed standard with three coat varieties, a fourth being recognized in 1897. However, the Lakenois remains unrecognized in the United States. The question of coat colours and types has remained a cause of lively debate, but the type has always been fairly settled.

MALINOIS This variety has short hair over most of its body, very short on the head and lower legs. There is more fullness around the neck and on the back of the thighs and the tail. It is fawn overlaid with black.

LAKENOIS This variety has a rough, dry, tousled coat, never long enough for the tail to look like a plume. It is fawn, overlaid on the muzzle and the tail with traces of black.

BREED QUALITIES

All of the Belgian Shepherd types are trainable, reliable characters, making good guard dogs as long as they are not left alone too much. They are often used in police work, with the Tervueren also employed as a sniffer dog. Surprisingly well suited to apartment living, they are relatively inactive indoors, but this does not mean outdoor pursuits can be skimped; the Tervueren is perhaps the most active, but all working dogs thrive on interesting exercise.

Of the four, the Groenendael is the most popular, followed by the Tervueren. These two have a reputation for being slightly snappy, perhaps due to breeding for use in security work, and are less suitable as family pets than the others. The lighter, short haired Malinois is less often seen, and the curly-coated Lakenois is quite rare. All are fairly healthy, although skin allergies, eye problems, and dysplasia are seen.

TERVUEREN Sporting a rich fawn coat overlaid with black, this type and the Malinois have a dark mask. Six areas must be black: the two ears, the two upper eyelids, and the two lips.

GROENENDAEL This type is a uniform shade of black. It has a long, smooth coat over the body, forming a ruff at the throat and a 'jabot' or apron over the chest.

Bearded Collie

ORIGIN United Kingdom
HEIGHT 50–56 cm (20–22 in)
WEIGHT 18.0–30.0 kg (40–66 lb)
EXERCISE LEVEL
COAT CARE
REGISTERED KC, FCI, AKCs
COLOURS Grey, black, fawn, brown, either solid or with white

A long coat and gentle expression give the impression that this breed is a big softie, and it does have a gentle, reliable personality. But beneath the coat is a lean body packed with spirit and energy.

 BLACK
 CREAM
 GREY
 DARK BROWN
 BLACK AND WHITE

BREED ORIGINS

According to the breed legends, a Polish sea captain traded three of his Polish Sheepdogs to a Scottish shepherd for a valuable ram and ewe in the early 16th century. When these dogs interbred with the local herding stock, the Bearded Collie breed was born. There may have been two sizes of the breed originally: a smaller, lighter one for gathering and herding in the highlands, and a heavier type for droving in the lowlands. They were used for centuries, variously called Highland Sheepdog, Highland Collie, and Hairy Moved Collie. The breed was described in the late 19th-century book *Dogs of Scotland* as 'a big, rough, "tousy" looking tyke, with a coat not unlike a doormat'. They may have been involved in the creation of the Old English Sheepdog.

Although shown at the turn of the 20th century, the breed then all but vanished. After World War II a Mrs Willison started its revival, and by the 1960s it was once again recognized and even exported to the United States, although it is still not common.

BREED QUALITIES

That long, high-maintenance coat is no fashion accessory; the weatherproof outer layer covers an insulating undercoat. The owner of a Beardie must be willing to go out in all weathers, because nothing will dissuade this dog. It is renowned for its 'bounce' and apparently boundless energy, and it needs access to an outdoor space.

The breed is also famed for its cheerful, enthusiastic, humorous personality, and a tail said to never stop wagging. It thrives on human company, pines without it, and makes an excellent family dog; despite its loud bark, it is not a good watchdog. Intelligent and sometimes headstrong, it benefits enormously from training, and enjoys tracking, competitive obedience or agility trials, or simply performing tricks. Although prone to hip dysplasia, this is a generally healthy breed that lives to about 12 years.

WELL HIDDEN Although set high, the ears are pendent and lie very close to the head, giving such a smooth line that they cannot be discerned at all on a well-groomed dog.

Border Collie

ORIGIN United Kingdom
HEIGHT 46–54 cm (18–21 in)
WEIGHT 14.0–22.0 kg (31–49 lb)
EXERCISE LEVEL
COAT CARE
REGISTERED KC, FCI, AKCs
COLOURS Any solid or mixed colours, white never predominating

This intensely intelligent and boundlessly energetic breed can be hugely rewarding to own. With an active, attentive owner, it is a superb dog; with an inactive or absent owner, it is a problem.

 BLACK
 CREAM
 GREY
BLUE

BREED ORIGINS

Developed in the border country of England and Scotland as a working sheepdog, today this remains the most popular herding breed. Although the breed was known since the 18th century, it was only recognized by its present name in 1915.

Centuries of breeding for ability rather than looks have created a supremely intelligent, fast, and responsive dog of great stamina. This is the ultimate breed for anyone who wants to compete in agility trials, or for an active family with older children who enjoy daily games with a canine companion. It is a perfectionist and will do almost anything for praise, so is highly trainable. The only difficulty is likely to be feeding its voracious appetite for activity, so couch-potatoes need not apply. If left alone for long stretches of the working day, Border Collies will become bored,

miserable, and destructive, and the negligent owner may find that they are snappily herded around their own home.

COLLIE LOOKS Although any colour is allowed, and there is a smooth-haired variety, the Border Collie is most often seen as a classic black-and-white dog with a long, insulating coat – although this is shorter in puppies.

Dog trials

Border Collies can perform outstandingly in this alternative to the 'beauty contest' dog show. There are classes devoted to tunnels, gates, jumps, and slaloms, as well as obedience classes, and herding trials for working lines. To a Collie, this is not a chore, but what it lives for. Anyone considering a Border Collie should visit a dog trial and ask themselves honestly if they could keep up.

German Shepherd Dog

ORIGIN Germany

HEIGHT 55–65 cm (22–26 in)

WEIGHT 22.0–40.0 kg (49–88 lb)

EXERCISE LEVEL

COAT CARE

REGISTERED KC, FCI, AKCs

COLOURS Black, grey, black with reddish-brown, brown; yellow to light grey markings

The Deutscher Schäferhund, also once called Alsatian, has served in wars, achieved Hollywood fame, and spawned two offshoot breeds, the Shiloh Shepherd and the White Swiss Shepherd Dog.

 BLACK

 GREY

 DARK BROWN

 BLACK AND TAN

CHANGING LOOKS Breed standards have shifted over the decades, emphasizing smaller dogs with shorter, darker coats.

Security work

The German Shepherd was used as a military dog in World War I, and taken home by soldiers returning to the United Kingdom and United States. Since then it has proved itself unparalleled in intelligence and trainability, and 'police dog' became a synonym for the breed.

BREED ORIGINS

The 'wolf-like dog of the country around the Rhine' was noted by Roman historian Tacitus nearly 2,000 years ago, but the German Shepherd is usually dated to the 1890s and credited largely to Max von Stephanitz. He owned Horand von Grafrath, the founding male, reputed to have a recent wolf cross in his parentage. Thuringian dogs gave the upright ears and wolf-like appearance, while Württemburger dogs were used for their temperament and speed.

BREED QUALITIES

Today, North American dogs have a very sloping stance, quite distinct from the more level European lines. Dogs from the old East Germany are said to resemble the original most closely, and working dogs are largely drawn from east European lines. Hip and digestive disorders remain a problem despite the best efforts of good breeders, and while some individuals make excellent family dogs, caution is advisable.

EVER READY The large pricked ears and clean-cut, tapering head mean that even at rest these dogs look alert and primed to spring into action.

Old English Sheepdog

ORIGIN United Kingdom

HEIGHT 56–60 cm (22–24 in)

WEIGHT 29.5–30.0 kg (65–66 lb)

EXERCISE LEVEL

COAT CARE

REGISTERED KC, FCI, AKCs

COLOURS Grey, blue, with limited white markings

Famous in much of the world as the 'Dulux dog', this profusely shaggy breed has a personality to match its cuddly looks. This is a loyal and adaptable companion.

GREY

BLUE

BREED ORIGINS

First bred selectively in the 19th century, mostly in southwestern England, the Old English may be descended from continental breeds such as the Briard, or even the Polish Lowland Sheepdog. Usually docked, it was also called the Bobtail. It was originally an aggressive and snappish character, but careful breeding has rendered it a biddable family dog, although it still makes a good guard.

SHAGGY DOG Square and thick-set, this is a sturdy breed with a rolling gait. A monthly clipping helps to keep it tidy.

Puli

ORIGIN Hungary

HEIGHT 36–45 cm (14–18 in)

WEIGHT 10.0–15.0 kg (22–33 lb)

EXERCISE LEVEL

COAT CARE

REGISTERED KC, FCI, AKCs

COLOURS Black, black with rust or grey shadings, fawn with black mask, white

This lively and intelligent little dog, originally a herder, is the best-known of the Hungarian breeds. Aided by its eye-catching coat, it has successfully made the shift to family companion.

BLACK   CREAM   GOLD

BREED ORIGINS

This breed's ancestors were probably large stock-guarding dogs that came to Hungary with the Magyars around 1,000 years ago. Black dogs were preferred, probably because they are easy to spot among sheep. The smaller Puli emerged as an agile herder, while the larger Komondor was used for guarding. Today the Puli makes an adaptable companion and guard dog, and does well in obedience trials.

CORDED COAT
Once it is worked into pencil-thick cords, the coat needs no daily grooming but it does require regular bathing and drying. The Puli is remarkably adaptable to a wide range of climates, and enjoys swimming – it is also known as the Hungarian Water Dog.

Rough Collie

ORIGIN United Kingdom
HEIGHT 50–60 cm (20–24 in)
WEIGHT 18.0–30.0 kg (40–66 lb)
EXERCISE LEVEL
COAT CARE
REGISTERED KC, FCI, AKCs
COLOURS Sable, sable and white, blue merle, tri-colour

One of the world's most popular breeds, this looks too elegant for herding work, although it retains its original abilities. First made fashionable at home by Queen Victoria, in the 20th century it became familiar to a wider audience as 'Lassie'.

BLUE

BLACK, WHITE AND TAN

BREED ORIGINS

For centuries, this was an obscure Scottish herding dog, producing both long- and occasional shorthaired dogs. It was somewhat smaller than it is today, with a less luxuriant coat and shorter nose. Then it was crossed with Borzois, giving a taller, leaner build and an aristocratic face, and has been at home in the show ring ever since.

BREED QUALITIES

Intelligent enough to work as a rescue and guide dog, this amiable breed makes a good family dog, but occasional snappish individuals do occur. Its popularity makes it essential to buy a pup screened for eye defects and hip problems from a reputable breeder.

COLLIE COAT This is an active breed that needs plenty of free running, but the spectacular coat is the greatest commitment. Daily grooming is needed, with more thorough attention weekly. In Europe the Rough and Smooth Collies are recognized as separate breeds; in North America one breed with two coat lengths is recognized.

Welsh Corgis

ORIGIN United Kingdom

HEIGHT 25–32 cm (10–13 in)

WEIGHT 9.0–12.0 kg (20–26 lb)

EXERCISE LEVEL

COAT CARE

REGISTERED KC, FCI

COLOURS Red, sable, fawn, black and tan, white allowed (Pembroke); all colours (Cardigan)

Although the Pembroke and the Cardigan Corgi remain distinct breeds with their own standards, they are very similar, a result of crossbreeding between them until the 20th century.

 BLACK

 RED/TAN

 BLACK AND WHITE

 BLACK, WHITE, AND TAN

 BLACK BRINDLE

BREED ORIGINS

Romantics claim that Corgis arrived with the Celts over 2,000 years ago. Others believe they are descended from Swedish Vallhund stock arriving with the Vikings a little over 1,000 years ago, although it may be that the Vallhund is descended from Welsh dogs. The name corgi is recorded in *A Dictionary in Englyshe and Welshe* published in 1574, as 'Korgi ne gostoc, Corgi or curre dogge', meaning working or guarding dog.

This was primarily a cattle-droving breed or 'heeler', left unemployed by transportation developments in the 20th century. Only when the future Queen Elizabeth acquired her first Corgis did the breed come back to popularity, this time as a companion breed.

BREED QUALITIES

Heelers had to be bold enough to run behind the feet of the cattle and nip their heels, low and robust enough to roll away from the resulting kicks, and determined enough to go back for more. These qualities make them lively companions, but too stubborn and snappish to be good family dogs.

CARDIGAN CORGI The ears of the Cardigan type are large and the nose less pointed than that of the Pembroke, although never blunt. The coat is hard and short or medium in length.

PEMBROKE CORGI Sturdily built but smaller than the Cardigan type, the Pembroke has a foxy, pointed face and a medium length coat. Pembroke Corgis often have naturally short tails; those with long tails were traditionally docked.

Akita

ORIGIN Japan

HEIGHT 60–70 cm (24–28 in)

WEIGHT 34.0–50.0 kg (75–110 lb)

EXERCISE LEVEL

COAT CARE

REGISTERED KC, FCI, AKCs

COLOURS White, white and red, fawn, or brindle; any colour (United States)

The largest of the Japanese breeds, this originates in Akita prefecture on the island of Honshu. It has developed along quite different lines in Japan and Europe and in the United States.

GOLD AND WHITE

TAN AND WHITE

BLACK BRINDLE

BREED ORIGINS

Used for hunting and fighting in the 19th century, after World War II, the Akita was low in numbers and included German Shepherd crosses. In Japan, breeders worked to restore the old breed, but hybrid dogs were taken home by American soldiers. The breed is now a Natural Monument in its homeland. All Akitas are staunch, fearless fighters that need experienced owners.

DIFFERENCES The American Akita is larger than the lines from Japan and Europe, and is allowed in a wider range of colours. The two types are not mutually recognized.

Alaskan Malamute

ORIGIN United States

HEIGHT 58–65 cm (23–26 in)

WEIGHT 34.0–39.0 kg (75–86 lb)

EXERCISE LEVEL

COAT CARE

REGISTERED KC, FCI, AKCs

COLOURS White with shades of grey or red

This was the preferred sled dog of North America for thousands of years. Its name comes from the Mahlemuts, the Alaskan tribe that kept it. Packs have been used in many polar expeditions.

BLACK AND WHITE

TAN AND WHITE

BREED ORIGINS

Recent genetic research confirmed that this is one of the world's oldest dog breeds. It is an intelligent and tireless pack dog. Loyal, affectionate, and gentle, Malamutes need plenty of work if they are not to become bored and destructive.

PRACTICAL STANDARDS Malamutes' sizes can vary widely, but the breed standards are healthy sizes ideal for pulling work in a matched team.

American Eskimo (Standard)

ORIGIN United States
HEIGHT Over 38 cm (15 in)
WEIGHT 9.1–16.0 kg (20–35 lb)
EXERCISE LEVEL
COAT CARE
REGISTERED AKCs
COLOURS White

Not to be confused with the larger white Canadian Eskimo Dog recognized in the United Kingdom, this spirited spitz comes in Standard, Miniature, and Toy sizes, packing all the punch of a typical sled-puller in a compact parcel.

BREED ORIGINS

Despite its name, this breed is not actually descended from Eskimo or Inuit dogs, but white spitz dogs brought by European settlers and descended from the German Spitz; anti-German feelings during World War I led to a swift change of identity. Despite its diminutive appearance, this dog has earned its keep: it won popularity performing in the Barnum and Bailey Circus, and

does well in obedience and agility classes. It makes a noisy watchdog, and may not be appreciated by close neighbours. Some individuals are shy or overly aggressive, but in general this is a good family dog.

SNOW DOG This is a healthy and long-lived little dog that lasts into its teens. The thick double coat is fairly easy to groom, but there is a tendency to brown tear staining on the face.

Australian Kelpie

ORIGIN Australia
HEIGHT 43–51 cm (17–20 in)
WEIGHT 11.0–20.0 kg (24–44 lb)
EXERCISE LEVEL
COAT CARE
REGISTERED FCI, AKCs
COLOURS Black, blue, red, fawn, chocolate, black and tan, red, red and tan

Australia's most popular working dog, this breed is known and shown around the world. In the United Kingdom it is only eligible for trials, but it excels in these, showing its collie heritage.

 BLACK   BLUE    RED/TAN   DARK BROWN   BLACK AND TAN

BREED ORIGINS

There have always been tales that the Kelpie contains dingo blood, and dingo crosses might have been made but not admitted; however, the breed's remarkable trainability makes this claim dubious. Collies from northern England provided much of its stock, with a black-and-tan bitch named Kelpie giving fresh genes and the breed name. Kelpies are tenacious, intelligent, and enthusiastic workers,

described as workaholics. They might be regarded as Australia's Border Collie, and need a similar level of commitment to an active and interesting life if they are not to be bored, snappy, and destructive.

BEAUTY OR BRAINS? Today the Kelpie is split into working and show lines. Those who breed working Kelpies for their abilities have less regard for looks.

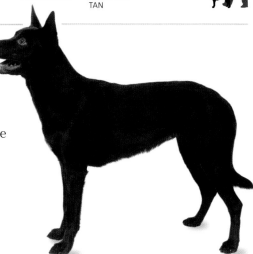

Bernese Mountain Dog

ORIGIN Switzerland
HEIGHT 58–70 cm (23–28 in)
WEIGHT 40.0–45.0 kg (88–100 lb)
EXERCISE LEVEL
COAT CARE
REGISTERED KC, FCI, AKCs
COLOURS Tri-colour

The Berner Sennenhund is the largest of the four tri-coloured Swiss mountain or cattle dogs, and the only one with a long coat. Historically used for herding and pulling carts, it is now a well-established companion breed.

BREED ORIGINS

The origins of these breeds are ancient, and Roman mastiffs are among the likely ancestors. The number of foreign dogs brought into Switzerland in the 19th century threatened the native breeds' survival: together with the Appenzell, Entelbuch, and Great

Swiss, this breed was saved by the efforts of breeders led by Professor Albert Heim. It is a powerful but affectionate and reliable breed. Sadly, many die young through cancer; the average lifespan has fallen in recent years to somewhere around seven years.

BIG AND BOLD Despite its size and sturdy build, the Bernese has historically been a surprisingly agile breed.

Boxer

ORIGIN Germany
HEIGHT 53–63 cm (21–25 in)
WEIGHT 24.0–32.0 kg (53–70 lb)
EXERCISE LEVEL
COAT CARE
REGISTERED KC, FCI, AKCs
COLOURS Shades of fawn, brindle; solid or with white

More accurately known as the Deutscher Boxer, this breed is often seen with cropped ears in the United States. The natural look shows its playful, intelligent – if stubborn – nature far better.

RED/TAN GOLD BLACK BRINDLE

BREED ORIGINS

The Brabant Bullenbeisser and similar hunting breeds are the immediate ancestors of the Boxer; their task was to seize large game and hold onto it until the huntsmen arrived, hence the broad, shortened muzzle. Bred by huntsmen for their working qualities, they were variable in type. In the late 19th century, breeders created this physically consistent type for showing. Highly trainable and popular for military and police work, they are nonetheless clowns at heart, and make good family dogs.

TALL TAILS The Boxer was traditionally docked, but this has now changed in Europe. It was feared that the tail would prove variable, but the standard for a high but not curled-over tail has now been set.

British Bulldog

ORIGIN United Kingdom
HEIGHT 30–36 cm (12–14 in)
WEIGHT 23.0–25.0 kg (51–55 lb)
EXERCISE LEVEL
COAT CARE
REGISTERED KC, FCI, AKCs
COLOURS Solid fawn, red, brindle, or with a black mask or white

Recognized by registries simply as the Bulldog, this iconic breed is as British as the John Bull character that it so often accompanied in patriotic cartoons.

TAN AND WHITE

BLACK BRINDLE

BREED ORIGINS

The name 'bulldog' has been in use since the 17th century, but the term originally described crosses of bear-baiting mastiffs and tenacious terriers. Bred to hang on to a bull for all they were worth in a fight, they had the short, broad jaw also seen in German Bullenbeissers that performed the same role in the hunt. But these early dogs were lighter, more athletic examples than the breed we have today, with a true fighting dog temperament.

When bull-baiting was banned in the 19th century, those who rescued the breed from oblivion created a new type of dog, not only much heavier set, but utterly reformed in character.

BREED QUALITIES

Today's Bulldog is almost without exception tolerant and gentle. It might be said that it simply had no energy for aggression: breathing disorders and heart trouble plagued the breed. Of late, responsible breeders have begun to reject the extreme looks that exacerbated these conditions, and Bulldogs can now look forward to healthier and longer lives. Their characters are more lively, but still as sweet.

GOING TO EXTREMES The large heads of Bulldogs mean the breed has a high incidence of caesarian births, while the deep folds on the face need scrupulous care to keep skin problems at bay. But for their fans, there is nothing to beat the Bulldog breed.

Cane Corso Italiano

ORIGIN Italy

HEIGHT 60–68 cm (24–27 in)

WEIGHT 40.0–50.0 kg (88–110 lb)

EXERCISE LEVEL

COAT CARE

REGISTERED FCI, AKCs

COLOURS Black, shades of grey or fawn, brindle

Also used for herding and hunting, this breed is primarily a guard. Its name translates approximately as Italian guard dog; it is also called the Cane di Macellaio, Sicilian Branchiero, and Italian Mastiff.

BLACK

GREY

GOLD

BLACK BRINDLE

BREED ORIGINS

The ultimate ancestor of the Corso is the Roman mastiff. The lighter examples of this type were used not only as military attack dogs, but in large game hunting. A natural continuation, the Corso has been kept throughout Italian history and across the country, although in most recent times, the highest numbers have been found in southern Italy. A quiet, intelligent breed that is loyal and protective of its home and family, the Corso needs sound training to ensure that it is not overly suspicious around strangers.

ROBUST BUILD Traditionally docked and often seen with cropped ears, the breed now sports a more natural look in Europe. It does suffer the same health concerns as other large breeds, particularly with regard to joints.

Chow Chow

ORIGIN China
HEIGHT 45–56 cm (18–22 in)
WEIGHT 20.0–32.0 kg (44–70 lb)
EXERCISE LEVEL
COAT CARE
REGISTERED KC, FCI, AKCs
COLOURS White, cream, fawn, red, blue, black

Whether smooth or rough coated, the Chow Chow looks like no other breed. It is one of the most ancient of all breeds, and has a varied history covering every role from working dog to dinner.

 BLACK
 CREAM
 RED/TAN

BREED ORIGINS

Genetic research confirms the Chow as an ancient type. In Asia it was used for hunting, sled-pulling, herding, and guarding, while its fur was valued and its flesh was eaten. It came to the West from China in the 19th century. This breed is still more than capable of fulfilling its historic guarding role, although it has not found favour as a herding or hunting dog in the West. Although breeders have been working to produce a Chow with more of a laid-back, family-dog nature, it remains for the most part an independent, stubborn, and slightly suspicious character. Early socialization and a strong owner are vital with this breed.

CONSTANT CARE The Chow is prone to a range of joint problems. The coat is also a serious commitment, as it sheds heavily.

Dalmatian

ORIGIN Croatia or India
HEIGHT 54–61 cm (21–24 in)
WEIGHT 25.0–30.0 kg (55–66 lb)
EXERCISE LEVEL
COAT CARE
REGISTERED KC, FCI, AKCs
COLOURS White with black or liver spots

Instantly recognizable, famous for one hundred and one reasons, the Dalmatian or Dalmatinac has in its time been a hunting dog, a herder, a ratter, and a carriage dog.

BREED ORIGINS

Dogs like this have been known in Dalmatia, now Croatia, for 4,000 years. But the Bengal Pointer, a similar dog from India, was known in the United Kingdom in 1700: which is the ancestor of the breed we know today is not certain. Deafness and urinary stones are health issues, and males especially can be aggressive – early training is vital, as well as a long daily run.

LOOK DEEPER The smart coat and fame of the breed attract many owners, but some are just not prepared for the time and energy demanded, particularly by a young dog.

Dobermann

ORIGIN Germany

HEIGHT 60–70 cm (24–28 in)

WEIGHT 30.0–40.0 kg (66–88 lb)

EXERCISE LEVEL

COAT CARE

REGISTERED KC, FCI, AKCs

COLOURS Black, brown, blue, or fawn, with tan

More often called the Doberman Pinscher in North America, this breed bears the name of its original creator. It has been tremendously popular as a guarding breed and won notoriety as much as fame, not all of it deserved.

BREED ORIGINS

German tax-collector Louis Dobermann created this dog in the 19th century as a bodyguard. He may have used the best of the dogs that came through his care as a part-time dog catcher, including some of the breeds used to create the German Shepherd; the Dobermann has also been used in police and security work.

A macho image and unscrupulous over-breeding have caused problems.

Some lines became aggressive or prone to fear-biting, so check the breeder's history. Although this is not suitable as a family dog, it should not be left entirely alone as a guard dog either: it needs plenty of interaction from an experienced owner. Health problems include cervical spondylitis, Von Willebrand's disease, bloat, hip dysplasia, and congenital heart disorders, so a veterinary check is essential before buying.

DOBERMANN STYLES Weimaraners, Manchester Terriers, Rottweilers, and German Pinschers may have influenced Dobermann looks. European dogs are now seen in their natural state, with long tails and soft ears, while American dogs are still usually docked and have ears cropped to points.

Giant Schnauzer

ORIGIN Germany
HEIGHT 60–70 cm (24–28 in)
WEIGHT 32.0–35.0 kg (70–77 lb)
EXERCISE LEVEL
COAT CARE
REGISTERED KC, FCI, AKCs
COLOURS Black, salt and pepper

Known as the Riesenschnauzer in Germany, this breed makes a set with the smaller Schnauzer and Miniature or Zwergschnauzer. A powerful breed with a dominant tendency, it is said by its devotees to be worth taking time and trouble over.

BREED ORIGINS

This was originally a herding dog, and common on farms across southern Germany as far back as the Middle Ages, although when it was first shown it was under the name Russian Bear Schnauzer. The costs of feeding such a large breed meant it eventually gave way to smaller breeds, but it enjoyed a revival of popularity in the late 19th century working to control livestock as a butcher's dog. This breed is too territorial and dominant to be recommended as a family companion, and can be spectacularly destructive if neglected or bored. Given an active, involved, and experienced owner, a Schnauzer can excel as a guard or sporting dog. Giants are prone to cancer, bloat, epilepsy, and hip dysplasia.

BORN TO BE BOSS With its stocky build and its strongly boned face, the Schnauzer is designed to inspire respect.

Great Dane

ORIGIN Germany
HEIGHT 79–92 cm (31–36 in)
WEIGHT 50.0–80.0 kg (110–176 lb)
EXERCISE LEVEL
COAT CARE
REGISTERED KC, FCI, AKCs
COLOURS Fawn, brindle, blue, black, white with black or blue

German Mastiff is a better translation of this breed's other name, Deutsche Dogge: this breed has nothing to do with Denmark. Once a hunting dog, war dog, and guard, it is now mostly a companion.

BLACK   BLUE   BLACK BRINDLE

BREED ORIGINS

The origins of this breed are obscure; it is probably descended from Alaunts, mastiffs brought to Europe by the Alans in the 5th century. A match for wild boar, bears, and wolves, these were crossed with Greyhounds to create more powerful but agile dogs called 'Dogge' in Germany. The Deutsche Dogge was born out of an amalgamation of the various types in the late 19th century.

BREED QUALITIES

Today's breed is a gentle giant, relaxed around children and other dogs, quiet and relatively inactive indoors, which is fortunate given its size: a cluttered home is not recommended. Although adults are relaxed and dignified dogs, the energy and ungainliness of young Great Danes is legendary. This breed is also renowned as a champion drooler.

SIZE MATTERS The giant is particularly prone to joint problems and tail injuries.

Labradoodle

ORIGIN Australia
HEIGHT 33–65 cm (13–26 in)
WEIGHT 10.0–40.0 kg (22–88 lb)
EXERCISE LEVEL
COAT CARE
REGISTERED None
COLOURS Wide range of solid colours

This is the standard-bearer for today's fashionable crossbreeds. In Australia, the Labradoodle has a breed standard with three sizes and is on the way to being regarded as a 'purebred'.

 BLACK CREAM BLUE GOLD DARK BROWN

BREED ORIGINS

In the 1990s, breeder Wally Conron began crossing Labradors and Poodles, aiming to create a non-shedding guide dog suitable for allergy sufferers. This is a work in progress, but Australian breeders hope to achieve a reliable coat while retaining a broad gene pool and an intelligent, biddable nature from the parent breeds. Elsewhere, Labradoodles are often first-generation crosses and highly variable.

CRUCIAL COAT The non-shedding coat is not fixed in early generation Labradoodles. To meet the breed standard in Australia the coat must be single.

Leonberger

ORIGIN Germany
HEIGHT 65–80 cm (26–32 in)
WEIGHT 45.0–75.0 kg (100–165 lb)
EXERCISE LEVEL
COAT CARE
REGISTERED KC, FCI, AKCs
COLOURS Cream to red with a dark mask

This dog takes its name from the town of Leonberg in Baden-Württemburg, where it was created as a hybrid from established breeds. Despite outrage from other breeders, skilled marketing by its creator saw the Leonberger become a status symbol.

BREED ORIGINS

In the early 19th century, a local politician Heinrich Essig created this majestic breed from a Newfoundland and a St Bernard. Its strength, calmness, loyalty, and obedience ensured its eventual acceptance. Reduced in numbers by two world wars, it is a much-loved family dog today, although it is sadly short-lived; cancer is a common cause of death, as in some other giant breeds.

LEONINE LOOKS The Leonberger is said to have been inspired by the town's heraldic emblem, the lion, but early dogs were black and white since they were bred from a Landseer-type Newfoundland.

Neapolitan Mastiff

ORIGIN Italy
HEIGHT 60–75 cm (24–30 in)
WEIGHT 50.0–75.0 kg (110–165 lb)
EXERCISE LEVEL
COAT CARE
REGISTERED KC, FCI, AKCs
COLOURS Solid black, blue, grey, solid or brindled fawn to red

The ancestor of many mastiff breeds, the Mastino Napoletano is distinguished by its loose, drooping skin, a relic from its distant past as a fighting dog.

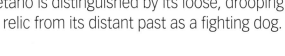

BLACK   GREY   BLUE   RED/TAN   BLACK BRINDLE

BREED ORIGINS

This is probably the most direct descendant of the great Roman Mastiff, described in the first century by Columella as a perfect house guard. On the verge of extinction after World War II, it was saved through the efforts of Dr Pierro Scanziani and Mario Querci. Instinctively protective and dominant, it makes a good guard if given early and thorough obedience training and socialization.

INNER BEAUTY
Messy eaters and champion droolers, these are not for the houseproud. Cropped ears and docked tails have given way to natural looks in Europe.

Newfoundland

ORIGIN Canada
HEIGHT 66–71 cm (26–28 in)
WEIGHT 50.0–69.0 kg (110–152 lb)
EXERCISE LEVEL
COAT CARE
REGISTERED KC, FCI, AKCs
COLOURS Black, brown, white with black

The ancient Molossus of the eastern Mediterranean gave us all the mastiff breeds we have today. They range from fighting dogs, through guardian breeds, to the gentle giant that is the Newfie.

DARK BROWN   BLACK AND WHITE

BREED ORIGINS

The Newfoundland's origins are uncertain enough to attract romantic legends. Nomadic Indian dogs, Viking bear dogs, and the Labrador are all cited as ancestors, as are crosses in the 18th century between local dogs and mastiffs owned by passing fishermen. Whatever its roots, the Newfie was invaluable to fishermen, pulling boats, carrying fishing lines to shore, and retrieving anything – or anyone – that fell overboard. Today, transport and communications improvements have left the breed without an obvious working role, but it has easily made the transition to much-loved family companion.

ABLE BODIED Many people have owed their lives to the Newfies' water rescue skills. Their weight-pulling abilites also saw them haul supplies through blizzards during World War II.

Poodle (Standard)

ORIGIN Germany
HEIGHT 38–60 cm (15–24 in)
WEIGHT 20.5–32.0 kg (45–70 lb)
EXERCISE LEVEL
COAT CARE
REGISTERED KC, FCI, AKCs
COLOURS Any solid colour

This breed's origins are acknowledged in its name, from the old German word *pudeln*, 'to splash'; it is called the Caniche, or duck dog, in France. This practical retriever can be a smart companion.

 BLACK
 CREAM
 BLUE
 GOLD
 DARK BROWN

BREED ORIGINS

This breed can be traced back at least to the Middle Ages, and probably arose in Germany, eastern Europe, or even Asia. It is officially recognized as French, however, and in France it developed into the modern sizes of Standard and the smaller Miniature and Toy types. It worked in French circuses, its intelligence and trainability making it hugely popular, and as a truffle hound. This is a healthy, able, adaptable breed, and certainly no fluffy toy.

CONTINENTAL AND LION CLIPS Although these look ornamental, their original purpose was to reduce the resistance of the coat in the water but leave the chest and the leg joints insulated.

SHORT CLIPS All-over clips are now allowed for showing. This simpler look is far easier for most owners to maintain, and allows the breed a little more of its natural dignity in everyday life.

STANDARDS FOR STANDARDS The allowed sizes for the different Poodle classes vary between registries, with FCI starting at a threshhold 8 cm (3 in) taller than others.

Pyrenean Mastiff

ORIGIN Spain
HEIGHT 72–80 cm (28–32 in)
WEIGHT 55.0–75.0 kg (121–165 lb)
EXERCISE LEVEL
COAT CARE
REGISTERED FCI
COLOURS White with grey, golden yellow, brown, black, silver, beige, sand, or marbled

A herd- and farm-guarding breed, the Mastin del Pireneo, sometimes called the Mastin d'Aragon, could take on bears and wolves. This robust, trainable breed makes a good guard for rural households.

GOLD AND WHITE

BLACK AND WHITE

TAN AND WHITE

BREED ORIGINS

Phoenician traders probably brought the first mastiffs to Spain from Asia thousands of years ago. This dog developed in the southeastern Pyrenees, and guarded both flocks and the home. A large breed with a deep voice, a strong protective instinct, and inherent reluctance to back down, it is not ideal for urban life. Sometimes aggressive towards other dogs, it controls its power.

UNDEREXPOSED BREED This is a solid, imposing dog, but never gives the impression of being overly heavy or slow. It is one of the rarer mastiff breeds, perhaps overshadowed by – or confused with – the Pyrenean Mountain Dog.

Pyrenean Mountain Dog

ORIGIN France
HEIGHT 65–80 cm (26–32 in)
WEIGHT 55.0–75.0 kg (121–165 lb)
EXERCISE LEVEL
COAT CARE
REGISTERED KC, FCI, AKCs
COLOURS White, white with very limited grey, pale yellow, or orange patches

Originating on the French side of the Pyrenees, this dauntless, intelligent breed is called the Chien de Montagne des Pyrénées in France and is also known as the Great Pyrenees in some registries.

GOLD AND WHITE

BIG AND BOLD The sheer size and weight of this breed make it unsuitable for city living. Like other large breeds, it is susceptible to joint problems, and it can develop skin problems in the heat.

BREED ORIGINS

Probably descended from ancient Asian mastiffs, this dog is recorded as a herd- and home-guarding breed by the Middle Ages, and was found at the French royal court in the 17th century. Nearly extinct in the early 20th century, it is now established across Europe and North America. Early examples were markedly wary, but breeding for companionship has mellowed its character.

Rhodesian Ridgeback

ORIGIN South Africa
HEIGHT 60–69 cm (24–27 in)
WEIGHT 32.0–36.0 kg (70–80 lb)
EXERCISE LEVEL
COAT CARE
REGISTERED KC, FCI, AKCs
COLOURS Light wheaten to red wheaten

The only registered breed indigenous to southern Africa, the Rhodesian is characterized by the stripe of hair that grows forward along its spine, which also gives the breed its name. It was believed unique in this trait until the discovery of the Thai Ridgeback.

BREED ORIGINS

Dogs with this characteristic ridge of hair, kept for hunting by the Hottentots, interbred with settlers' hounds and mastiffs in the 19th century. The resulting breed was used in pairs or trios to find lions for hunters, and an old name for the Ridgeback is the African Lion Hound. With changing attitudes to wildlife, the breed has moved into the home, and it makes a loyal guard dog or companion. It is a dignified breed that can be aloof with strangers, and it prefers to have its owners to itself, rather than sharing them with disruptive children or other dogs.

KEPT IN TRIM The first standard for the Ridgeback, written in the 1920s, was based on that of the Dalmatian. It placed the emphasis on agility and elegance, producing a breed of great endurance and speed.

Rottweiler

ORIGIN Germany
HEIGHT 58–69 cm (23–27 in)
WEIGHT 41.0–50.0 kg (90–110 lb)
EXERCISE LEVEL
COAT CARE
REGISTERED KC, FCI, AKCs
COLOURS Black and tan

Originally a cattle dog and hauler of carts, later a guard, military dog and police dog, the Rottweiler was never, as is sometimes asserted, a fighting dog. This belief is just part of the sometimes unfavourable, often unfair reputation this breed has gathered.

Dangerous dogs?

Rottweilers are intelligent and highly trainable, and a well-socialized Rottie in the hands of an experienced and sensible owner is a fine dog. However, there is no denying that they are protective, assertive, and can show a temper.

BREED ORIGINS

The Rottweiler's earliest ancestors were probably Roman mastiffs; an ancient military route ran through the town of Rottweil in southern Germany. They were popular on farms, and were also known as 'Rottweil butchers' dogs' because of their usefulness in controlling animals at slaughter, pulling carts, and guard duties. Numbers declined greatly in the 19th century, but they were saved by proving their efficiency

CATCH THEM YOUNG How a breed like a Rottweiler is brought up has a great effect on its behaviour. Puppies that are constantly exposed to human play, children, and other animals are very different from guard dogs kept outside.

when tested for their potential as police dogs. Now they are recognized as guards around the world, but seen with less favour as companions. Their size and weight alone make them a better choice as a guard than as a family dog around small children.

BIG AND BRAVE Powerful and impressive in build, the Rottweiler unfortunately suffers the dysplasia problems almost inevitable in larger breeds. The tail was customarily docked in the past, but is now left natural in Europe.

St Bernard

ORIGIN Switzerland

HEIGHT 65–90 cm (26–36 in)

WEIGHT 45.0–136.0 kg (100–300 lb)

EXERCISE LEVEL 🐕

COAT CARE ✂✂

REGISTERED KC, FCI, AKCs

COLOURS White with reddish-brown patches or mantle

Regarded as the Swiss national breed, these massive dogs are also called St Bernhardshund or Bernhardiner, and have been known as Saint Dogs – still sometimes used in North America – Alpenmastiff, and Barry Dogs.

BREED ORIGINS

These dogs are descended from Swiss farm breeds, but their original ancestors were Roman mastiffs. They probably arrived via the most ancient pass through the Western Alps, the Great St Bernard Pass. In 1049, monks founded a hospice there named after St Bernard of Menthon, and since at least the 17th century, mastiffs lived there as companions and guards, hauling carts and creating paths through deep snow. They became legendary rescue dogs after Napoleon's army went through the pass in 1800.

BREED QUALITIES

These lugubrious-looking dogs are gentle, friendly, loyal, and obedient. Their size makes them unsuitable for many homes, but their ponderous movements mean they are unlikely to bowl children over. Like many large breeds, they are prone to bloat and joint problems.

START SLOW Big dogs like the St Bernard take as much as 18 months to become fully physically mature. Exercise should be carefully monitored while their bones are still growing.

LESS IS MORE There are two coats: this shorthaired or *stockhaar* has a dense double coat and was more used for work in the snow. The medium-length, straight to slightly wavy coat of the longhair could gather icicles.

Samoyed

ORIGIN Northern Russia/Siberia
HEIGHT 46–56 cm (18–22 in)
WEIGHT 23.0–30.0 kg (50–66 lb)
EXERCISE LEVEL
COAT CARE
REGISTERED KC, FCI, AKCs
COLOURS White, cream, white and biscuit

Called the Samoiedskaïa Sabaka in their native land, but affectionately known as the Sammy, these smiling dogs were the working companions of the nomadic, reindeer-herding Samoyed peoples. They were once generally called Bjelkier or Voinaika.

BREED ORIGINS

Samoyedic peoples have been in Siberia for some 2,000 years. Their dogs were essential to their lifestyle, just like the Malamute in Alaska or Lapphund in Finland. They would herd reindeer, sometimes pull sleds, and sleep alongside their owners for warmth. Over the centuries, they acquired an almost mythical reputation for their abilities and loyalty. Pioneering Norwegian explorer Fridtjof Nansen took a team of 28 over the polar ice in the 1890s, and his praise of the breed influenced other explorers to use it, including Amundsen when he reached the South Pole in 1911.

BREED QUALITIES

These dogs always lived close to their owners, and as a result thrive on human company, with a friendly greeting for all. Established as good-natured family dogs in many countries, they are full of energy and need an active life to keep them occupied. They can suffer an inherited kidney problem.

COLD PROOF The double coat is water repellent on top, impenetrably woolly beneath. Black skin resists snow glare, and the tail covers the nose when sleeping, warming the inhaled air.

MAN'S BEST FRIEND With a smiling face and a nature that 'displays affection to all mankind', this is a companion, not a guard.

Shar Pei

ORIGIN China
HEIGHT 45–50 cm (18–20 in)
WEIGHT 20.5–27.5 kg (45–60 lb)
EXERCISE LEVEL
COAT CARE
REGISTERED KC, FCI, AKCs
COLOURS Any solid colour except white

This breed is named in China for its harsh coat: Shar Pei means 'sand skin'. But when the breed became fashionable in the West in the 1980s, it was the wrinkles that caught the imagination.

BLACK   GREY   BLUE   RED/TAN   GOLD

BREED ORIGINS

The Shar Pei may have existed for over 2,000 years, kept on farms for hunting and guarding. More recently it was used in fights, and it can be stubborn and aggressive. The communist regime nearly saw the demise of the dog, but exports from Hong Kong in the 1970s saved it. There are hereditary problems with skin allergies and ingrowing eyelashes: choose breeders carefully.

FIGHTING COAT
There are two lengths of coat: the short horse coat seen here and the longer brush or bear. Loose skin and a prickly coat were good defences in dog fights, but some Shar Peis are more dramatically wrinkled than others.

Shiba Inu

ORIGIN Japan
HEIGHT 34–41 cm (13–16 in)
WEIGHT 7.0–11.0 kg (15–24 lb)
EXERCISE LEVEL
COAT CARE
REGISTERED KC, FCI, AKCs
COLOURS Red, red overlaid with black, black and tan, white

This is the smallest of Japan's native breeds, and its name describes it in minimal terms: *shiba* means 'small', and *inu* – or sometimes *ken*, another reading of the same *kanji* – simply means dog.

RED/TAN   BLACK AND TAN

BREED ORIGINS

Small dogs of this type have been present in Japan for millennia, and used to hunt small animals and birds. Pure specimens became scarce through crossing with imported English gundogs in the 19th century. In the 1920s, work to conserve them began, and in 1937 the breed was designated a Natural Monument. A quiet and loyal breed, they can be aloof with strangers.

ANCIENT PATTERN
In all colours, the Shiba Inu has a pattern called *urajiro* or 'white beneath'. The coat is light on the underparts and has light areas on the sides of the muzzle and the cheeks.

Siberian Husky

ORIGIN Siberia
HEIGHT 50–60 cm (20–24 in)
WEIGHT 16.0–27.5 kg (35–60 lb)
EXERCISE LEVEL
COAT CARE
REGISTERED KC, FCI, AKCs
COLOURS Any colour

One of the lighter sled-pulling breeds, the Siberian Husky has become more famous as a breed in Alaska than in its original homeland. For a time it was the ultimate racing dog.

 BLACK
 GREY
 GOLD AND WHITE
 TAN AND WHITE

BREED ORIGINS

These dogs were used for centuries by the Chukchi people of Siberia for sled pulling and reindeer herding. DNA analysis has confirmed it as one of the oldest breeds in existence. It was brought to Alaska by fur traders for arctic races, and used by Peary in his trip to the North Pole in 1909, but won most publicity and popularity in the 1925 serum run to Nome, or Great Race of Mercy, when teams of sled dogs carried diphtheria antitoxin to the isolated town of Nome, travelling 1,085 km (674 miles) in a record-breaking five and a half days to halt an epidemic.

BREED QUALITIES

Lighter than most other sled-pulling breeds, the Husky is characterized by a seemingly effortless gait and enormous stamina. These qualities mean it is a breed for the active, and left alone it can be destructive. They are generally cheerful dogs, gentle and friendly.

LOOK LIVELY Huskies are good-natured, but their intelligence can incline them to mischief, so owners need to be as alert as their dogs.

SIBERIAN LOOKS The breed has a tendency to blue in one or both eyes, but this is by no means universal. The thick coat is fairly tangle free, but needs plenty of combing when it moults.

INDEX

Gardening School

RHS Gardening School

Authors: Simon Akeroyd and Ross Bayton

First published in 2018, this revised and updated edition first published in 2021

by Mitchell Beazley, a division of Octopus Publishing Group Ltd,

Carmelite House, 50 Victoria Embankment, London EC4Y 0DZ

www.octopusbooks.co.uk

An Hachette UK company

www. hachette.co.uk

Published in association with the Royal Horticultural Society

Distributed in the US by Hachette Book Group

1290 Avenue of the Americas, 4th and 5th Floors, New York, NY 10104

Distributed in Canada by Canadian Manda Group

664 Annette St., Toronto, Ontario, Canada M6S 2C8

ISBN: 978 1 78472 810 6

A CIP record for this book is available from the British Library

Printed and bound in China

Conceived, designed and produced by The Bright Press

an imprint of The Quarto Group

The Old Brewery, 6 Blundell Street,

London N7 9BH, United Kingdom

T (0)20 7700 6700

www.QuartoKnows.com

Design: Studio Noel

Illustrations: Sarah Skeate

Mitchell Beazley Publisher: Alison Starling

RHS Publisher: Rae Spencer-Jones

RHS Consultant Editor: Simon Maughan

The Royal Horticultural Society is the UK's leading gardening charity dedicated to
advancing horticulture and promoting good gardening. Its charitable work includes
providing expert advice and information, training the next generation of gardeners,
creating hands-on opportunities for children to grow plants and conducting
research into plants, pests and environmental issues affecting gardeners.
For more information visit www.rhs.org.uk or call 0845 130 4646.

Gardening School

Everything You Need to Know to
Get the Most from Your Garden

SIMON AKEROYD & ROSS BAYTON

CONTENTS

Chapter 5

Growing Fruit and Vegetables   124

Chapter 6

Growing Under Cover   162

Chapter 7

Propagating Plants   176

Chapter 8

Problem Solving   192

Chapter 9

Planting Design   214

Chapter 10

The Gardening Year   238

1. THE BASICS OF GARDENING

For thousands of years humans have manipulated the natural environment around them for their own benefit. From the first small patches of forest cleared to grow food crops to today's grand estates, gardens have been intimately connected to the growth of civilisation and the improvement of the human condition.

Most of today's gardeners do not garden out of necessity, as in the past, but for a wider variety of reasons. Aesthetic pleasure, better health, status, stimulation and, paradoxically, relaxation are all answers given in response to the question 'Why?', and it is clear that gardens are as much of a necessity in the modern world as ever, even if most no longer provide household essentials.

Gardening is the closest many of us will come to creating a work of art. No paintbrushes are required, except perhaps for pollinating runner beans and painting fences. Instead, gardeners have to combine aesthetic judgement with science and manual labour to achieve their goals. But with a little planning, some basic knowledge of botany, a sensible range of tools and techniques, an understanding of the environment and the weather, and a modicum of plant knowledge, gardeners can create their own living masterpiece, a reflection of themselves and their lifestyles.

No two gardens are alike. No two days in the garden are the same. No two years will be the same. The thread that holds everything together is the effort that you, the gardener, puts in.

HOW WE USE GARDENS

Throughout history people have created gardens for relaxation, pleasure and the cultivation of plants. Many ancient civilisations placed great importance on the cultivation and creation of gardens, and these spaces played significant roles in defining their cultures. Historic stories set in garden contexts, such as the Hanging Gardens of Babylon or the Garden of Eden, show that societies have always viewed gardens as valuable to their cultural identity.

← Socialising and Relaxing

Nowadays, in our diverse and multicultural society, there are numerous uses and reasons for gardens, depending on your lifestyle. For the majority of people, a garden is for relaxation and pleasure. It is an outdoor space to be enjoyed and although there are some gardens that are literally just a space for socialising, most garden owners also enjoy caring for a green space and cultivating plants.

← Self-sufficiency

Growing your own food is a very popular incentive for gardening. You might take on an allotment or create a kitchen garden at home purely for the cultivation of edible crops to feed yourself, family and friends. Some gardeners grow their own because they believe the crops are better for you and have more flavour than those you can buy; others do it to save money on their grocery bills. Home-grown produce also benefits from being lower in food miles and so better for the environment. And you can find many more varieties of vegetables and fruit in the pages of a seed catalogue than on the shelves of a supermarket. However, most people grow their own food simply for the pleasure of producing something from seed, watching it mature and harvesting it from their own garden.

Other reasons for gardening include encouraging and helping wildlife, or making collections of particular plant enthusiasms. And of course you may simply enjoy the creative challenge of designing an outdoor space and keeping it attractive as the seasons turn.

↑ Community Space and Allotments

Gardens can also be used as a space for sharing ideas and for community involvement. There are hundreds of community gardens around the country where like-minded people make and maintain an outdoor space that can be shared with others. Community gardening offers a great opportunity to meet people, get fit and enjoy being outdoors. It's ideal for people who don't have their own garden, but also for others who are keen to learn more about practical gardening and to get involved with their local community.

Allotments bridge the gap between private garden and shared space; allotment owners are each responsible for their own parcel of land, but also work as part of the allotment community – and allotment owning also offers the ideal opportunity to get outside, cultivate some land, grow plants and meet other people.

KEY THINGS TO CONSIDER

Whatever you intend to use your garden for, whether filling it with flowers, planting a kitchen garden, creating a place to socialise with friends, or all three, it's important to assess its potential before starting work. What outdoor space a house or flat has is one of the main factors when people choose what they're going to rent or buy, and there are important practical considerations to take on board when you're looking at a new garden.

▲ *Making the most of limited space, this balcony is lined with troughs planted with climbers and foliage plants as well as colourful bedding.*

How much space is there?

You probably don't have much choice when it comes to size – if you only have a small courtyard or balcony then an orchard or large herbaceous border is out of the question. However, you can get creative in even a small space. Most plants can be grown in pots and there might be the possibility of growing a 'green roof' on top of a bin storage area or other outbuilding; the latter is a great way of growing plants without taking up any additional space.

Is it overlooked?

Privacy and seclusion are important considerations when starting to plan a garden. Most people want to enjoy relaxing in their garden without being overlooked, so if you want to create a quiet, private place outside, think about how you will achieve this at least in part, if not all, of your space. Fences, trellis, pergolas and plants can all help you to make this work.

Do you have good access?

Think about the access to your outdoor space. Can you get to the back garden without having to carry everything through the house or flat? If you can't, this may restrict what you can achieve: getting large quantities of soil and other materials into the garden will be difficult.

Do you need hard landscaping?

If you have elaborate plans for your garden you may need help to build walls, paths, raised beds, a pond, and so on. Professional gardeners and contractors are expensive, so budgeting is important. If you are putting in non-temporary structures you may need planning permission, too, so check with your local authority before commissioning any work. If you're doing the work yourself, check out where the services are. Underground electricity, gas and water pipes and cabling will need to be identified before you set to with a spade, mattock or mini-digger.

Other considerations

There are other important aspects you should think about. All gardens need water: is there an outside tap? Is there a water butt? If you don't have either, can you install one or both? Bringing water to a garden from an inside tap is often impractical and, in some cases, impossible.

To get the full picture of what you'll be able to grow, you'll also need to assess your soil; work out which way your space faces, how much light it gets, and when, and how much shelter it has from wind. Finally, you need to know where it fits in the landscape: that is, to have a broad idea of its micro-, meso- and macroclimates. All of these are explained in the following pages, which help you to get to know the space you've got and get an idea of its potential.

▲ *Raised beds are ideal for growing vegetables in, but forward planning and budgeting are required to get the right look and feel.*

LIGHT AND ASPECT

Some plants love to spend their time basking in the sunlight while others prefer to dwell in the cooler, shadier recesses of the garden. Knowing which is which is key for the gardener – there are always plants that will thrive in your garden, whether it is in sunshine or shade; the skill is to pick the right plant for the space. So before rushing off to the garden centre and exchanging your cash for some beautiful plants, it is worth looking at where the light falls in your garden.

▲ *Lower light levels in a garden can offer exciting opportunities to create mini woodland gardens with attractive plants at the base of larger trees.*

Which way does your garden face?

The sun rises in the east, reaches south at about
midday and sets in the west, so a south-facing
garden will receive the most amount of light during
the day and a north-facing garden will receive the
least. An east-facing garden will only receive the
sunshine in the morning when it is cooler than
later on in the day, whereas a south-west-facing
garden will receive the afternoon and early evening
sun, which is usually the warmest time of the day.

To figure out which way your garden faces, you can
either observe it on a clear day and see where the
sun is at various times or you can use a compass.
Lay the compass flat on your hand. The red arrow
will always point to magnetic north, so if you face
the direction of the arrow, you will be facing north,
your back will be facing south, east will be to your
right and west to your left.

Light and shade

Any upright, from a house to a tree, a pergola or a
hedge, will cast shade into a garden when the light
is behind it. Some of these things are within your
control – if you want to get more light into your
garden, a tree might be pruned, for example, or a
pergola moved – but others aren't, in which case
you will need to work with the shade by picking
suitable plants.

Remember, too, that the height of the sun varies
during the year. In the winter the sun is low in the
sky and a north- or east-facing garden will get very
little light, particularly if there are houses or trees
in the way. In summer, however, the sun is much
higher in the sky, and even a north-facing garden
may get more seasonal light if the sun is high
enough to shine above the obstruction.

Tricks you can use to create more light include
using light or reflective materials in your garden.
Surrounding walls and fences can be painted
pale colours, white gravel can be used on paths,
and you might make a water feature or pond.
Some gardeners use mirrors on fences and walls,
too (although bear in mind that these can prove
hazardous for birds if they're not carefully placed).

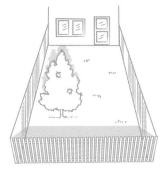

South-facing garden (midday)

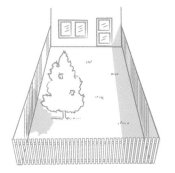

West-facing garden (midday)

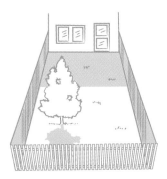

North-facing garden (midday)

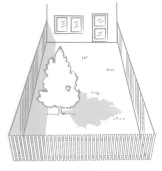

East-facing garden (midday)

MOISTURE AND TEMPERATURE

Two of the key ingredients needed for plants to grow well are moisture and warmth. Where you live in the world determines the types of plants you can grow.

Succulents are plants suitable for dry, arid conditions and can survive without being watered for long periods.

Temperature range

There can be a huge range in temperature in different parts of the same country. In England, for example, compare the warm climate of South Devon in the south-west, where many subtropical and tender plants thrive, with the cooler temperatures of North Yorkshire in the north, where the growing season is shorter and early frosts limit the range of plants you can grow.

Gardens in the west of the UK tend to warm up earlier in the spring than those in the east, meaning that they may often be at a different stage of seasonal growth from one another. This will not only affect when plants will flower but also when you can sow seeds or transplant seedlings out of doors.

When planning what plants to grow in your garden, research the temperatures in the area, so you know what will and won't thrive there. Most plant labels tell you whether they are hardy or not, which will help you decide whether they are suitable for your plot.

Precipitation and the water table

The moisture in your area also determines what plants can be grown in the garden. There are generally two factors that will affect this. First, the amount of rainfall. This can be affected by unexpected factors – if, for example, you live near a range of mountains, your area may have a higher annual rainfall. Second, the water table in your garden will also affect its overall moisture levels. The deeper the water table, the drier the garden.

Even some plants originating from hot countries will appreciate regular watering or rainfall throughout the growing season.

CLIMATE AND LOCATION

Where you live geographically has a massive bearing on what you can and can't grow. However, it's not only dependent on the overall temperature and rainfall of your region, known as the macroclimate; there are other factors within your area that affect temperatures, rainfall and the survival of plants, and these are known as the mesoclimate and the microclimate.

▲ The warm macroclimate of vineyards in the Loire Valley, France enables more grape varieties to be grown than in cooler regions.

Macro, meso and micro

To understand the difference between the three, take the example of a vineyard in the famous wine-producing Loire Valley. The overall climate of that region in mid-west France would be referred to as the macroclimate – in other words, the 'larger, overall climate' for the Loire Valley. And the reason the region is famous for wine is because generally in that area the climate is suitable for ripening grapes. However, within the Loire Valley there are various villages and vineyards all with their unique locations on top of a hill, in a valley, by a river, on a south slope or a north one, and so on. These variations dictate the mesoclimate of the vineyard, which fluctuates within the overall macroclimate for the Loire Valley. This is why some vineyards produce better grapes and therefore better wines than others.

Finally, if you then took just one of those vineyards you might identify one patch of vines that receives more sunlight, or is warmer because it is protected by something such as a nearby rock, and that makes that specific patch of vines produce more grapes than vines further down the row. It's these unique small variations that make the microclimate that determines the plants' ability to produce grapes.

← Macroclimate

Numerous factors affect a macroclimate. In global terms, macroclimates are affected by their distances from the equator and the polar regions, but on a smaller scale, proximity to mountain ranges, hills, valleys, lakes or the sea will all make a difference. In the UK, the Gulf Stream, a warm sea current that travels up from Mexico, increases the temperatures in certain areas of the country. It is possible to grow subtropical plants as far north as the west coast of Scotland due to the climatic effect of the Gulf Stream.

↑ Mesoclimate

At a more local level, there are lots of significant influences that will affect the plants that can be grown. Whether you are in a city or the countryside will affect the temperature and shelter of your garden; most urban areas are a few degrees warmer than rural ones. South-facing slopes will be much warmer than north-facing ones, too.

Clumps of trees and woodlands can act as windbreaks and slow down the cooler air. Valleys are often warmer than the tops of hills or mountains, but they can also trap cold air, making them frost pockets. Nearby lakes or bodies of water can reflect sunlight and make an area warmer.

↑ Microclimate

This is the area that a gardener can really influence or improve. For example, more light can be allowed into a garden by pruning trees, while hedges can be planted to protect plants from prevailing cold winds. South-facing walls or fences can be used to train fruit trees on, providing them with shelter and warmth as they bask in the midday sun. Alternatively, areas of shade can be created by planting trees.

WIND AND WINDBREAKS

Strong winds can have a devastating effect on plants in the garden. There's a reason why trees either don't grow or have highly distorted shapes on exposed hillsides: all plants dislike strong winds. Most gardeners want upright, healthy trees and shrubs in their gardens. If there's a strong prevailing wind, this can be difficult, so it's important, first, to assess how windy a garden is, and, second, how best to protect plants from the wind's effects.

Assessing the wind

The simplest method of working out the direction in which the wind most commonly blows in your garden (the prevailing wind) is to plant a flag in a key area and watch how it flies every day over a few weeks. Another good indicator is to look at any existing trees and shrubs and see if they are leaning one way or the other.

In urban surroundings, the wind is often of less concern, because there are so many blocks in its path, but in the countryside, and particularly in coastal settings, wind can be a major problem for establishing and maintaining plants. Apart from anything else, it can be very hard to establish a plant if the wind is constantly rocking it, as this prevents the plant's roots from developing and anchoring in the soil.

Creating a windbreak

If your garden is in an exposed environment, the best course of action is to create a windbreak to protect the plants. The most obvious historical example is the walled garden, which many large houses built in order to create a sheltered, warmer environment to ripen fruit and produce earlier

crops. In most modern gardens a hedge windbreak is the most practical solution. For a windbreak to be successful, it must allow the wind to filter through it. A solid structure, such as a wall or fence, can cause turbulence on the lee side, exaggerating the power and strength of the wind.

Remember, you don't want to stop air movement entirely. A gentle breeze is useful in the garden, as the movement of air can help prevent the build-up of diseases.

Hedges grown as windbreaks can be either evergreen or deciduous, bearing in mind that the latter will be less effective in winter. Trees or shrubs that are tough and resilient to strong winds, such as laurel, privet, beech, hawthorn, blackthorn, Griselinia and hornbeam, are the choices that work best.

Of course, a windbreak doesn't have to be a hedge. It can be a mix of different types of trees and shrubs, planted around the garden in spots where they will slow the wind down and gradually dissipate its strength.

← Hedges are suitable for windbreaks as they gently filter out the prevailing wind, therefore protecting plants behind them.

← Grow plants in pots so that they can easily be moved to provide extra shelter when needed in gardens with changing wind directions.

← Walls will provide protection from prevailing winds, but be aware that the speed of the wind just above the structure also increases.

← Trellises are effective windbreaks but will be even better if they have plants growing on them to provide extra protection.

ASSESSING YOUR SOIL

The old saying goes, 'the answer lies in the soil', and there is a lot of truth in it. Plants can be pernickety things; if the soil conditions aren't right, they simply won't perform, and in the worst-case scenario will end up dying. Establishing what kind of soil your garden has is therefore key to assessing it properly and you should do it right at the start, before too much other planning has begun.

So what is soil?

Soil is the result of the breakdown of rocks over thousands of years into tiny particles of minerals. Mixed in with it are the remains of long-dead plants and animals, as well as soil bacteria and fungus, a mixture together referred to as humus or organic matter. There is also water and air. If you happen to have moved into a recently built house, you may also have to deal with building rubble in the soil.

For simplicity, there are essentially three different elements in soil – sand, clay or silt. Few soils are made up of purely one element – they are usually a mix with one or more elements dominant. Most desirable of all is a loamy soil, which is basically a fairly even mix of all three elements. Loamy soil drains well, but holds on to nutrients and moisture well, too.

↑ Sand

Sandy soil is a blessing if you do a lot of digging, as it is very light to move about. It also warms up quickly in springtime, meaning it is easier to grow early crops of vegetables or flowers. The downside of sandy soil is that, compared with, say, clay, it has large particles, meaning that it doesn't hold on to moisture, organic matter or nutrients. This can result in an impoverished soil which needs to be topped up with fertilisers regularly — such as bone meal, blood, fish and bone, and chicken manure — and bulky organic matter. These additions will also help sandy soil to retain the moisture.

↑ Clay

Anyone who has ever had to garden on heavy clay soil will know how back-breaking it can be to dig and cultivate. Clay soil is very dense, due to its tiny particles, and although this means that it is better able than sand to hold on to nutrients and moisture, it can drain poorly when it rains and goes rock-hard when dry. Adding lots of organic matter will improve drainage and alleviate the hard-baked problem in summer. In springtime, clay soil can be slow to warm up due to its dense texture and its tendency to hold on to moisture.

↑ Silt

Silty soil has medium-sized particles and, although it can be sticky like clay when wet, it drains faster. It holds on to nutrients and moisture better than sand.

SOIL TEST

As a quick test of soil type, take a small handful and see if you can roll it into a ball. If you can, it is clay or silt; if you can't, it's a sandy soil.

Now try to roll the ball into a sausage shape. If it will roll, it's clay; if not, it's more of a silty soil. Silty soil generally has a slightly gritty-but-silky texture, while sandy soil feels much coarser.

Acid or alkaline?

Finally, you need to know the pH value of your soil. PH is the standard scientific measurement used to work out soil's acidity or alkalinity. The reality is that you can't really change the pH of your soil; ideally you should try to select plants suited to the conditions. Although you can tweak it with soil additives to change pH levels, be aware that the soil will quickly revert to its original state. To suit the widest range of garden plants, the ideal pH is between 6 and 7.5. If your heart is set on a plant that won't like your natural soil, bear in mind that it will still be possible to grow it in a container, where you can give it the soil it prefers.

A few very specific groups such as blueberries, camellias or rhododendrons need acidic conditions. Neutral is pH 7, so basically anything below this is classified as acidic, whereas anything higher is alkaline.

Simple pH soil-testing kits are available in most garden centres or online. Take a few samples of soil from random areas in your garden. With each sample, place it in the container provided with the kit, add the solution (also provided with the kit), give it a shake and wait for the solution to change colour. Compare the colour to that on the chart provided to judge what the pH is. Usually a yellow or orange colour denotes acidic soil, light green is neutral and dark green is alkaline.

If your garden soil is alkaline, you can still grow plants that prefer acid conditions, such as blueberries, by planting them in a container full of the acidic soil that meets their needs.

THE LAYERS OF THE SOIL

TOPSOIL
Most plants grow in the topsoil, which is dark in colour and which contains the highest amount of decomposed organic matter, or humus. The depth of topsoil can vary, but is usually around 30–50cm (12–20in).

SUBSOIL
Underneath the topsoil is the subsoil, which is harder, much more difficult to cultivate, and will contain less humus and fewer nutrients than the top layer. It is usually a different colour and texture to the topsoil, so is easy to identify.

BEDROCK
Below the subsoil is the bedrock, the stony layer which can't be worked.

If you want to see how deep your topsoil is, you can either dig out a small pit or use a soil augur, a tool which can be pushed into the ground and which will bring up soil samples from different depths. If the topsoil layer proves to be very thin, you may need to add some — plants will struggle to grow in shallow topsoil.

2. UNDERSTANDING PLANTS

As gardeners, caring for plants is our major concern. We aim to provide ideal conditions for growth, then reap the benefits in various forms: beautiful blooms, fantastic foliage and bumper crops of fruit and vegetables. To make the most of your plants, however, it is essential to know a bit about how they work. Not only does this enable you to identify the various parts of any plant – crucial when pruning – but you'll also understand what your plants need in terms of water, sunlight and soil nutrients, so that you'll be able to give them exactly what they want.

Understanding plants not only equips you to meet their needs, but also helps you to choose which plants to use in different situations. Plant habit is the difference between a huge tree and a dainty herb – both are useful but they need to be matched to spaces that fit their size. How long individual plants will live is also a key part of planning – at one end of the scale, perennials may live for many years; at the other, annuals grow, flower and die within a year. You'll probably want to include both quick-result plants and slower burners in your garden.

HOW PLANTS EVOLVED

As gardeners, we tend to think of gardening as working with a set of ingredients. But plants are key ingredients in a much bigger picture which we may think less about: they release the oxygen we breathe and provide most of the food we eat. So it's worth considering exactly what constitutes a plant and how the different plant groups are related.

The two groups that comprise all life on Earth were originally classified as 'kingdoms' by the 18th-century Swedish naturalist Carl Linnaeus. He called them Animalia and Vegetabilia. The latter was later renamed Plantae. Over time, however, it became apparent that not all members of Plantae were closely related, and various organisms were split off into other groups. These included fungi, lichens, slime moulds, some algae and protozoa. Today, plants are defined as living things that produce their own food by means of photosynthesis, and whose cells are each surrounded by a protective wall. Plants range from microscopic algae, each consisting of a single cell, to massive, multicellular trees, some of the largest living organisms on Earth.

Photosynthesis occurs in tiny structures called chloroplasts, which can be found in mesophyll and guard cells. The cuticle and epidermis help to reduce leaf water loss.

Upper epidermis

Palisade mesophyll

Cuticle

Spongy mesophyll

Guard cells

Lower epidermis

Green energy

Photosynthesis is a chemical reaction that takes place inside plant cells, within structures known as chloroplasts. These contain green pigments that harness the energy in sunlight and use it to fuse water and carbon dioxide, forming simple sugars and oxygen. The sugars, which may be combined and stored as starches, feed the plant. Apart from a handful of parasitic plants that lack leaves, all plants rely on photosynthesis for food. A few other non-plant groups also practise photosynthesis, though the chemical pathways may be different. It's hard to overstate the importance of this process; not only does photosynthesis produce plant food, which ultimately feeds all other life, but oxygen, the reaction's by-product, forms the most important component of the air we breathe.

The production of oxygen via photosynthesis paved the way for the development of life on our planet and, over time, such life became more complex. Plants evolved, taking numerous different forms. Some of these eventually became extinct, but several independent lineages remain today. Derived from some of the earliest plants, mosses and liverworts lack roots and absorb moisture through all parts of their bodies. Ferns and clubmosses, which developed later, have a vascular system to transport water and reproduce by means of dust-like spores. In contrast, conifers and other gymnosperms produce seeds. Flowering plants, or angiosperms, developed later than all these groups, and combine several advanced features that have enabled them to spread across the world; they make up around 90 per cent of all land plants.

Flower power

The evolution of flowers probably occurred in conjunction with the evolution of insects. Non-flowering plants such as conifers rely on wind to transport their pollen, but the results are inevitably hit-and-miss: much of the pollen does not reach its target. In making use of a huge range of crawling and flying insects and, later in the evolutionary order, other creatures such as birds, bats and primates, each different type of flower ensures that most pollen will reach another of the same type efficiently. As individual insects and flowers adapted to each other's needs, so more plant and insect species evolved, resulting in the great wealth of flowering plants – and matching diversity of pollinating insects – that we see today. Gardeners are major beneficiaries of this diversity; it means that we can find attractive plants for any environment or situation. Selective breeding has supplemented the natural range, too. These cultivated varieties were chosen for positive characteristics, such as larger blooms, tastier fruit or disease resistance.

Many flowering plants utilise insects, such as this honeybee, to transfer their pollen from flower to flower, ▼ resulting in pollination and seed production.

PLANT ANATOMY

It's invaluable for gardeners to have a basic map of plant anatomy in their heads. That way, whether you're pruning a rose, harvesting seeds, taking cuttings or simply trying to identify a weed, you'll never get lost. When naming the parts of a plant, it's easiest to start at the root and work your way up to the flowers.

Roots and stems

Plant roots have two roles: to anchor the plant, and to absorb water and nutrients. In a typical root system, the larger roots provide physical support, while much smaller roots, especially thread-like root hairs, absorb the most moisture. Roots can be thick and fleshy or thin and fibrous, and some are adapted for nutrient storage (see page 35). While most roots are subterranean, some plants such as tree-living epiphytes, including many orchids, have aerial roots which emerge from their stems.

Stems are both the skeleton and the vascular system of a plant. They support the foliage and flowers, but also transport water up from the roots and food down from the leaves. Most grow upright, but some, known as prostrate stems, travel along the ground, while others – pendulous stems – hang downwards. Some perennials also store nutrients in thickened horizontal stems called rhizomes. In trees and shrubs, stems thicken over time forming woody trunks.

The parts of a flowering plant

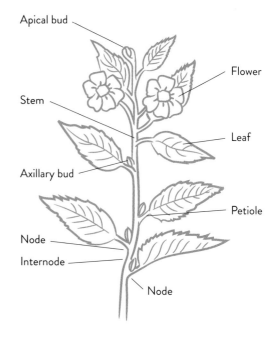

- Apical bud
- Flower
- Stem
- Leaf
- Axillary bud
- Petiole
- Node
- Internode
- Node

Leaves

Plant leaves are in many ways the original solar panels; they're broad, flat and arranged to face the sun, from which they absorb the energy needed to power photosynthesis. Most are composed of two parts: the petiole and the lamina. Petioles, or leaf stalks, attach the foliage to the stem at a point known as a node. The lamina, or blade, can vary in its form, texture and colour. The shapes of the leaf tips (apices), edges (margins) and bases are also changeable.

Most plants have a single petiole at each node, growing on alternate sides of the stem, but some have pairs of leaves at each node ('opposite'), or multiple leaves at each node ('whorled'). Some leaves lack a distinct petiole and the lamina joins directly to the stem. Others have leaf-like structures, called stipules, at the base of the petiole. Leaf arrangement is an important feature in identifying a plant.

When examining leaves, it's important to check whether they are simple (undivided) or compound (fully divided into leaflets). Confusingly, the leaflets of some compound leaves can resemble simple leaves. To be sure, follow the petiole until you reach the stem; a leaf will have a bud or growth point at the node, whereas a leaflet will not. Compound leaves may have their leaflets arranged like fingers on a hand (palmate) or like a bird feather (pinnate).

Flowers and fruits

Most plants reproduce by transferring pollen from one flower to another, where it fertilises ovules. The fertilised ovules develop into seeds, which are dispersed within a fruit formed from the flower's ovary. Flowers are composed of four types of organ arranged in rings: sepals, petals, stamens and carpels. The sepals, which together form the calyx, protect the flower in bud. The petals, which, grouped, are called the corolla, attract pollinators. Stamens are made up of a stalk, or filament, and a head, the anther, which produces pollen, and the narrow connecting point between the two is called the style.

From this basic structure comes an infinite variety of forms, with floral organs varying in shape and number. Flowers typically include both stamens (male) and carpels (female), but may also be unisexual, with male and female flowers on the same plant (monoecious) or separate plants (dioecious). In many plant groups, numerous flowers are clustered together to form an inflorescence. Once the ovules are fertilised, they develop into seeds while the surrounding ovary forms a fruit. Plant fruits are adapted in different ways to aid in the dispersal of seeds away from the mother plant. As a result, some are fleshy and attract hungry animals, while others use wings, hooks or hairs to help their dispersal.

The parts of a leaf

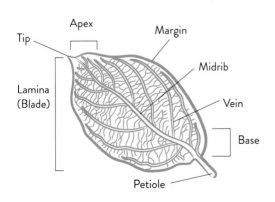

The parts of a flower

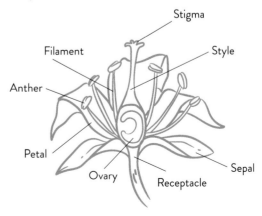

HOW PLANTS GROW

Plants grow and develop in a different way from animals. In animals, growth happens in youth, largely halting in adulthood. Plants, however, grow throughout their lives, and some reach both great size and extreme age. Most plant growth originates in growing points at the stem and root tips, known as meristems. Plant cells also have a much greater ability to regenerate damaged tissues than animal ones.

For most plants, life begins as a seed which contains both an embryo and a store of nutrients that will fuel the growth of the young plant. As temperatures rise in spring, seeds absorb water from the soil, swelling up before the first root, the radicle, emerges. While the root grows downwards, the first stem, or hypocotyl, appears and begins to grow upwards towards the light. Once above the soil surface, leaves develop. When they have expanded, the seedling can begin to harness the energy of the sun.

Seeds vary greatly in size and shape, often depending on the amount of nutrients they store. At one end of the scale are the dust-like seeds of orchids which, unusually, have no nutrient store at all, leaving orchid embryos to rely on symbiotic fungi to provide their first meal. At the other, the seed of the double coconut palm (*Lodoicea maldivica*), easily the world's largest, weighs in at almost 20kg (44lb). Containing a bumper crop of nutrients, it feeds the embryonic palm while it grows enough to emerge from a dense canopy of parental leaves.

Primary growth

Plant stems and roots develop from growing points called meristems, which are responsible for plant growth and which contain stem cells capable of developing into any part of the new plant. As the stem elongates, small clusters of cells are left behind by the meristems, creating buds that can develop into branches or side shoots. In most cases, these buds remain dormant, because the growing

The meristem at the tip of a plant produces hormones that inhibit the growth of lateral buds.

Meristem

Lateral bud

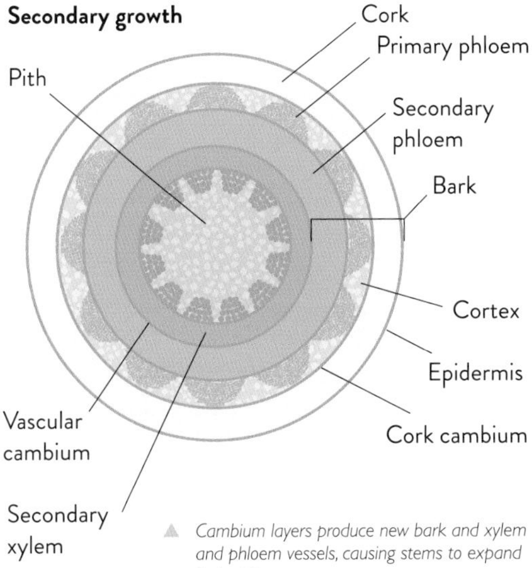

Cambium layers produce new bark and xylem and phloem vessels, causing stems to expand their girth.

point at the top of the stem releases a hormone, from a class known as auxins, that inhibits the growth of side shoots.

This last bit of biochemistry is the reason gardeners sometimes pinch out the tips of young plants to encourage bushy growth. Removing the top (apical) meristem halts the flow of hormones, allowing side shoots to form and the plant to thicken. Encouraging bushy growth is good practice for bedding plants, shrubs and hedging, but should be avoided when growing trees where a single stem or leader is desired.

Secondary growth

The extension of stems and roots is known as primary growth; secondary growth is the thickening of stems and roots that you see in all woody plants, including trees. The stems of all woody plants contain two different sorts of vessel: xylem, which transports water from roots to leaves, and phloem, which moves sugars formed in the leaves down the stem. They are divided by a layer of meristematic cells called cambium, and this layer generates new xylem and phloem, gradually thickening the stems. To stop the bark from bursting as the stem widens, another cambium layer (called cork cambium) produces new, expanded layers of bark. Each year, new layers of xylem and phloem are laid down and the outer walls of xylem cells gradually accumulate a polymer called lignin. The cells eventually die, but the tough, lignin-filled walls remain, creating a network of water-transporting tubes. Xylem is also the primary component in wood, lending rigidity to stems and allowing for the development of tall trees, shrubs and vines. When a tree stem is cut, the xylem can be seen in the rings that allow tree age to be determined.

New directions

While much plant growth results from new cell production, individual plant cells can also expand and grow. When exposed to light from one direction, cells on the dark side of the stem extend while those on the sunny side stay the same. This is what causes windowsill plants to arch towards the light. This process, known as positive phototropism, is also controlled by auxin hormones. Some vines perform a reverse manoeuvre, known as negative phototropism – they grow away from the sun because they are looking for a trunk to support them as they climb, and the shadiest areas are directly below trees.

Some flowers, such as the osteospermums shown below, can follow the sun and track it from east to west, allowing their blooms to warm up quickly and thus attract more pollinating insects.

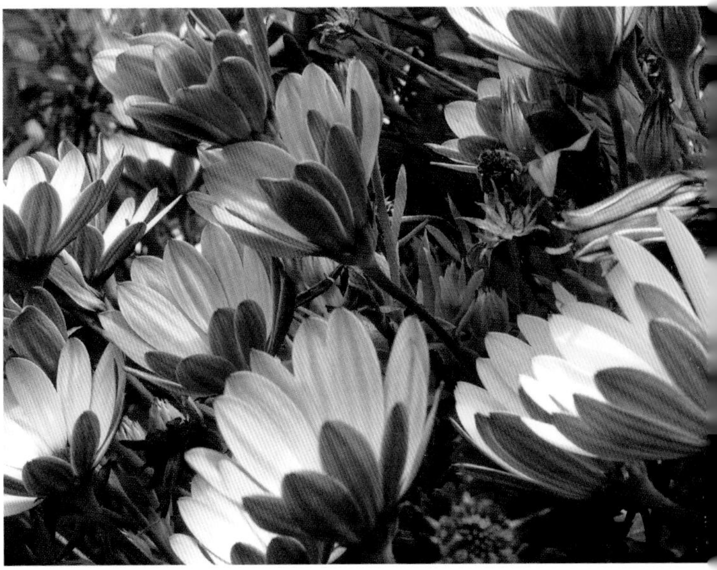

HOW PLANTS MULTIPLY

A crucial stage in the life cycle of any plant or animal is the creation of the next generation. Most plants do this by flowering and forming seeds, but some exceptions use other means. As a gardener, it's useful to have a broad understanding of the different ways in which plants reproduce. You'll need it when you want to 'make' more plants from those you already have, and sometimes, by manipulating the process, you can also improve the plants you grow.

Plant reproduction can be divided into two broad categories: sexual and asexual. The former involves the transfer of genes between plants; when flowers are pollinated, genetic material in pollen combines with genetic material in the ovules to form seeds, which are genetically distinct from the two parent plants. Asexual reproduction does not involve genetic transfer and any offspring are identical to the parent. The propagation techniques that gardeners use, such as division, cuttings and layering, are forms of asexual reproduction, but plants can also reproduce in this way without any human intervention.

Flowers, fruits and seeds

The blooms of flowering plants may look beautiful to us, but we are not their intended audience. Scent and colourful petals exist to entice animals so that they will transport pollen from one flower to another. Some plants have modified flowers to attract specific pollinators. Butterflies prefer broad blooms with floral tubes, while many bee-pollinated flowers have lines on their petals to guide the insect in. The flowers of grasses and many trees, including birch and oak, are pollinated by the wind, so have no need to be showy. Having a unique pollinator ensures pollen is delivered to the right address – another flower of the same species – but many plants take their chances; they have unspecialised blooms and welcome all comers.

Once the ovules of the receiving plant are fertilised, they develop into seeds. The tissues surrounding the seeds also change, becoming fruits. Like flowers, many fruits have evolved to attract the animals that ultimately disperse the seeds. Fleshy fruits advertise with vivid colours and the promise of a sweet treat. Other seeds lack fleshy coatings, but use spines or hooks to hitch a ride, and yet others have wings or even explosive pods which can help to disperse them without the help of animals.

The fragrant, tubular flowers of buddleja are attractive to many species of butterfly.

Plants produced without flowers

▼ *Flowers are not the only way in which plants swap genes. In conifers, pollen is transferred between male and female cones by the wind. Seeds develop within the female cones and are later released, blown by wind, or falling to the ground and travelling inside a hungry animal.*

▼ *Asexual reproduction sidesteps the transfer of genes, creating genetically identical offspring. Strawberries and many grasses develop new plants at the tips of horizontal stems called stolons.*

▼ *Several shrubs and trees, such as sumach (Rhus), poplar (Populus) and rice-paper plant (Tetrapanax), can develop new stems from surface roots some distance from the main stem.*

▲ *Many bulbs and corms form offsets, called bulbils and cormels. These are usually made below the ground, but a few types of lily (Lilium) produce bulbils on their stems above ground, while in some onions (Allium), they form among the flowers.*

▲ *Some species, such as piggyback plant (Tolmiea menziesii) and mother-of-millions (Kalanchoe delagoensis), develop miniature plantlets on their leaves, while in orchids like Phalaenopsis, plantlets, called keikis, form on the stems or inflorescences.*

▲ *Ferns do not produce seeds, but release dust-like spores from fertile sites on their leaves. These grow into green, fleshy structures called prothalli, which release sperm that swim across the ground, using flagella, seeking another prothallus. When they find one, eggs held within the structure are fertilised, and a new fern develops as a result.*

WHAT PLANTS NEED

To grow and thrive, plants need water, soil nutrients and carbon dioxide from the air, along with enough sunlight to fuel photosynthesis. Gardeners don't need to worry about providing CO_2, but do need to ensure that plants get enough light, water and nutrients. It's useful to know how plants make use of these basic ingredients.

The sugars that are produced by its chemical reaction are not only used by plants as fuel, but in due course nourish the animals that eat them, so photosynthesis is the crucial starting point for most food chains. In addition, we need the oxygen it produces as a by-product to breathe.

Photosynthesis occurs in plants within tiny structures called chloroplasts, located within the cells of the leaves and other green parts. Chloroplasts contain chlorophyll, a pigment that absorbs energy from light, powering the photosynthetic reaction. Water absorbed by the plant's roots and carbon dioxide, which enters the leaf through pores called stomata, are combined to create simple sugars and oxygen. Plants either generate energy by burning these sugars in the process of respiration, or convert them into starches for storage. While carbon dioxide is freely available, gardeners need to make sure that the plants in their care have access to light and plenty of water to ensure healthy growth.

Water

Photosynthesis is not the only use plants have for water; it also provides physical support. Plant cells filled with water are firm, but if they dry out water pressure decreases and the plant wilts. The amount of water a plant needs depends on many factors, including soil type, climate and the plant's geographical origin. Freely draining soils, such as those rich in sand, don't hold water for long and plants living in them desiccate quickly. Those growing on heavier clay soils are less likely to suffer from drought.

Of course, climate is an important consideration; in humid weather, plants lose less water by transpiration, while in dry or windy conditions, water loss spikes. Native plants are likely to thrive in your garden, as they're adapted to local weather conditions. On the other hand, plants from further afield may struggle. Those that originate in tropical forests, for example, are adapted to high humidity and may not be happy when grown in drier habitats, while desert plants may readily survive drought, but can be killed by excess water during winter.

Soils and nutrients

The water that plants absorb from the soil contains a range of chemical elements. While these may not have a direct role in photosynthesis, many are essential for growth. The best known are nitrogen (N), phosphorus (P) and potassium (K), but many others, including calcium (Ca), magnesium (Mg) and iron (Fe), are crucial (see page 91). You can supplement these minerals by applying targeted fertilisers, but improving the soil with added organic matter will also help.

Many plants enhance the efficiency of their roots by forming a relationship with fungi in the soil. Known as mycorrhizae, these fungal threads in the soil share water and nutrients with plant roots in return for a portion of the sugars produced by photosynthesis. A handful of plants have responded to soil nutrient deficiencies through a more direct method; carnivorous plants living on poor, peaty soils trap insects and absorb nutrients directly from their bodies.

Sunshine and showers

Photosynthesis uses the energy of the sun to produce sugars. Plant pigments (primarily chlorophylls) absorb light energy and transfer it, allowing the chemical reaction to go ahead. Sunlight, when it reaches plants, is composed of a range of different wavelengths, including those that correspond to the different colours of the rainbow. Chlorophyll pigments mostly absorb blue and red light, but reflect green, and thus plants appear green to our eyes.

Almost all plants need light to live; only a handful of species can do without it, and these are typically colourless parasites that rely on green plants or fungi to sustain them. The amount of light needed by different plant species varies hugely and many have specifically adapted to low- or high-light environments.

Plants should be positioned where they will receive enough light, taking into account orientation, local weather and anything that casts shade.

Water is essential for photosynthesis. When plants open their pores, or stomata, to absorb sufficient carbon dioxide, water vapour escapes, a process known as transpiration.

To reduce their water losses, some plants conceal their stomata within tufts of hair, under a layer of wax or by curling their leaves. Many succulent plants close their stomata during the day to reduce transpiration. They open them at night, when cooler temperatures limit water loss.

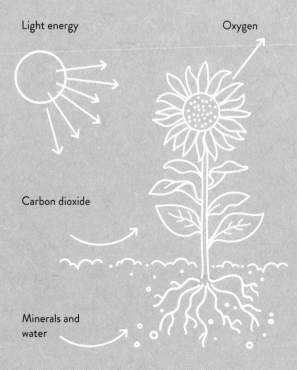

Light energy

Oxygen

Carbon dioxide

Minerals and water

HOW TO READ PLANTS

Unlike people, plants cannot tell us when something is wrong – you have to learn to 'read' them for problems. The key is regular and close inspection of their stems, leaves, flowers and general habit. Plants do communicate, you just need to learn how to look.

Ongoing scientific studies demonstrate that plants communicate with one another using the complex language of biochemistry. Chemicals released into the air by leaves can alert neighbouring plants to the presence of pests. But you don't need to be a scientist to understand some of the messages your garden plants are issuing. Changes in their habit can reveal that necessities such as light and water are in short supply, while variations in leaf colour may indicate nutrient shortage, pest attack or viral infection.

← Wilt

Perhaps the most obvious visible cry for help is when plants wilt. The likely cause is drought and the damage is readily repaired with a watering can. Confusingly, though, some plants wilt when they've had too much water. The popular houseplant African violet (*Saintpaulia*) hates excess moisture, which can kill the roots and resulting in wilting — once this has happened, the plant isn't usually salvageable, though leaf cuttings may provide replacements. Several fungal diseases also cause wilting, notably the unimaginatively named clematis wilt.

← Phototropism

Another whole-plant movement results when they receive insufficient light. Known as positive phototropism (see page 31), plants naturally grow towards a light source, which can result in leggy, inclined plants of poor habit. Move such specimens to a brighter spot. When grown in the absence of light, plants are typically yellowish-white with elongated stems, a condition called etiolation – as in that forgotten potato sprouting in the pantry.

← Leaf Condition

Leaves are prime communication devices as changes in shape or colour are easily seen. Unexpected holes suggest hungry pests or diseases, such as shot hole, while weird distortions can indicate viral infection, herbicide exposure or cold damage.

Leaves change colour before they fall, but also in response to nutrient deficiency, and the colour changes can indicate which mineral is lacking. Yellow leaves with green veins, a condition called chlorosis, indicate iron deficiency. Yellow mottling can result from viral infection or mite infestation. Collect or photograph leaf colour changes and use them when diagnosing the problem.

← Visitors

Watch out for visitors to your plants, too — some may bring news about the health of your plants. Small birds such as blue tits are attracted to colonies of aphids, so watch out for them and be ready to clear up their leftovers. When birds or badgers dig up patches of lawn, it's likely there are chafer larvae feeding on the grass roots. White butterflies are a sign of trouble in the vegetable garden; their caterpillars are likely munching your brassicas.

UNDERSTANDING PLANT NAMES

Giving names to newly discovered plant species is one of the most important tasks in botany. Not only do names offer a helpful way to separate species, but without them it's impossible to know just how many species there are. Once named, the plant also has a label to which the results of scientific studies can be added. An internationally standardised naming system exists for this purpose.

The Royal Botanic Gardens, Kew currently have over a million plant names in their online Plant List. Despite this, it's thought that there are only around 400,000 plant species on Earth – the huge discrepancy results from botanists in different countries unwittingly giving the same species different names. Fortunately for horticulturists, the number of garden-worthy plants suitable for growing in the UK is even fewer; the Royal Horticultural Society's Plant Finder lists a mere 70,000 to choose from.

Latin binomials

In 1753, Carl Linnaeus decided to bring order to the study of living things by giving every different one a name made up of two words, genus and species. Much like our first name and surname, except that in Linnaean classification the 'surname' (genus) always comes before the 'first name' (species). This binomial system worked so well that it was soon widely adopted, and it remains the system we use today. It's extraordinarily useful, once you've got used to the fact that all scientific names are in Latin.

Why Latin? Because, counter-intuitively, it keeps things simple. Take, for example, the horse-chestnut tree, a native of the Balkans that's widely cultivated across Europe. In France, they call it *marron d'Inde*, in Germany *Gewöhnliche Rosskastanie* and in Italy *castagna amara*. And in the UK it's also known as Spanish chestnut. Confused? You might have been, but fortunately, there is only one Latin scientific name – *Aesculus hippocastanum*. At the time Linnaeus chose Latin for his naming system, it was the universal language spoken by scholars. But even today, gardeners from different countries can easily communicate using Latin plant names. The system works.

Describing plant variation

Gardeners have been busy over the years, cross-breeding and 'improving' plant species so that they make better garden plants. In nature, too, plant populations vary from place to place, so the normal binomial may not be sufficient to describe a local variation. In such cases, additions are made to the standard name to explain what the variant is:

Subspecies: A distinct, naturally occurring variant of the typical species. For example, *Armeria maritima* subsp. *elongata* has wider leaves and longer bracts than *Armeria maritima*.

Variety: Like a subspecies, but with fewer physical differences. For example, *Sorbus aucuparia* var. *xanthocarpa* differs only in its yellow fruits from the red-fruited species.

Cultivated variety (usually shortened to **Cultivar**): Variants that are selected in cultivation, or produced by cross-breeding one plant with another. Cultivar names can be in any language, but are not usually Latin and are therefore not in italics; they are enclosed within inverted commas. For example, *Clematis macropetala* 'Lagoon' is a selected form of *C. macropetala*, while *Clematis* 'Betty Corning' is a cultivar of uncertain parentage.

Hybrid: When two different species cross-breed, the resultant offspring is a hybrid, denoted by an '×' between the genus and species name, as in *Rosa × alba*. If two species in different genera cross, a much rarer situation, then a hybrid genus name is created with the '×' at the start of the name, as in × *Fatshedera lizei*, a cross between *Fatsia* and *Hedera*.

Family, genus and species

The binomial system not only provides internationally understood names but also indicates relationships – plants with the same genus name are thought to be closely related. Remembering that the genus is like a surname, and that it comes before the species, the rose genus (*Rosa*), for example, can be split into several unique and individual species, including *Rosa banksiae*, *Rosa carolina* and *Rosa rubiginosa*. This naming system developed so that related genera (plural of genus) could be grouped together into families. Thus, the rose family (*Rosaceae*) includes genera such as *Crataegus* (hawthorns), *Malus* (apples), *Prunus* (cherries) and *Rosa* (roses). Above the family are several additional layers of classification, though these are rarely useful in everyday horticulture. Latin plant names always appear in italics (or underlined if handwritten), with the first letter of the genus capitalised and the species name all in lower case.

◀ *A fragrant, near-thornless rambler, Rosa banksiae 'Lutea' is one of several forms in the distinctive Banksiae group, originally from China.*

The lilac flowers of the Clematis cultivar 'Betty Corning'. ▶

39

TREES AND SHRUBS

Forming the backbone of any garden that is large enough, trees and shrubs give structure and privacy, together with a broad palette of options, including eye-catching bark, foliage, flowers and fruit. Decorative trees anchor any border design, while fruits such as apples, pears and plums supply a harvest. Many shrubs, including ornamental camellias, rhododendrons and lavenders are both high-impact and low-maintenance. Careful pruning can also transform many woody plants into hedges or clipped ornamental shapes.

Trees and shrubs are perennial plants, which means they can live for many years. Some trees are extraordinarily long-lived – one Great Basin bristlecone pine (*Pinus longaeva*) in California is the planet's oldest single tree at over 5,000 years old – but at the other end of the scale, some shrubs, including lavender and rosemary, may have a useful lifespan of around only five years. All trees and shrubs have woody stems, but trees are typically larger with a single trunk, while smaller shrubs are branched from the base. In most cases it is easy to spot the difference, but some woody plants defy classification. The tree-like *Rhododendron arboreum* in the Himalayas, for example, has been recorded at over 30 metres (100 feet) tall, but branches much like a shrub.

Types of tree

Trees are classified in several ways. They may be evergreen, holding on to most of their leaves year-round, or deciduous, shedding their leaves in autumn. The difference is one of timing – evergreens shed leaves gradually throughout the year, while deciduous trees drop them all in one go.

Trees may also be described as broad-leaved or coniferous. Conifers, also called softwoods, typically have needle-like foliage and a conical growth form, most are evergreen, and their seeds are formed in cones. Broad-leaves, or hardwoods, have flat, wide leaves and a much-branched growth form. They can be evergreen or deciduous, and produce seeds within dry or fleshy fruits.

▲ Conifers often have needle-shaped leaves and a conical growth form.

Broad-leaves often have flat, wide leaves and a much-branched growth form.

Tree families

Another way to view tree classification is in terms of family relationships. Some plant families are entirely woody – the birch (*Betulaceae*), oak (*Fagaceae*) and pine (*Pinaceae*) families are good examples. Others contain a mixture; the rose family (*Rosaceae*) includes trees (apple, rowan, cherry), shrubs (roses, cotoneaster) and herbaceous perennials (meadowsweet, cinquefoil).

Size matters

When picking garden trees, the most important factor to consider is their full-grown size. You'll often find this quoted in catalogues and at point of sale as a height after ten years' growth. Overgrown trees will dominate a garden, taking up all the sunlight and soil moisture, and can also be expensive to remove. If you choose carefully, though, there are many garden-worthy small trees available.

Shaping trees and shrubs

Gardeners can transform woody plants into almost any shape by pruning. Common box (*Buxus sempervirens*) can reach nearly 9 metres (30ft) tall if left untouched, but for most gardeners, it will be used as a low hedge or topiary. Major forest trees such as beech (*Fagus sylvatica*) and western red cedar (*Thuja plicata*) can form well-behaved hedges with regular trimming.

▼ *Choose garden trees carefully, selecting species that won't outgrow their space. Large trees such as oaks are best suited to parks, while smaller rowans fit many gardens.*

SHRUB SHAPES

In general, shrubs are woody plants with multiple stems, though this definition includes a lot of variation. A good example of a typical shrub is pieris, which has a short, single trunk that branches low to the ground to form a network of stems. But some shrubs, such as Kerria and lilac (*Syringa*), generate multiple stems at the base from underground suckers. A similar effect is produced when certain shrubs, like willows (*Salix*) and dogwoods (*Cornus*), the latter particularly valued for their colourful stems, are cut to ground level each spring.

A few shrubs, including hardy fuchsias and Cape figwort (*Phygelius*), maintain woody stems in warm regions but are cut to ground level when it's cold, acting almost like herbaceous perennials.

Smaller shrubs, including lavender (*Lavandula*), rosemary (*Rosmarinus*) and sage (*Salvia*) are sometimes known as subshrubs, a term that also encompasses plants that are woody only at the base or whose branches grow low to the ground.

Most shrubs branch near the base.

Suckering shrubs form thickets.

Subshrubs are small but woody.

CLIMBERS AND WALL SHRUBS

Though often woody like trees and shrubs, climbers or vines have long stems that originally evolved to stretch through forest trees to reach sunlight above. Some species cling to tree trunks, while others creep across the forest floor. Wall shrubs don't climb but can be trained in a garden to cover vertical surfaces. Many such plants are often vulnerable to low temperatures and benefit from the extra heat radiated by sun-warmed walls.

Vines and other climbers use trees and shrubs as climbing frames, allowing them to access more light. Walls, fences, pergolas and obelisks can all serve as substitutes to support decorative climbers, while others can be allowed to ramble along hedges or provide ground cover. And they're not only decorative; vine plants may offer an edible harvest too – their crops include grapes, kiwis, blackberries, peas and beans.

Many wall shrubs are sprawling species that need reinforcement if they're not to fall over. They'll look better if tied in to a wall or fence, and this also protects them from strong winds. Some usually free-standing trees, too, can be trained against a wall where they appreciate the shelter and extra warmth. In colder areas, peaches, apricots and cherries may crop better when wall-trained.

Annual or perennial?

As a designation, 'climber' only refers to the growth habit of the plant, not its longevity. Most are woody perennials, either evergreen (ivy, akebia) or deciduous (grapes, Virginia creeper), but there are other types. Sweet peas and many morning glories are annuals, living only for one season, while runner beans and cup-and-saucer vine (*Cobaea scandens*) are tender perennials and are killed by winter frost, so are usually treated as annuals in

colder climates. Brewer's hop (*Humulus lupulus*) and everlasting pea (*Lathyrus latifolius*) are herbaceous perennials, dying back to ground level each winter, and regrowing the following year.

Queen of climbers

In temperate gardens, the genus *Clematis* is probably most gardeners' favourite when it comes to climbers. Not only does it contain many varied species, suited to a range of locations, but huge numbers of cultivars have been developed, greatly expanding the range of flower colours and forms. *Clematis* will grow in full sun or partial shade and climb using the stalks of their leaflets, which grasp in a similar fashion to tendrils.

Clematis range from tiny alpine plants, under 10cm (4in) tall, such as *C. marmoraria*, to massive vines such as *C. rehderiana* that will happily occupy a tree. Most are deciduous, but several species are evergreen, including the attractive *C. urophylla* and *C. cirrhosa*, and some are non-climbing herbaceous perennials. Garden clematis fall into three groups (see page 103): those that flower in late spring and require little pruning (Group 1), those that bloom in early summer and require light pruning twice a year (Group 2) and finally late-summer flowerers that are pruned hard in spring (Group 3).

▲ Clematis climb by twining their leaf stalks around a support.

Star jasmine (Trachelospermum jasminoides) is a useful evergreen climber for a sunny wall, producing masses of fragrant flowers in summer. ▶

METHODS OF SUPPORT FOR CLIMBING PLANTS

There are many ways to support a climbing plant –
trellis, horizontal wires, obelisks – but your choice
depends on how the plant attaches itself.

Most climbers naturally grow through other plants
and can be encouraged to clamber into garden trees
and shrubs, so long as they don't overwhelm them. As
wall shrubs are not true climbers, their long, flexible
stems must be tied into position. Always install robust
frameworks for climbers and wall shrubs, as they are
often long-lived and difficult to disentangle if an aged
trellis or too-light wires collapse.

*Twining climbers, such as runner beans
and wisteria, naturally wind their stems
around other plants, so prefer vertical
wires, wooden posts or trellis.*

*Climbing roses and blackberries use
thorns to fasten themselves and are
best tied into horizontal wires.*

*Grapes and cucumbers form tendrils that cling,
so netting works well.*

*Ivy and climbing hydrangea produce aerial roots along the stems,
so attach themselves to tree trunks and walls.*

HERBACEOUS PERENNIALS

This large group is a staple of most gardens. Herbaceous perennials are available in so many varieties that one or other of the group can be used almost anywhere, from pots to hanging baskets, ponds to bog gardens, rockeries to woodland glades. It's in grand herbaceous borders, however, where they're most impressive. Herbaceous perennials are justly popular as they can be real showstoppers, generally requiring very little in the way of seasonal care.

A perennial is any plant that lives for three or more years, while the term 'herbaceous' indicates that the plant is not woody. Most herbaceous perennials emerge from underground roots in spring, grow, flower, then set seed, before dying back to the roots in winter. There are exceptions to this pattern, though; barrenworts (*Epimedium*), elephant's ears (*Bergenia*), *Heuchera* and several others retain some or all of their leaves throughout the winter. The underground root system of perennials can be fibrous or fleshy – some plants, such as the bearded iris, have swollen, horizontal stems called rhizomes. (For other subterranean rootstocks, such as bulbs and corms, see pages 50-53.) The boundary between herbaceous perennials and shrubs is not always clear; tree poppies (*Romneya*), for example, can develop into woody shrubs in warmer climates, but behave like herbaceous perennials in cooler areas, dying back to ground level in winter. And members of the family crop up in the vegetable garden, too – for example, asparagus, artichokes, rhubarb and strawberries.

Year-round colour

As many of the most familiar perennials flower in summer, you might think that they had little to offer at other times of year, but there's a perennial, sometimes more, in bloom for every month of the year. When choosing border plants, think of the seasons as the different acts of a play, then plan to ensure there are performers on stage at all times. Draw your borders on paper, noting both the physical arrangement of plants and their peak seasons of interest. Don't be afraid to overlap; several spring bloomers, such as bloodroot (*Sanguinaria canadensis*), *Corydalis flexuosa* and showy toothwort (*Cardamine pentaphylla*) have all but disappeared underground by summer, so their spots can be filled by plants that flower later.

Herbaceous peonies rival roses with their stunning blooms, but unlike roses, which have woody stems, these herbaceous perennials disappear underground over winter, re-emerging in spring. ▶

While perennials are grown mainly for their flowers, many also have other appealing features. When you spot the vivid crimson new growth of peonies and bleeding heart (*Lamprocapnos*), say, and the first spears of *Hosta* and Siberian iris, it's always exciting: the first shoots of spring.

The foliage of bear's breeches (*Acanthus*), Chinese rhubarb (*Rheum*) and umbrella plant (*Darmera*) hold their own with architectural forms, while the colourful leaves of coral bells (*Heuchera*) rival any flower. In autumn, bluestars (*Amsonia*) and *Mukdenia* outshine many deciduous trees with their vibrantly coloured leaves. Fruits and seeds also have a beauty all their own; the umbrella-like seed heads of fennel, lovage and most other members of the carrot family (*Apiaceae*) last well into winter and pair well with ornamental grasses. Chinese lanterns (*Physalis*), stinking iris (*Iris foetidissima*) and cuckoo pint (*Arum maculatum*) produce decorative displays of fleshy fruits, too.

Extending the season

Choosing the right plants will ensure a long season of colour, but there are other ways to keep the show on the road. The 'Chelsea chop' is a pruning technique that delays flowering in herbaceous perennials. Around late May (which is when the RHS Chelsea Flower Show takes place, hence the name), prune your perennials back by up to half. They respond by flowering later in the season, often forming smaller flowers, but many more of them. If you have several clumps of the same perennial, chop half of them and leave the rest, and you'll have the best of both worlds. Spring is also a good time to divide perennials; consider planting spare divisions in pots, then use them to fill bare patches in your borders by dropping the pots into the gaps. Many perennials respond well to deadheading by forming additional flowers, though if your plant also produces decorative fruits or seed heads you may want to hold back.

Ferns

This group of non-flowering plants are best known as woodland dwellers who like shade. Their leaves, or fronds, unfurl from crozier-shaped buds and come in a variety of forms. The most familiar are green and feather-like, but fronds can be undivided, as in hart's tongue (*Asplenium scolopendrium*), finely divided with membranous leaflets, as in maidenhairs (*Adiantum*), or even mottled with colourful patterns, as in painted lady (*Athyrium niponicum* var. *pictum*). Some are evergreen, others deciduous, and their habits vary considerably. Tree ferns have stout trunks composed of roots, while many polypodies climb through trees with creeping stems. Vigorous ostrich fern (*Matteuccia struthiopteris*) rapidly spreads across damp soil, while dainty *Blechnum penna-marina* makes a far more restrained ground cover. A few, such as lip ferns (*Cheilanthes*), will even tolerate arid conditions.

Most hardy ferns are easy to grow, given full to partial shade and a soil rich in organic matter. They are, of course, good choices for growing in the shade, and pair well with woodland species such as *Hosta*, *Heuchera* and *Trillium*, all of which will benefit from a thick mulch. In spring, before the new fronds emerge, trim off any dead or winter-damaged leaves. In dry weather, supplementary watering is appreciated, but otherwise ferns are low maintenance.

Grasses and bamboos

Not long ago, the only grasses seen in British gardens tended to be either solitary specimens of pampas grass (*Cortaderia selloana*) or lawn turf. But ornamental grasses have now thoroughly infiltrated our borders. Grasses and bamboos together form the plant family *Poaceae* (sometimes called *Gramineae*), but in the garden, plants with grassy leaves from both the sedge (*Cyperaceae*) and rush (*Juncaceae*) families also fall into the ornamental grass category. Bamboos are evergreen grasses with underground rhizomes and attractive upright canes (culms). Some species are well-behaved, forming neat clumps, while others spread rapidly underground, invading nearby territory. Always choose your bamboo with care and, if you pick a spreader, invest in a bamboo barrier which, sunk into the ground, will keep it within bounds.

Ornamental grasses also vary in habit, some developing into neat tussocks or clumps, while others will run – so choose carefully. Their foliage ranges in colour from blue through vivid green to red and yellow; some varieties are even striped. Grass flowers are not colourful, but the plants' grace in movement more than makes up for this, and grasses are a great addition to borders, where they contrast well with other perennials and have a long season of interest. Prairie gardens that combine tall grasses and perennials evoke the natural landscape and are very much in vogue.

Alpines and aquatics

In terms of water needs, these two groups sit at opposite ends of the spectrum. In mountainous regions, alpines grow high above the treeline, although plants in the group also occur at lower altitudes, in the Arctic. They typically survive in thin, stony soils and hate excess moisture. Aquatic plants, on the other hand, grow partially or fully submerged in freshwater ponds, lakes and streams. Both groups have their uses in the garden: alpines make great container plants and can also be used to fill cracks in walls or spaces in specialist rockeries, while well-planted ponds attract wildlife and make a great focal point.

However you choose to use plants from either group, you need to remember their water preferences. Ensure excellent drainage for alpines by incorporating plenty of grit and sand into the soil before planting. Raised beds and planters drain more freely than borders, so may be a better choice. When choosing aquatics, check the water depth given on the label. Deepwater plants, such as many waterlilies, should be planted near the bottom of the pond, while most marginals only need their roots to be submerged.

Alpines, such as this Androsace koso-poljanskii, *thrive when grown in raised beds. As they are often rather petite, this makes them easier to observe up close.*

*While often lacy and divided, fern leaves can also be bold and entire, as with the glossy fronds of European native hart's-tongue (*Asplenium scolopendrium).

Miscanthus *is a group of ornamental grasses with an upright habit and attractive feathery seedheads.*

ANNUALS AND BIENNIALS

Trees, shrubs, climbers and herbaceous perennials have something in common – they are all perennial and may live indefinitely, though the strict definition of a perennial includes plants that live three years or more. When choosing and planting them, care must be taken to ensure both that they will be happy in their intended location and that they will not outgrow it. But with annuals and biennials, this is rarely a consideration. They live fast and die young!

Annuals, biennials and bedding plants come in an abundance of colours and forms, so you can build a beautiful border without using perennials or shrubs.

- Annual plants complete their life cycle within one year. Sunflowers, sweet peas and nasturtiums, to take just three examples, germinate from seed in spring, grow and flower through summer, then set seed before winter. With an even shorter lifespan, ephemerals run to seed in a matter of weeks. They include both weeds such as thale cress (*Arabidopsis thaliana*) and groundsel (*Senecio vulgaris*) and desert plants that survive drought as dry seeds.

- Biennials take two years to complete their cycle, spending the first developing a crown of leaves, then flowering and going to seed in the second. Foxgloves (*Digitalis*), honesty (*Lunaria annua*) and parsley are examples.

- Popular bedding plants, such as pelargoniums, petunias and begonias come into a slightly different category – many are perennial, but frost-tender, so don't last long in cold climates. They tend to be used for seasonal planters and hanging baskets, and are also often seen used *en masse* filling in space, for example in public parks or on roundabouts, a scheme known as carpet bedding.

From borders to meadows

Annual plants can either be grown direct outside, scattering the seed over a prepared area of soil, or sown individually in pots or seed trays. Which technique you choose depends not just on their hardiness, but also on how happy they are to be moved as seedlings, and how fast they grow. Hardy annuals, which are usually native to temperate areas of Europe and North America, are best sown direct into the soil. Not only is this less work, but it also avoids the need for a greenhouse or cold frame and is best suited to annuals that dislike transplanting, such as poppies. Sweet peas, though hardy, are often sown in pots in autumn to protect them from cold weather (and hungry mice), but also to ensure they flower earlier the following year. Tender species, such as morning glories (*Ipomoea*), should be sown indoors and transplanted after the danger of frost has passed. Biennials are mostly hardy and will self-seed if left after flowering. Sow direct outdoors or in containers in a cold greenhouse.

With their quick turnaround, annuals are useful gap fillers in garden borders. If you've got a patch of ground that hasn't found a purpose, too, sow a mix of annuals to give you some colour and discourage weeds until you decide on a permanent design. Seed mixes that contain a range of hardy annuals, such as poppies (*Papaver*), cornflowers (*Centaurea*) and corncockles (*Agrostemma githago*), offer a handy shortcut to creating a flowering meadow. They'll provide a riot of colourful flowers throughout the summer, then set seed in autumn, ensuring at least a partial show the following year. Slightly different from a traditional wildflower meadow, which is made up of a mixture of grasses and perennial wildflowers, annual meadows are easier to establish and require little care. Additional seed may be required to boost the blooms in subsequent years.

Using bedding effectively

Most bedding plants can be grown from seed, but they're tender, so if you want to grow them in quantity, you need a greenhouse. Instead, many gardeners simply buy bedding plants in trays from nurseries. To get them to perform at their best, they'll need both water and fertiliser. Add fertiliser granules and water-retaining gel crystals to container compost when planting up troughs or hanging baskets, as this will reduce the need for additional watering and feeding. Never allow bedding in containers to dry out, and deadhead spent flowers regularly to keep the plants blooming. Most bedding plants will only flower well in full sun; if you need options for partial shade, choose begonias and busy lizzies (*Impatiens walleriana*), as these will still flower with less light.

BULBS, CORMS AND TUBERS

In spring, much of the colour in our gardens comes from bulbs and other perennial plants with underground storage structures. From the earliest snowdrops, through crocus and daffodils, to the grand finale of tulips and alliums, spring bulbs give gardeners a lot of bang for their buck. Like herbaceous perennials, many bulbs gladly flower again in subsequent years and some multiply readily, so they're a good investment. What's more, very little care is required to get the most from many bulbs.

Bulbs, corms and tubers are all storage devices, allowing plants to build a reserve of nutrients during better times in readiness for tougher conditions ahead. Many of the species that use them hail from regions with stark changes between the seasons – for example, the Mediterranean Basin – so that the plants can grow during brief wet periods before entering dormancy as temperatures rise.

Snowdrops (Galanthus nivalis) are one of the first bulbs to bloom, sometimes pushing through late winter snows. They come up every year and gradually spread. ▶

BULB, CORM, TUBER

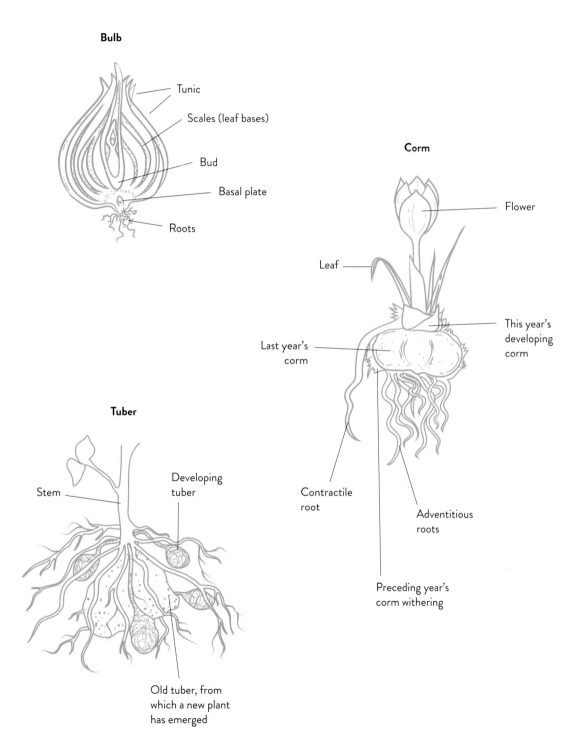

Bulb

Tunic

Scales (leaf bases)

Bud

Basal plate

Roots

Corm

Flower

Leaf

This year's developing corm

Last year's corm

Contractile root

Adventitious roots

Preceding year's corm withering

Tuber

Stem

Developing tuber

Old tuber, from which a new plant has emerged

Bulbs are composed of fleshy, scale-like leaves, which form layers, like those you find within an onion. Bulbous plants include daffodils, tulips, lilies and amaryllis. Corms are short, squat stems. They do not show layers if cut in half and are often surrounded by papery tunics that are formed from their dried-out leaves. Plants that develop from corms include crocuses, gladioli and freesias. Tubers arise both from underground stems – a category including potatoes and cyclamen – or roots, a group including dahlias and sweet potatoes. Rhizomes are stems that grow horizontally just below or on the surface of the soil. Some, including those of bearded iris and root ginger, are swollen with stored nutrients, while others, including lily of the valley, are slender, travelling further to expand the plant's territory.

Seasonal bulbs

There's a bulb flowering at almost every time of year, but in the temperate Northern Hemisphere, it's spring that is peak season. In part this is because many of our most popular garden bulbs are plants that originated around the Mediterranean and they flower after the winter rains, but before it gets too hot. Most spring bulbs belong to one of three plant families: *Liliaceae* (lilies, tulips, fritillaries), *Amaryllidaceae* (snowdrops, daffodils, alliums) and *Asparagaceae* (bluebells, squills, hyacinths). All

of these should be planted the previous autumn, allowing them to root before winter. Also worth planting in autumn are the corms of *Crocus* and autumn crocus (*Colchicum*), and tubers of winter aconites (*Eranthis*), anemones and cyclamen.

Summer-flowering bulbs are planted in spring and perhaps the best known are the true lilies (*Lilium*). Others worth seeking out are summer hyacinth (*Galtonia candicans*) and swamp lily (*Crinum* x *powellii*). Planted in spring, *Gladiolus* and *Montbretia* corms will grow into elegant border plants or can be used as cut flowers, while tuberous begonias and rhizomatous cannas make exotic-looking bedding plants. Dahlias have a huge and devoted following and offer a huge range of flower colours and shapes, sometimes with colourful foliage too. Size-wise, they go from giants like *Dahlia imperialis* to plants that don't grow much above ankle height, which are useful for containers or bedding. Pot up tubers indoors in spring or buy pot-grown plants after the final frost has passed.

Finally, while there are few bulbs that flower outdoors in winter, amaryllis (*Hippeastrum*), paper-white daffodils (*Narcissus papyraceus*) and forced hyacinths enliven the dark days indoors. Forced bulbs have been treated so that they flower earlier than is typical of their type.

◀ Some Crocus species bloom in autumn, but most flower in spring and with their small size, they're ideal for use in pots, mixed in with winter bedding.

Bulb	Sun/ Shade	Moisture	Hardiness	Height (cm)	Spread (cm)	Plant (cm)	Flower
Autumn crocus (*Colchicum*)	●	◡	H5	50	10	Jul–Aug	Aug–Sept
Cannas (*Canna*)	●	●	H1	180	100	Mar–Apr	Jun–Oct
Crocuses (*Crocus*)	●	◡	H6	10	10	Sep–Oct	Jan–Feb
Daffodils (*Narcissus*)	●	◡	H6	5–50	5–15 (most)	Sep–Oct	Feb–May
Dahlias (*Dahlia*)	●	●	H1	30–150	30–200	Apr–Jun	Jul–Sep
Fritillaries (*Fritillaria*)	●	◡	H5	10–100	10–30	Sep–Oct	Mar–May
Gladioli (*Gladiolus*)	●	◡	H1–H4	50	10	May–Jul	Jul–Sep
Hardy cyclamen (*Cyclamen*)	◗	◡	H6	5–13	8–15	Sep–Mar	Sep–Mar
Hyacinths (*Hyacinthus*)	●	◡	H6	20–30	7.5	Sep–Oct	Mar–Apr
Lilies (*Lilium*)	◗	◡	H6	80–150	10–50	Sep–Oct	May–Sept
Snowdrops (*Galanthus*)	◗	◡	H6	12	5	Apr–May	Jan–Mar
Tulips (*Tulipa*)	●	◡	H6	15–75	15 (most)	Oct–Nov	Mar–May

Situation

● Full sun preferred

◗ Partial shade preferred

Watering

● Moist but well-drained

◡ Well-drained

Hardiness

On a scale of 1 to 6

In autumn, garden centres stock up on spring bulbs, corms and tubers, both packaged and sold loose. Whichever you buy, always inspect bulbs carefully, checking that they feel firm and have no signs of damage. Beware when handling hyacinth bulbs as they can cause irritation to human skin; some nurseries offer disposable gloves for this purpose. If you opt to buy online, choose a reputable mail order company or online nursery to ensure you get quality stock.

It's crucial to get spring bulbs into the soil before the ground freezes and it really helps to plant them at the right depth. Most bulbs and corms need to be planted at a depth three times the height of the bulb. Many tubers and rhizomes prefer shallower lodgings; always check the instructions. Buy pot-grown bulbs in spring to fill any gaps and choose your summer-flowering bulbs at the same time.

ROSES

All the other plants in this book are divided up into groups depending on their growth habit – trees, shrubs, climbers – but one genus warrants a section all its own: *Rosa*, the roses. With voluptuous flowers in almost every colour, and often sweetly scented, these long-lived shrubs and climbers are excellent garden plants. What's more, the immense variety available ensures that there's a good rose for almost any garden situation.

Wild roses occur naturally across Asia, Europe and North America. The many thousands of different cultivars available today have all been bred from these wild species, of which there are around a hundred varieties. Several other plants are commonly known as roses – you'll find them in *Hibiscus*, *Hypericum*, *Cistus* and many other genera – but true roses are restricted to *Rosa*.

Rose cultivars are so numerous that they've been divided into a series of categories. Some describe the plant's habit, like shrub, climbing and rambler, while others reference the arrangement or shape of the flowers – think *polyantha* or *floribunda*. Still others reflect the parentage of the plants, such as damask, China and centifolia roses. Given the long history of hybridisation in garden roses, many cultivars belong to more than one group. Hybrids and cultivars are the most popular garden roses, but some of the original species remain worthy of cultivation, with attractive foliage (*Rosa glauca*) or colourful hips (*R. moyesii*).

Roses are often good and effective mixers in a border, mingling with a whole range of other plants.

The versatility of roses means you can use them in your garden in many ways. ▶

Choosing roses

The traditional practice of growing roses in dedicated beds or borders, often in regimented rows, has largely been replaced as gardeners with smaller plots sought to mix their favourite rose in with their perennials and other plants. Not only does this have a more relaxed effect, but it also has the benefit of reducing the risk of pests and diseases, which can blight large groups of roses planted together.

First, choose the habit you need: do you want a climber for an archway, a small plant for a container, or a shrub to add height to a border? Roses can also offer ground cover; their flowers and fruits can attract wildlife, or they can be clipped into informal hedges.

Next, think about maintenance; disease-resistant varieties reduce the need for pest control, while species roses and landscape cultivars call for less pruning than many popular hybrids.

SPECIES TO TRY

For climbing into trees
▼ R. 'Paul's Himalayan Musk' (rambler) AGM

For fragrance and flowers
▼ R. Gertrude Jekyll = 'Ausbord' (shrub) AGM

▲ *For attractive foliage*
   R. *glauca* (shrub) AGM

▲ *For a shady or north wall*
   R. 'Madame Alfred Carrière' (noisette) AGM

Roses may have a single ring of petals (single, left) or many additional petals (doubles) as in, for example, Rosa 'Faith', shown above.

Keeping roses healthy

All plants can suffer from pests and disease, but roses sometimes seem to attract more than their fair share, especially where they are grown in quantity.

• Chemical control of many of these problems is possible (see page 210), but careful stewardship can reduce the need for spraying.

• Try to mix other shrubs and perennials in with your roses, as many of these are not susceptible to rose diseases and so will not act as a reservoir for them. Flowering annuals and perennials also attract insects such as hoverflies, whose larvae consume aphids and other rose pests.

• Carefully inspect roses on a regular basis, as rapid identification and removal of diseased material can halt their spread. Always gather fallen leaves and flowers that have fallen from sick plants. Do not compost them, as pests and spores can linger in organic material.

• Never plant a new rose on a site previously occupied by roses, as the young plant may be affected by a somewhat mysterious ailment known as replant disease, which can result in a lack of vigour in the new rose, and in extreme cases may even kill it.

• Finally, as most cultivated roses are produced by grafting stem cuttings onto a rootstock, always make sure that the stock is planted below soil level. If not, it may begin to produce its own shoots or suckers, which are more vigorous than the grafted material and can take over the plant. These shoots, which often have different foliage from your chosen rose, are seldom as attractive as the plant you chose.

Most garden roses are produced by grafting a stem from a cultivar onto the rootstock of a species. ▶

3. PRACTICAL GARDENING

The essential elements of a garden are the living things grown in it, and like all living things plants need the right conditions and care to flourish. It's the gardener's job to turn a drawn or visualised plan into a planted-up plot, and to make sure that the garden is given the best possible start.

As usual, preparation is the key to ensuring you're successful. First take note of the essentials – the type of soil in a garden, how much sunshine it gets and when, how susceptible it is to wind or frost – then take them into consideration in your planning and put the knowledge you've gained to good, practical use.

Having the right tools to hand for necessary jobs is a critically important part of gardening, ensuring that you can work efficiently – the right tool for the job will save you, the gardener, an awful lot of time and effort. Preparing the ground thoroughly, making the right choice of plants, and knowing how and where to plant them will also go a long way to ensuring your long-term success.

TOOLS AND EQUIPMENT

Having the right tools for the job is essential, allowing you to work efficiently and to get the job done right. Gardeners are offered a vast range of different tools, with literally dozens of variations on, for example, a basic spade or trowel. Some options are really only for specialists – if you worked as a full-time groundskeeper, for example, you might want some of the numerous turf and grass-care tools, but the average gardener really doesn't need them. Arm yourself with some of the key basics, though, and you'll be equipped to deal with most of the jobs that the average garden throws at you.

Buying tools

Price is a major consideration when buying new tools. As always, you tend to get what you pay for: tools at the higher end of the price spectrum are usually made of higher-quality material. The best hand tools are made from stainless steel, which is light and has a polished surface which is easy to push into the soil. They'll also keep for longer than those made with cheaper metal alloys.

Size and weight matter – always handle gardening tools before buying, because everyone has different preferences as to what feels good in the hand and is comfortable to work with. Finally, remember to check out car boot sales and other secondhand suppliers when you're buying tools, particularly if you're on a tight budget. You'll sometimes find a bargain at a fraction of the original cost.

USEFUL GARDEN TOOLS

Tined cultivator A hand tool with sharp prongs at the working end. It's pulled through the ground, and is used for breaking up surface compaction or capping that can prevent moisture from penetrating the top few centimetres of soil. It can also be used to control weeds and in some cases to create a tilth for seed sowing, although a rake will give a better finish. It is possible to get long- or short-handled versions; the latter is more useful for getting in closer around plants, but you need to do more stooping when you're using it. Many tined cultivators have removable/interchangeable heads.

Trowel An essential hand tool. Wider-bladed versions make a larger hole and are used for planting small plants, such as annuals or bedding. Versions with narrower blades are useful for planting bulbs or smaller seedlings. Longer-handled versions which give better leverage in heavier soil are also available.

Hand fork Used for weeding smaller beds. The small size enables weeds to be dug out with minimal damage to surrounding plants, and reduces the amount of bending down if you need to weed raised beds. Longer-handled versions make the work less back-breaking, and offer better leverage in heavier ground conditions.

Watering can and rose Plants die for lack of water more than any other cause, so having the right kit to keep them watered is important. There are numerous hoses and irrigation systems available, but probably the cheapest, simplest and most useful tool you can have is a watering can. A fine rose on the end of the spout allows you to water your delicate seedlings with fine droplets of water.

Trug A large plastic trug is a useful tool for collecting up garden waste as you work your way round the garden. Large, lightweight buckets or heavyweight bags with handles can be used as alternatives for collecting and carting away garden rubbish. The more ornamental (and usually smaller) wooden trugs are popular for collecting harvested crops such as fruit or vegetables.

Dibber No gardener should be without a dibber. They are essentially small pointed rods, between 15–25cm (6–10in) long, that are pushed into soil or compost to create a hole for sowing. Some have a D-shaped handle. There are lots of different types on the market, but if you're on a budget, a pencil or a small pointed stick will do the job.

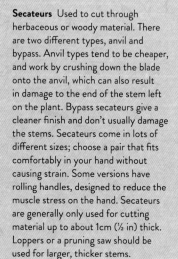

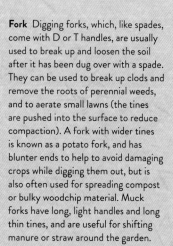

Rake The everyday garden rake is a long-handled tool used to prepare seed beds and break the soil down to a fine tilth suitable for sowing. The tines also remove any unwanted debris. The back of the rake can be used to tamp down the soil over a sown drill or to rake seed gently into the top few centimetres of the soil if you are sowing grass or a wildflower meadow. 'Landscape rakes' with a slightly longer head are also used for levelling soil. Spring-tine rakes have thin, wiry tines and are used on lawns to remove thatch from around the base of the grass blades.

Secateurs Used to cut through herbaceous or woody material. There are two different types, anvil and bypass. Anvil types tend to be cheaper, and work by crushing down the blade onto the anvil, which can also result in damage to the end of the stem left on the plant. Bypass secateurs give a cleaner finish and don't usually damage the stems. Secateurs come in lots of different sizes; choose a pair that fits comfortably in your hand without causing strain. Some versions have rolling handles, designed to reduce the muscle stress on the hand. Secateurs are generally only used for cutting material up to about 1cm (½ in) thick. Loppers or a pruning saw should be used for larger, thicker stems.

Fork Digging forks, which, like spades, come with D or T handles, are usually used to break up and loosen the soil after it has been dug over with a spade. They can be used to break up clods and remove the roots of perennial weeds, and to aerate small lawns (the tines are pushed into the surface to reduce compaction). A fork with wider tines is known as a potato fork, and has blunter ends to help to avoid damaging crops while digging them out, but is also often used for spreading compost or bulky woodchip material. Muck forks have long, light handles and long thin tines, and are useful for shifting manure or straw around the garden.

Wheelbarrow Used for transporting material around the garden. Most have just a single wheel. Barrows are usually made of plastic or stainless steel and come in a range of sizes. Choose one that, first, you can manage without causing strain on your body and, second, that is narrow enough to wheel down your paths and between your beds.

Leaf collectors Large pairs of plastic 'hands' are useful for picking up leaves that have been raked into piles. Alternatively, two short pieces of thin timber planking can do a similar job. It is possible to get plastic 'hands' on the end of handles, which saves back-breaking work in the autumn when collecting all the falling foliage off the lawns and out of the flower beds.

Border spade/fork Smaller than the standard spade and fork, these scaled-down versions are useful for making smaller holes and giving you more precision when working in among borders and flower beds. Their smallness makes them lighter and therefore not as tiring to use if you're going to be working with them all day.

Mattock This robust gardening tool is shaped similarly to a pickaxe, but while one end has an axe-like blade for chopping through hard, woody roots, the other is blunter and chunkier and is used for chopping through compacted soil.

Gloves A thick, robust pair of gloves is essential when you are digging out brambles, pruning roses or working with any other types of spiky or prickly plants. Thin gloves are more suitable for light weeding and other general gardening jobs.

Hoes There are numerous types of hoe for garden use. The Dutch hoe is used to slice through weeds just below the surface of the ground. The long handle saves the gardener from having to stoop, while the narrow blade makes it easy to work between rows of small vegetables or other plants. It should only be used on annual weeds, as perennials will reshoot from where they are severed. Draw hoes are used by pulling or drawing the blade towards the user and they penetrate the ground deeper than Dutch hoes. The curvy shape of the blade gives the draw hoe its other name, the swan-necked hoe, and means that you can use it in a small chopping motion. The edge of the draw hoe can be used to draw out a drill for seed sowing, or the entire blade pulled through the ground to make a shallow trench. Short-handled versions of the draw hoe, called onion hoes, are used for weeding at close proximity in and among plants.

Spade In the horticultural world, it isn't as simple as just calling a spade a spade. There are lots of variations available; understanding the nuances will make a huge difference to your efficiency. A spade has a D or T handle, named for their respective shapes. The length of the shaft also varies: longer ones give you more leverage, but are trickier for shorter people to use. Some spades have a straight handle, whereas others have a slight angle, again to make it easier to lever out and cut through sods of soil. The tread on the top of the blade, sometimes called the shoulder, varies in width too. Most spade blades have a blunt or square end, but some have pointed ends, making them easier to insert into compacted soil. It's important to handle a spade before you buy it. Try out the length of the handle, to make sure it doesn't force you to stoop or stretch too much when digging, and look at the breadth of the tread, considering if it will be comfortable when pushing it into the ground.

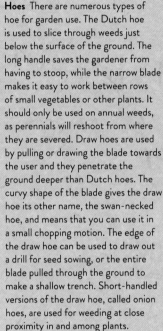

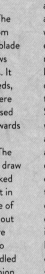

Shovel While spades are generally used for digging, shovels are used for shifting bulky material such as wood chippings or sand. The same broad considerations apply to shovels as to spades — they, too, vary in size, weight and length.

Garden string One of the most useful bits of equipment in the garden. Pulled between two sticks, it helps you achieve a straight line when sowing vegetables or ornamental plants, and can be used as a guide for cutting out lawns or laying paving.

Daisy grubber This is a weeding tool with a short handle attached to a long, narrow, two-pronged blade, designed to prise out long-rooted weeds without disturbing the surrounding soil.

GROUND PREPARATION

A lot of the hard work that goes into creating a garden happens before any plants are even put into the ground. Preparing the ground properly is essential to get your garden off to the best start possible. Badly prepared ground will cause bigger problems later on, with weeds getting out of control and poor, malnourished soil.

The type of soil you have in your garden will ultimately determine the types of plants you can grow, unless you have plans to excavate much of the existing soil and import huge amounts in. Most gardeners opt to work with their existing soil conditions, and match garden design and plants to complement them. Fortunately, there are thousands of plants that will suit every imaginable condition, from boggy and rocky to dry and arid and everything in between. Whether or not you intend to work with existing conditions, however, it is still important to make improvements and do some soil preparation before you plant.

Weed removal

Weeds are almost always part of the picture when you first start work in a new plot. Whether you believe in the 'no-dig' method or the traditional method of digging over the ground, perennial roots of weeds will still need to be removed before planting. Once the new plants have gone into the ground, it is much harder to eradicate weeds. Do remember that if you are working in winter, weeds may not be evident because herbaceous material has died back. This often happens when gardeners take on an apparently clear allotment in winter, without realising that weed roots lie beneath the surface, waiting to appear as soon as the weather warms up.

The easiest way to eradicate weeds is to spray with a systemic weedkiller (usually containing glyphosate) and wait a few weeks for the chemical to be taken down from the green chlorophyll in the leaves and into the roots. For really pernicious weeds, such as ground elder, bindweed and perennial nettle, it may need a few sprays before it has the desired effect. A bed left like this for a few weeks or months before planting is known as a stale bed.

◄ *Ensure that all weeds have been removed from the soil before starting to plant.*

Many gardeners prefer not to use chemicals, and you can dig out or smother the weeds instead, although if you want to avoid a recurrence of the problem, you do need to ensure that you get rid of every bit of root, and some can go down as far as a metre (3ft) below the surface. Thorough, methodical digging does work. Large stones and rocks should also be removed at this stage, as they will impede the development of plants when they're trying to establish. Other options include covering the soil to exclude light for a year or two, and a flame weeder for annual weeds.

If you are unfortunate enough to have Japanese knotweed in your garden, you may need to contact a specialist contractor to remove the rhizomes before considering any sort of planting. Spraying glyphosate doesn't seem to be very effective, and plants sometimes need injecting. Some contractors will dig out the entire area, sieve the soil to remove the rhizomes and return the 'cleansed' soil to you.

Weed suppression

If you aren't going to be planting for a while, any bare soil should be covered with a weed-suppressing membrane to prevent the germination of any new weeds. This will also help to warm up the soil, so that when you are ready to sow or plant, the plants or seedlings will establish much faster than if the soil had been left uncovered. If using landscape fabric, avoid the lighter type (spun material), which tends to rip. Heavy-duty woven fabric is much more durable. Whatever you use make sure it is well pegged or weighted down so that it doesn't blow away in high winds.

Preparing the soil

When perennial weeds have been removed from the soil and it has been dug over with a spade (see page 129), the ground can be lightly forked to break up big clods, then further reduced with a garden or landscape rake so that the soil becomes a fine tilth suitable for sowing or planting into. The rake can also be used to level the ground, removing any bumps and hollows. On really steep ground, it may be necessary to terrace the ground and to create level beds along the slopes. The ground can also be raked to re-contour areas to create different levels in the garden.

▲ Heavier, woven weed-
▲ suppressing membranes work more effectively than the lighter variety.

▲ Landscape rakes are useful for levelling uneven ground and for breaking up lumps of soil into a fine tilth for sowing.

IMPROVING THE SOIL

The condition of the soil that plants grow in is probably the most important factor in whether they will thrive or struggle in a garden. There is a wide range of different products that can be incorporated into the soil to improve it. It is worth spending time improving the soil before you plant, because new plants will benefit from good soil from the moment they are planted. There are basically two types of products you can add to the soil: fertilisers and mulches/composts.

Fertilisers

These are often incorporated into the soil prior to sowing or planting. This is known as base dressing. Adding them after the soil has been planted up is called top dressing. Fertilisers can be organic or inorganic, and come in numerous different forms, including powder, granules and liquid.

For general planting it is usually best to use a balanced fertiliser, but if you wanted to customise towards one element, you can. To incorporate more nitrogen (for green, leafy growth) for example, you could feed with chicken pellets, or to add more phosphorus (to encourage strong root growth), you could add bone meal; blood, fish and bone, or superphosphate. Something with a high potassium level, such as a tomato feed, will encourage flowering and fruit. As plants have different mineral and nutrient requirements at different stages of growth, the best compromise is a controlled-release fertiliser, which, although it's quite an expensive option, will release varying amounts of either nitrogen, potassium or phosphorus depending on what point in the season it is. If you're using a base-dressing fertiliser, it should be applied to the surface just before you plant, to ensure it doesn't wash off the bare soil.

▲ Mixing fertilisers into the soil or compost prior to planting is an effective method of boosting the available nutrients for plants.

Nutrient content

Fertilisers will usually be labelled with the letters NPK, alongside a number. This shows their nutrient content. N stands for nitrogen, P for phosphorus and K for potassium. The number next to them shows the ratio of the nutrients – so, for example, NPK 1:1:3 on a fertiliser label would indicate that it is higher in potassium than nitrogen or phosphorus.

Applying mulches and compost

Fertilisers feed your plants with nutrients and minerals, but they won't improve your soil texture. To tackle this, you need to use bulky organic matter, such as garden compost or well-rotted manure. Incorporating bulky material is best done a few weeks before planting to allow levels to settle.

Adding animal manure is one of the best ways to improve soil texture, and it will also add a certain amount of nutrients, which will be released slowly into the ground. These days it would seem you can get almost any type of animal manure if you're willing to look hard enough – alpaca, kangaroo or even lion manure have been offered for sale. For most gardeners, though the first choice is usually horse manure – it's the richest – followed by pig or cow manure.

Garden compost is another form of rich, bulky organic matter that will boost the humus matter in your soil, and it's free, if you have the space to maintain a compost heap. Mushroom compost is readily available and is effective, but has a high lime content, so avoid using it around acid-loving plants. Leaf mould can also be used – it has poor nutrient levels but is a good soil conditioner.

Rotting down manure

Always make sure that animal manure is rotted down before you use it, because the nitrogen it contains can scorch the plants when fresh. The way to rot down fresh manure is to stack it in a heap, add lots of water to help decomposition, then cover it with plastic sheets to warm it up and speed up the rotting stage. The manure should be ready to add to the ground after a few weeks. Alternatively, some people mix some manure in with their compost heap, where it will have longer to rot down, and may even help the progress of other composted materials.

Adding plenty of rotted manure prior to planting will add some nutrients and, more importantly, improve the quality
▼ *of the soil.*

DIGGING AND THE 'NO-DIG' METHOD

The process of digging over soil has been carried out for thousands of years and is considered to be one of the key cultivation techniques for improving the ground prior to planting. However, some modern gardeners advocate an alternative technique called the 'no-dig' method, which has also been shown to provide good results in the garden.

SINGLE DIGGING TECHNIQUE

Use a spade for digging over the soil. Work methodically over the soil to ensure the whole area is cultivated. Marking the area out with a string helps to ensure all the ground has been worked over.

Digging is hard work. To avoid straining your body, try to keep your back straight while you dig, and don't overload the spade; only load it with manageable amounts. If possible, schedule digging an area in short sessions over a few days, rather than trying to do all the work in one long shift.

Whichever method of digging you are following, always remember to dig out perennial roots as you go.

Single digging is enough for most allotments or flower beds.

DOUBLE DIGGING TECHNIQUE

Double digging is useful where the subsoil is compacted and needs breaking up. Follow the steps for single digging, shown, but additionally fork over the floor of each trench to the depth of the tines, and dig some extra organic matter into the bottom. Avoid mixing the soil from the lower trench (subsoil) with the topsoil from the upper trench.

① Mark out trenches with string.

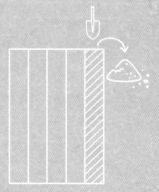

② Dig out the soil a spit deep (the depth of the spade blade) and save it for the final trench.

3 Move over to the next trench along, marked out with string, and start digging out trench two, putting the contents into trench one and mixing in organic matter as you go.

4 When you finish, trench two will be empty. Dig out trench three alongside it, and use the soil you're digging to backfill trench two, adding organic matter as you go.

5 Continue this process until the whole plot has been covered, filling the final trench with the soil from trench one. Finally, rake the bed level and leave to settle for a few days before planting.

THE 'NO-DIG' TECHNIQUE

If you're thinking that the digging techniques recommended sound too much like hard work, don't despair. There is another school of thought that not only saves all that back-breaking work but also argues that digging actually damages the existing soil structure and the natural activities of microorganisms, bacteria and earthworms. Instead, the 'no-dig' technique recommends that the soil should be left undug and, instead, layers of organic matter, such as compost, should be regularly added to the surface, and left slowly to become incorporated into the soil layer beneath, as rain and the activity of earthworms gradually channel it below ground. Soon a healthy, natural substrate will be created for plants to thrive in. Seeds are sown or plants planted directly into the top layer of the organic matter. It may be necessary occasionally to use a fork to remove perennial weeds.

A layer of well-rotted compost or other organic matter is added directly over the soil surface and left. An empty bed should be left for some weeks before planting; if you want to practise the no-dig method on a bed that is already planted, simply lay the layer of organic matter carefully around the plants, avoiding direct contact with their stems.

Gradually rain will start to water the organic matter down through the soil, and the activities of worms and bacteria will start to mix the layers naturally, resulting in enriched soil with an improved structure.

Compost or soil

Fertiliser

Loose straw

Fertiliser

Parcels of lucerne hay

Newspaper

The layers of a typical no-dig bed

Trenching

Last of the techniques is trenching, which is the ultimate in ground preparation, but is only necessary for extremely compacted subsoils. You start as for single digging, with a trench a spit deep, but then dig out another trench within the first, to the same depth but only half the width. The trench will look as though it has a step in it.

The base of the lower trench is then forked over and organic matter added, then the soil of the upper half of the trench (the step) is moved over into the lower, leaving a new 'low' layer exposed on the other half of the trench which, in its turn, is dug over and has organic matter added. Then a second trench is dug alongside the first, to the 'step' depth of the first. Soil from this trench is added to the first trench as you dig, to bring it up to ground level, and the sequence is repeated until the whole area has been covered.

Why dig?

Even if you choose to cultivate your crops using the no-dig method, there are still occasions when there are benefits to digging. First, if the ground is very compacted, or has never been cultivated before, the soil will need to be broken up to remove any 'pans' below the surface that will get in the way of the roots of trees, shrubs and even, in very shallow soil, herbaceous plants. Compacted soil also drains poorly, and digging helps to improve this.

Digging over the ground is a good way to incorporate well-rotted manure or other organic matter into the depth of the soil, encouraging tree and shrub roots downwards towards the water table. This will give them a chance of longer lives and will equip them better to survive periods of drought.

When to dig

You can dig over the soil at any time of year, but it is best to avoid extremes of weather, such as frosts, droughts or very wet periods, as this can harm the soil structure as well as create a difficult environment for working in. Many gardeners like to dig over the ground in late autumn, when most of the crops have been harvested. Not only does digging warm you up as the weather starts to get cooler, but traditional gardening lore claims that heavy clods of soil exposed on the surface will break down better when the winter weather arrives.

Digging will help to break up very compacted soil which may otherwise block
▼ *roots from growing freely downwards.*

Worms are a gardener's friend, as they aerate the soil, make it more friable and
▼ *pull nutrients down into the ground.*

CHOOSING AND BUYING PLANTS

Today, garden centres, nurseries and even supermarkets, along with many hundreds of online plant suppliers, are bringing a huge range of plants within the reach of gardeners. Despite the vast choice available, the basic rules of choosing good plants for your garden remain the same. However tempting the colourful displays, whether on tables and trolleys or on screen, long-term horticultural quality rather than instant eye appeal should be your overall goal.

How to choose the right plants:

• First and foremost, concentrate on plants that suit the conditions of your garden, and fit the place and the purpose you're buying for.

• If you are shopping in person, the chances are that you will be buying pot-grown specimens. Check that the plant is correctly labelled, looks healthy and is free of pests and disease or any other type of damage. Moss or liverworts in the pot may be a sign that the plant has been sitting around too long, and so is to be avoided if possible.

• If possible, gently remove the plant from its pot to check the roots (if not, at least check underneath to see if roots are growing through the holes. This may indicate that the plant is 'pot-bound', making it is less likely to establish successfully.)

• Check that the plant is a good representative of its type. Shrubs should be balanced and well branched, and trees should not look stunted or top-heavy (both are signs that the pot – and therefore the root ball – is too small). Pot-grown perennials should look healthy and vigorous, with strong growing shoots. If buying annuals or bedding plants, choose plants with plenty of shoots and buds rather than full flowers to ensure a longer seasonal display.

Bare-root plants

The great advantage of buying container-grown plants is that they can be planted at almost any time of the year, unless weather conditions are too extreme. However, it is also possible to buy plants either 'bare root' – that is, completely without soil – or 'root-balled', where the roots and some soil are lifted and wrapped before sale. Deciduous trees and shrubs, especially roses and hedging, are often sold bare root during the dormant period between October and April and are cheaper than pot-grown plants, though they require planting or at least heeling in (planting in a temporary situation before being moved to their permanent position) as soon as possible after delivery.

Ordering plants online or by post makes a visual check before buying impossible, so it is especially important to buy from reputable suppliers, most of whom offer guarantees of some sort and testimonials or customer reviews. Do your research beforehand to avoid disappointment.

PLANTING TREES AND SHRUBS

If you are planting a tree, you usually expect it to live for years to come, possibly even to be admired by future generations, so it's essential to give the tree the best possible start by planting it well. Although shrubs are shorter-lived than trees, it is still important to plant them correctly so they will look their healthy best in the garden.

Buying a tree from a garden centre or nursery is an investment for the future, and can be expensive – yet it is astounding how many trees die within just a few years due to being badly planted. The main mistakes are that a tree is planted too deeply, causing the base of the trunk to rot, or that the roots have been allowed to become pot-bound in the nursery and can't establish properly once planted, instead continue growing in a spiral and eventually strangling themselves. Another common reason for low success rates after planting is lack of water in the first few seasons.

One other key consideration when planting a tree is its location. Imagine how it will look in 10 years' time, 25 years' time… perhaps, if you're planting in a really big landscape, even in a century or two. Will it begin to block a view? Will it cause too much shade in your garden? Will it cause problems with your neighbours?

Also, check what conditions it likes and whether it will be able to cope with the surrounding environment. Some types, such as most *Acer*, prefer sheltered conditions away from exposed winds and out of direct sunlight which can desiccate their leaves. Other trees thrive in hot, direct sun and can tolerate harsh, windy conditions. Make sure the tree is suited to the plot.

A well-planted tree such as this cherry (Prunus incisia) should last a lifetime and look beautiful for many years to come. ▶

HOW TO PLANT A TREE OR SHRUB

Shrubs are planted in the same way as trees, as described below, but do check on the label for spacing requirements to ensure they are given enough room. Most probably won't need staking.

① Dig out a hole that is the same depth as the root ball and at least twice its circumference. To gauge the depth of the root ball, remove the tree from the pot and scrape away any loose compost to expose the top of the root system and the very bottom of the trunk, which will widen slightly as it meets the root ball (this is called the root flare). This is the point that should be level with the ground when planted, and the planting hole should be only as deep as necessary to allow for this. Lightly prick the bottom of the hole with the garden fork to encourage roots to go downwards.

② Check the root ball once removed from the pot. If it has been in a container for a while, the roots may be compacted and growing tightly around each other in the pot. These roots need to be vigorously pulled out to ensure that once the tree is in the ground, the roots grow outwards and don't continue to spiral around. If they don't spread outwards, they will be susceptible to drought as their only source of moisture and nutrients will be within the tiny planting hole. Long-term, this will also mean that the tree is unstable as the roots haven't reached out far enough to anchor into the ground.

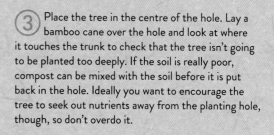

③ Place the tree in the centre of the hole. Lay a bamboo cane over the hole and look at where it touches the trunk to check that the tree isn't going to be planted too deeply. If the soil is really poor, compost can be mixed with the soil before it is put back in the hole. Ideally you want to encourage the tree to seek out nutrients away from the planting hole, though, so don't overdo it.

④ Ask somebody to hold the tree straight and start to backfill around the rootball with the soil you dug out, until the hole is filled in. Soil can also be backfilled by washing it into the hole with lots of water; this has the added bonus of getting lots of moisture to the roots on planting, and of minimising air pockets, ensuring roots and soil make good contact.

⑥ The tree will probably need staking for the first couple of years, particularly if it is top-heavy and in an exposed position. Use an angled stake at about 45 degrees to avoid damaging the root ball. Bang the stake into the ground with a mallet. The tree should be tied to the stake low down on the trunk, about an eighth of the way up. This will allow the trunk to flex in the wind, which will strengthen it like a muscle and ensure that the tree can stand on its own once the stake is removed, which should be after no more than two years. Use a tree tie with a protective pad between the trunk and the stake to prevent it rubbing.

⑤ Firm the soil in around the root ball using your foot, with your heel towards the outside of the hole and toes towards the trunk. Work your way round until the tree feels stable in the hole.

⑦ If you haven't already watered when backfilling, give the tree a good watering once it's in, to allow the soil to settle around it. Well-rotted manure or garden compost can be added around the surface of the hole to a depth of about 5cm (2in) to help retain moisture and suppress any competitive weeds. Ensure that the organic matter is at least 6cm (2½in) away from the trunk — if it's heaped up in direct contact, it may cause the tree to rot.

PLANTING ROSES

Roses are the most spectacular of shrubs, with a huge range of colour and fragrance to choose from, whether you pick a rambling rose to scramble over a pergola, an old-fashioned, heavily scented shrub type for a herbaceous border or a hybrid tea rose with spectacularly large flowers to grow in a pot. Whatever type you fancy, roses must be planted correctly to get them to perform at their best.

If roses are to be housed in a container they can be planted at any time of the year, but aim to avoid extremes of weather. The best time for planting in the ground is usually early to mid-autumn as the soil will be warm, which will give the plant the chance to establish itself before the onset of winter and ensure that it is ready to burst into growth in spring. Bare-root roses are only available from late autumn to late winter and should ideally be planted as soon as they are purchased. If this isn't possible, bury their roots in soil (heeling in) until you are ready to plant them.

Most roses prefer full sun, but some will tolerate part shade; check which variety you have when deciding on the location to plant it in. Expert advice from a reputable supplier is always helpful.

Roses like a rich, heavy soil, so if yours is infertile or sandy, dig large amounts of organic matter, such as well-rotted horse manure or garden compost, into the top 30cm (12in) of the soil before you plant. As a general rule of thumb, you should add about a wheelbarrow-full of organic matter to one square metre (1.2 sq yards) of ground.

Keeping roses happy and healthy

Roses, and most plants of the rose family (*Rosaceae*), suffer from a problem called replant disease, meaning that if other members of the family have previously been planted in the ground, then either you should choose a new location for a new rose or roses, or you should remove the soil of an area 1m (3ft) square, and the same depth, and replace it with new soil before planting. Using mycorrhizal powder around the root system may also help newly planted roses combat the problem.

Roses will be less stressed if they don't have to compete with weeds for nutrients, so – as is good practice with all planting – ensure that the area has been well weeded before you plant. If the new rose plants are bare root, soak the roots in a bucket of water for an hour or so before planting. If the roses are in containers, give them a thorough watering. As roses are hungry feeders, they will also benefit from a base dressing of a general-purpose fertiliser at about 100g per sq metre (3½oz per 1.2 sq yards). Don't use fertiliser if you are using mycorrhizal powder, however – research has shown that it suppresses the natural benefits of the fungus.

▲ Planting a rose correctly should help keep it looking healthy and producing an abundance of flowers.

HOW TO PLANT ROSES

- Dig out a planting hole (see page 74) for each rose, about the same depth as the root ball and approximately twice the circumference.

- If container-grown, remove the rose from its pot and give the roots a tug to ensure they won't continue to grow around in a circle but will instead grow outwards once planted. If the roots continue to grow inwardly it will make the rose plant susceptible to drought.

- Place the rose in the middle of the hole. Check the planting depth by placing a bamboo cane across the top of the hole and seeing where it touches the stem of the plant. If you're planting a bare-root rose, look for the grafting union (a bulge on the stem of the plant). In a heavy, moisture-retentive soil the union should be at, or just above, the soil level; in a sandy, free-draining soil the union should be at soil level or very slightly below it.

- If you are using mycorrhizal powder, add it to the planting hole at this stage.

- When you're happy with the height, backfill the area surrounding the root ball of the rose with a 50:50 mix of compost and the excavated soil from the hole. Gently firm the plant in by pushing the soil down with your fingertips, ensuring the soil goes between the individual larger roots rather than just sitting on top of them. Water the plants in well, or water as you backfill.

- If you are planting more than one rose, check the label for the spacing needed between plants, as this varies enormously depending on the variety and type of rose. Label each rose as you plant, or make sure existing labels are well attached to the stems, so you don't get them mixed up.

PLANTING A HEDGE

Hedges are wonderful natural features with multiple uses. In the garden, they can define boundaries, screen out unattractive features, create private areas, and bring structure and pattern to an overall design. They can also provide a rich habitat for wildlife.

Hedges can be grown in lots of different forms, from many different trees and shrubs. Evergreen ones will provide year-round screening, whereas deciduous hedges grown from species such as beech (*Fagus sylvatica*) will give you seasonal colour – a beech hedge will range from lime green in spring through to deep mellow buttery colours in autumn and then copper as it clings to its leaves into winter. Hedge height can range from 30cm (12in) or so, in a clipped knot garden for instance, to house-high in the case of some soaring species such as leylandii (*Cupressus* x *leylandii*) and other conifer

types. Whichever kind of hedge you want in your garden, however, the principles of establishing it will be the same.

Remember to water the plants for the hedge thoroughly before you plant them. If they are bare-root trees, it is worth placing their roots in a bucket of water for an hour or so first.

▼ *Evergreen hedges provide structure as well as all-year-round interest.*

79

HOW TO PLANT A HEDGE

① Hedges can consist of a single row of plants, but more often than not are planted as a double row in order to create a thicker structure. To do this, stretch out two parallel lengths of string along the line of your intended hedge. If you are using young, bare-root trees the rows should be 40cm (16in) apart; if you are using larger, container-grown trees, the rows may need to be further apart to allow enough space to plant their larger root balls.

② Mark where each hedging plant is going to be planted with canes. Plants should be about 40cm (16in) apart, but should be staggered. Start the second row 20cm (8in) away from the start of the first one, so that the planting has a zigzag effect between the rows.

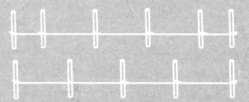

③ To plant a bare-root hedging plant, push a spade the full length of its blade (known as a spit depth) into the soil where the first tree is to be planted and simply push the handle forward about 20cm (8in) away from you. This will open up the soil slightly and create a gap. Slide the bare-root tree down the back of the spade and settle it into the gap and then gently pull the spade out of the ground, allowing the soil to close up around the plant. Firm the plant in by gently treading round it with your feet.
Repeat the process until all the plants are in the ground.

4 If you are planting a hedge with large, containerised trees, it is usually easier to dig out a trench along the two rows at the same depth as the height of the root ball. Remove the plants from their pots and place them in the trench, evenly spaced, remembering to stagger the second row to create a zigzag effect. Ask somebody to hold each plant upright as you work along the row, backfilling the trench and firming the soil in around the plants.

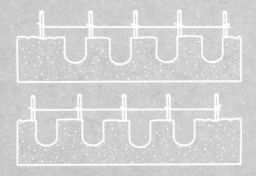

5 Plants should be thoroughly watered after planting. If you live in an area where rabbits or deer are a problem, you may need to put rabbit guards or wire fencing around the bases of the new plants.

6 To encourage the hedge to 'bush out', trim back the central trunks, or leaders, by a few centimetres to encourage lateral growth. Repeat this in successive years as the hedge plants grow, so that the hedge begins to fill out and create the desired shape and coverage.

PLANTING IN CONTAINERS

Almost any kind of plant can be grown in a container, as long as the gardener provides the right conditions and care. Planting in pots may be essential if you have no access to a garden or have very limited space, but it can also be a useful addition to larger gardens, when you need an extra burst of colour in summer or a stylish focal point. A surprising number of different vegetables and herbs are also perfectly happy grown in pots – set down by the back door or on a warm windowsill, they can be in useful proximity to the kitchen.

Choose containers that suit your taste as well as meeting the needs of the plant. Terracotta is a good classic choice, but stylish contemporary containers may sometimes be more appropriate in a modern setting, while lightweight plastic pots are often the most suitable for balconies and rooftops.

The size of the pot will obviously be dependent on the size of the plant: larger for trees and shrubs, smaller for herbs, annuals and perennials. As a rule, a container should offer enough space to fit the root ball comfortably, leaving some room for the roots to grow out and down.

A soil-based compost is appropriate for permanent plantings such as trees, shrubs and larger perennials. It will retain water, be heavy enough to ensure the pot's stability and can be revitalised each spring by top dressing. To top-dress pots, remove the top layer of compost and replace it with fresh compost and slow-release fertiliser.

Bedding plants, vegetables and annuals can be grown in ordinary multipurpose compost, which is easily replaced each season. For hanging baskets, choose a proprietary hanging basket compost, or mix slow-release fertiliser and water-retaining crystals into ordinary compost to ensure that the baskets are easy to maintain.

HOW TO PLANT IN CONTAINERS

- Ensure the container has adequate drainage – make holes in the bottom if necessary. Pot feet may also help to allow excess water to drain away and stop plants sitting in soggy, oxygen-deprived soil.

- Fill the pot with compost mixed with a granular fertiliser. If you are growing shallow-rooted bedding plants in a deeper pot, you can partially fill it with gravel before adding compost; for a tree or a shrub, however, the pot should be completely filled with compost.

- Leave a 5cm (2in) gap at the top of the pot so that water and compost won't spill over during watering.

- Position your plants, firm them in gently after planting and water well.

MAKING A LAWN

Gardeners often have a love-hate relationship with lawns. Most people appreciate the benefits of a lawn, whether for kicking a football about, or for lounging on, simply enjoying sitting out of doors. The pleasure may be countered by the regular mowing and maintenance needed. If you have the space, though, a lawn does create a lovely area in which to unwind in the garden.

There are two ways to make a lawn: one is to sow seed, and the other is to lay turves. Each method has pros and cons, as described below.

Laying turf

Advantages
• Instant effect – a lawn made of turves looks great almost as soon as it is laid. And it can be walked on just a few weeks after laying.
• Depending on soil condition, laying turf may require less soil preparation than for sowing seed.

▲ *Turf can be laid at any time throughout the year, although it's not advisable to do so during extreme weather conditions such as drought or frost.*

Disadvantages
• Rolls of turf are more expensive to buy than seed. If you don't have a van or pickup, you'll also have to pay for delivery, as turf is bulky to handle.
• Laying heavy rolls of turf is strenuous. Sowing seed is much lighter work.
• Turf is on a tight schedule. If you want it to be in top condition, it needs to be laid within a day or two of being delivered.

Sowing seed

Advantages
• Seed is much cheaper to buy than rolls of turf.
• Seed gives you a much wider range of grass to choose from. With rolls of turf there are often just two types: fine lawns and hard-wearing lawns.

Disadvantages
• Seed takes much longer than turves to become established, and there are problems to watch out for whilst waiting for the seed to germinate – you may need to check for weeds as it grows, for example, or net the lawn area to stop birds from eating the seed.
• Seed will only germinate in warmer weather, between spring and mid-autumn.
• Sowing seed requires a very fine tilth to get established, so there may be a good deal of soil preparation involved.

PREPARING THE GROUND

Prepare the ground by thoroughly digging it over to the depth of a spade's blade. If there are compaction and drainage issues, you may need to double-dig (see page 68). All stones and weeds should be removed. Organic matter, such as garden compost, should be dug into the top 15cm (6in).

(1) The ground should then be roughly raked, trodden down by walking over it and then raked again before leaving it for a couple of weeks to allow the ground to settle. If you lay turf or sow seed too soon, the soil won't have fully settled, and you will be left with an unstable surface, with hollows and bumps appearing all over your lawn.

(2) After a few weeks, return to the plot and walk over it again or use a light roller and rake it over a few times in different directions. Correct any hollows and bumps that may have appeared and break the soil down to a fine crumbly tilth. It is now ready for sowing or laying turf.

SOWING A LAWN

Choose a clear windless day, so the seed won't blow about.

(1) Mark out a grid of 1 metre (1 yard) squares using string.

(2) Measure out your rate (how much seed you need to sow – standard mixes often prescribe 50g per square metre (2oz per square yard), but check the packet instructions as the quantity may vary in different grass species). Sow half in one direction across the square, then the other half at 90 degrees to the first half.

(3) Rake the seed in very lightly so that it is just below the surface of the soil.

(4) Repeat this process in the other squares. Lightly water in the seed.

(5) It may be necessary to cover the lawn with nets or use vibrating strings to prevent birds from eating the seed.

(6) The lawn should be established in a few weeks – exactly how long depends on weather conditions. It will need watering during dry periods; if needed, as often as daily.

(7) Once the sward (the expanse of short grass) is thick enough, use a half-moon to cut the edge and give the lawn a clearly defined edge.

Sow half the seed in one direction across the square, then the other half at 90 degrees to the first half.

LAYING A LAWN

Turves can be laid throughout the year but will need lots of irrigation if laid in summer or during a dry spell. The rolls will quickly shrivel up if not kept well-watered. When laying turves, avoid walking on them directly – lay a plant of wood across them and stand on it to lay the next row. This will ensure that your weight is equally distributed along the turves and will help them bed into the soil better.

① Lay your first row of turf up against one edge of the intended lawn area. Tamp the roll down with the back of a rake to ensure the roots bind with the soil underneath.

② Make sure that the end of one roll and the start of the next one are tightly butted up to one another; turves will dry out quickly and shrivel up if the edges are exposed.

③ Stagger the next row, like brickwork, so that the rolls don't all end in a lined-up grid across the lawn.

④ Keep a bucket of loam (soil made up of clay and sand, containing humus) with you and as you work along each row fill any hollows that appear, to make sure you have a level surface.

⑤ Try to avoid placing short strips at the end of each row, as these will be susceptible to drying out. Instead, move a longer strip to the outside and use the smaller section to fill the gap between the two longer ones.

⑥ Once all the turves have been laid, use a half-moon to cut and trim the edges. Work off a plank so your weight is evenly distributed.

⑦ Fill any gaps between turves with a sandy top dressing made up of one part organic matter, three parts sand and three parts loam.

⑧ Fill any gaps between turves with a sandy top dressing made up of one part organic matter, three parts sand and three parts loam.

Place shorter strips in the middle of the row.

4. EVERYDAY GARDEN CARE

The ongoing care of a garden is both a challenge and a pleasure for most gardeners. Gardens are constantly changing, both day-to-day and seasonally. And by their very nature, they all require regular intervention to a greater or lesser degree. Even the most 'natural' garden has to be managed to some extent, or nature itself will quickly take over in its own extravagant way.

Depending on time and resources, gardens need maintenance to remain fit for purpose. Basic techniques are easy to learn, and include feeding, pruning and watering. Lawn and hedge care, too, are useful skills to have under your belt.

Learning and applying these techniques is the essence of good gardening, and they will stand you in good stead, whatever kind or size of garden you are looking after.

A garden is never 'finished', but there are constant small satisfactions to be enjoyed in its everyday care.

WATERING AND IRRIGATION

Water is just as important for plants as it is for us, and mostly rain water provides all that our gardens need. Paying attention to the water needs of plants is key to keeping your garden healthy. In fact, incorrect watering is one of the main causes of death in plants.

Water butts are increasingly popular among gardeners for collecting rainwater and therefore ▼ avoiding relying on expensive mains water.

The simplest test to see if a container plant needs water is to stick your finger in the soil or compost. If it feels dry to the touch, then the plant usually needs watering. However, be aware that some plants, particularly house plants, suffer if they are overwatered and prefer to stay on the dry side. If in doubt, get advice from the garden centre or check the label (it's always worth asking about water requirements when you buy an unfamiliar plant). When you do water, make sure the water is penetrating deeply into the soil surrounding the plant and not just running off.

In summertime, some container plants need watering as often as twice daily. If you're on a water meter this can get expensive, so think about whether you're in a position to harvest rainwater. The best way to do this is to channel it from the roof of a shed or garage into a water butt. There are plenty of options available in every garden centre, but a water butt doesn't have to be custom-made – bear in mind that any watertight container, such as a plastic dustbin, will work well.

Ways to cut water use

Using water wisely is very important. Here are a few things you can do to reduce your water waste:

• Avoid moving large plants from containers into the ground in summer as they will need watering once or twice a day until they are established. Instead, move them in autumn or early spring to cut the amount of watering required. By summer, they should have established a better root system and be able to source more water for themselves.

• Water in the evening or early in the morning. Avoid watering in the heat of the day, as most of the water will evaporate. Water splashing onto leaves under direct sunlight can cause water scorch marks, too.

SETTING UP A WATER BUTT TO HARVEST RAINWATER FROM A SHED ROOF

① Prepare your water butt by drilling a hole to fit the tap into, about 5cm (2in) above the base of the butt.

② Screw the tap into the hole, ensuring that the washer is on the inside of the water butt to guarantee it stays watertight.

③ Position the water butt next to the shed, placed where it won't get in your way when passing by. Raise it on bricks so there is enough room underneath to position a watering can under the tap.

④ Attach support brackets at the top of the sides of the shed, just below the roof, to support the guttering, ensuring that the guttering slopes slightly downwards towards the water butt.

⑤ Slot the guttering into the support brackets.

⑥ Attach a section of downpipe leading to the top of the water butt.

A lid on a water butt will reduce evaporation, and also deter mosquitoes from breeding in the water. If the one you've chosen has a lid without a hole (to fit the downpipe through), you may need to cut one yourself.

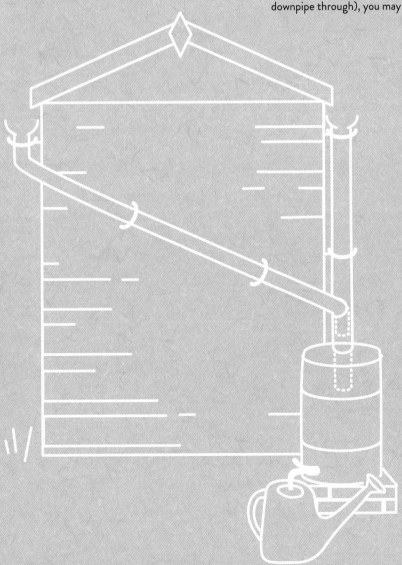

▲ *Plants in hanging baskets and containers will need more watering than those planted in the ground.*

• Use an irrigation system for your container plants or plants growing under glass. There are lots of different options on the market, including some that attach to the mains water system with pipes leading to all your plants, so that all you need to do is turn the tap on. Some systems have timers so that you can go away on holiday and not have to worry about your plants. There is also a weather-responsive solar system that senses when the sun is out and releases water when it feels the plants will need it.

The plants that suffer the most during dry periods are those in containers and hanging baskets, which need more frequent watering – sometimes as much as twice a day – than those in the ground. If you are going away for a day or two, move them into the shade to help them cope, and give them a good drink before leaving and immediately on your return.

• Mulch around your plants with organic matter. This helps to retain moisture.

• Push the soil or organic matter up around the plants to create a bowl shape around the stems. This will help to hold in the water when watering.

RIGGING UP A SEEP HOSE

Seep hoses are simple irrigation systems. They are useful in areas of the garden that are newly planted and that may need a bit of help to get them established in their first year. Although you can buy seep hoses, it is easy to rig up your own from an old piece of hosepipe, plus a tap attachment and a closed end piece.

(1) Use a knife to cut tiny holes into the hosepipe at 10cm (4in) intervals.

(2) Attach a closed end section at the end of the hosepipe to prevent water coming out.

(3) Lay it on the ground among your rows of vegetables or other plants.

(4) Attach the other end to the mains tap. Turn on the tap and check to see how much water is coming out of the holes.

If you attach your seep hose to a timer, you'll have a fully automated watering system. You can set it to water plants at night, when the water won't evaporate.

FEEDING AND FERTILISERS

Occasional feeds with fertilisers will help to keep your plants healthy and ensure they are getting the right nutrients. Regularly monitor your plants to check they are growing well; the first sign of a nutrient deficiency in a plant is often discoloration of the leaves.

Plants are remarkably clever organisms. They generate their own food from the soil, mixing ingredients together to make healthy nutrition that will sustain them during the growing season. The raw ingredients include mineral ion nutrients, which plants mix into a concoction with water and the carbon dioxide found in the soil, and absorb through their roots. In the horticultural world, mineral ion nutrients are divided into two groups, macronutrients and micronutrients. The latter are sometimes also called trace elements and the plants need them in much smaller quantities.

The nutrients plants need

These nutrients are essential for a plant's survival. If the soil it's planted in is nutrient-deficient, then either the soil will need to be replenished with fertiliser or the plant will need to be fed directly with a foliar feed.

The macronutrients plants need are nitrogen (N), phosphorus (P), potassium (K), magnesium (Mg), calcium (Ca) and sulphur (S), while the micronutrients include iron (Fe), manganese (Mn), copper (Cu), zinc (Zn), boron (Bo) molybdenum (Mb) and chlorine (Cl).

For a gardener, the three main macronutrients to be aware of are nitrogen, phosphorus and potassium. Nitrogen promotes green, leafy growth, phosphorus promotes strong root growth and potassium helps a plant develop its flowers, fruit

▲ Fertilisers come in several guises, such as powders, liquids and in this case pellets, which are used to feed plants.

and colour. Commercial fertilisers are often labelled with their ratio of NPK, a guide to the percentages of the three that they contain.

Plants that don't get enough of two key micronutrients, iron and manganese, may also suffer. This particularly applies to acid-loving plants – rhododendrons, camellias, magnolias and heathers among them – that are planted in non-acidic soil. A deficiency of iron and manganese will cause leaves to turn yellow between the veins, and the plant will need feeding around its roots to compensate – although it's worth noting that if a plant is in the wrong soil, the best way of all to solve the problem is to move it to more appropriate conditions.

Types of fertiliser

The choice of fertilisers can be bewildering; there are so many brands and types on offer. The three main groups, though, are as follows:

• *Bulky organic fertilisers*
Manure and garden compost fall into this category. Bulky organic fertilisers don't have as many nutrients as inorganic fertilisers – very roughly, you would need about a ton of well-rotted manure to provide the same amount of nutrients as just 30kg (66lb) of inorganic fertilisers. However, they do improve the soil in other ways: they contain micronutrients, encourage earthworm activity, increase moisture levels and improve soil structure. All of these are helpful to plants; in particular, better soil structure encourages good root development. Green manures are also an effective method for improving the nutrient content of the soil (see page 129).

• *Organic concentrated fertilisers*
These are made from plant or animal extracts. Bone meal, blood, fish and bone, and hoof and horn are all examples. They are bought as proprietary mixes and are available from most garden centres. They are effective feeds but are usually more expensive than inorganic fertilisers. However, they will generally last for longer in the soil.

• *Inorganic fertilisers*
These are also sometimes called synthetic fertilisers and are artificially made up to provide a more concentrated feed than organic ones. They generally provide a much faster feed of macronutrients to the plant, but don't remain in the ground as long. A middle way is to buy controlled- or slow-release fertiliser, which is designed to release nutrients gradually throughout the growing season.

How to apply fertilisers

The most common method of feeding the soil is to 'broadcast' the fertiliser. To do this on bare soil, prior to planting, measure the area you want to cover into a square-metre or square-yard grid, and mark the squares out using string or bamboo. Measure out the amount of fertiliser recommended per square metre (or yard) according to the product label. Evenly sprinkle the fertiliser over each square. Do this on a still day to avoid wind drift.

If plants are already established, scatter the fertiliser around the roots of the plants. This is sometimes called fertiliser placement. Don't use more than the recommended amount because this can damage plants and seedlings. Always wear gloves when handling fertiliser, and avoid breathing it in. You can usually leave the fertiliser on the surface, or very lightly rake it in. Phosphorus, however, is fairly immobile, and proprietary feeds of it may need digging in.

On larger areas, a drop-fertiliser spreader can be used, which spins or broadcasts the feed over the soil at a rate calibrated on the spreader.

Sprinkling fertiliser granules around the roots is a quick and effective method of feeding plants.

COMMON NUTRIENT DEFICIENCIES

Some of the more common deficiencies often need treating with fertilisers to help keep plants healthy.

PROBLEM	DEFICIENCY	SOLUTION
Pale green leaves and poor growth	Nitrogen	Apply a high-nitrogen fertiliser such as sulphate of ammonia or dried blood. Green manures grown in the soil the previous year can also help.
Yellow or brown leaves, particularly at tips and margins	Potassium	Feed with sulphate of potash, tomato feed or high-potash fertiliser.
Poor growth rate and yellow foliage	Phosphate	Feed with bone meal or superphosphate.
Yellowing or browning on leaf margins and between veins, often occurs on acid-loving plants growing in alkaline soil	Manganese and iron	Water with rainwater, not tap water. Mulch around roots with acid mulches, such as rotted pine needles. Feed with sequestered iron.
Distinctive interveinal chlorosis, blotches of yellow and brown	Magnesium	Foliar spray with Epsom salts diluted in water (210g in 10 litres/8oz in 18 pints of water).

Liquid feeds and foliar feeding

Liquid feeds are concentrates, usually in either powder or liquid form, that are diluted in water and used to water the roots of the plants. Tomato feeds are the most common example of this type of feeding. Avoid applying liquid feeds in the rain, as this dilutes them more and nutrients are washed away.

Foliar feeding is the quickest way to get nutrients into a plant, as the feed is absorbed directly through the leaves. The most commonly used example is a dilution of Epsom salts in water, which is sprayed directly onto foliage to treat for magnesium deficiency.

AN INTRODUCTION TO PRUNING

There is no mystery to pruning. Much of it is just common sense. Is a plant getting too big? Then it needs to be pruned. Has some of it died? Then the dead and damaged parts need to be removed by pruning. By and large, pruning applies to woody plants only: trees, shrubs and climbers. Some herbaceous perennials can also be pruned – for example when old flower heads are cut off to prolong flowering (deadheading) – but when people talk about pruning they are usually referring to woody plants.

Pear trees should be pruned at least once a year to keep them in shape and to ensure new growth.

Pruning basics

The object of pruning is most often to keep a plant to size, or to encourage it to grow in a particular direction (such as against a wall), or into a pleasing shape. Dead, diseased, damaged and crossing growth may also need to be removed from time to time to keep a plant healthy. Pruning is achieved by carefully selecting the parts that need to be removed, then removing them cleanly with a sharp pair of secateurs or a pruning saw.

When to prune

It is always a good idea to have a pair of secateurs in your pocket when working in the garden, since growth often needs cutting back here and there to keep plants looking tidy and remove any wayward shoots that might be blocking paths or obscuring views. The best results are achieved when the gardener shows restraint, undertaking major pruning only when it is necessary. Pruning can be carried out at any time of year, depending on the type of plant, but the predominant two seasons are winter (when the plant is dormant) and summer, when a lighter prune will remove excess growth.

HOW TO CUT

Prune at a 45-degree angle, just above a bud.

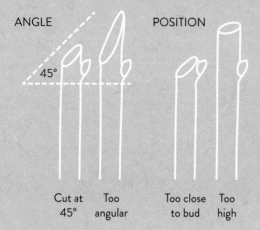

ANGLE

45°

POSITION

Cut at 45°   Too angular   Too close to bud   Too high

CORRECT USAGE

When using secateurs, keep the blade on top and the hook below.

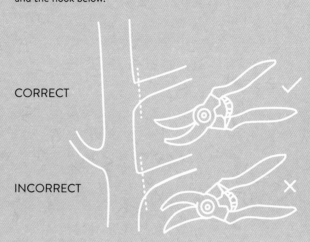

CORRECT

INCORRECT

Winter: Heavy pruning work is usually left to late winter, when deciduous trees and shrubs are laid bare and their branch structure is much more evident. New growth in spring will soon soften any hard cuts, so recovery times are faster. The aim of winter pruning is to control plants that are outgrowing their positions and to maintain an open network of healthy stems and branches that do not cross or rub.

Summer: Pruning jobs are usually kept relatively light in summer, although you may find yourself doing a lot of clipping and shearing just to keep pace with the rate of growth. Hedges need trimming, roses deadheading, topiary clipping, and wayward growth snipping off as and when. Light and often is the mantra.

Flowering shrubs

Left to their own devices, shrubs will soon outgrow their allotted space. The rule with flowering shrubs is to clip or trim them right after they have finished flowering, every year. In this manner, they will never need severe pruning (which might disfigure them) and they will have a whole year in which to recover and prepare themselves for the next display. Pruned too soon before flowering, you are likely to remove all the developing flower buds.

▲ *Secateurs*
◄ *Pruning saw*

PRUNING EVERGREENS

Evergreens provide wonderful all-year-round interest in the garden. Some can be trimmed into elaborate topiary shapes, while others provide effective screening from nearby houses, or are used to mask compost bins or stark-looking fences.

Fortunately, most evergreen shrubs can largely look after themselves, and require minimal pruning in order to show off their beautiful shape and foliage. There are some exceptions. Topiary, for example, needs tight clipping with a pair of hedging shears or a hedge trimmer a few times a year to keep it in shape. Some of the more vigorous evergreen hedges, such as the popular and infamous leylandii (*Cupressus* x *leylandii*) or rampant laurel bushes, may also need more frequent pruning to keep their growth habit under control. But by and large, evergreen shrubs don't need the same amount of pruning as deciduous or fruiting trees. This is partly because evergreens are mainly grown for their foliage and so don't require the hard pruning that encourages a display of flowers and fruit. Most evergreen shrubs only need pruning if they have lost their shape, have some diseased material that needs removing or have outgrown their space.

When to prune

The most effective time to prune evergreens is in late spring, after the risk of frosts has passed. This gives the shrub time to recover and regrow, and the wood to ripen, before there is any risk of the young growth being damaged by frosts late in the year. Pruning in winter and autumn can also leave the plant susceptible to the cold. In milder areas, the timing of pruning evergreens is less important, and they can often be pruned at most times of the year.

Pruning lavender

Lavender is one of the most popular evergreen shrubs but it quickly becomes leggy if it isn't pruned and kept in shape. Traditionally, lavender is cut twice a year, the first time after flowering – a very light pruning, just removing the flower heads. The theory is that enough foliage is left on the plant to protect its centre from cold temperatures in winter. The second prune is slightly harder and is done in springtime, cutting into the foliage from the previous year, ensuring that the plant is kept tidy and compact. Avoid cutting into the older wood, as it doesn't always regenerate.

Pruning topiary

Topiary works best when a plant is shaped from a very young age. It is possible to train a mature shrub, but it isn't always as effective, and some shrubs don't react well to the harder cuts that have to be made to get the shape started. The best way to start with a young shrub is to use a template, such as a sphere or pyramid. Place the structure over the plant and use a pair of shears to shape it gradually. It's best to do this initial shaping in spring, after the risk of frosts. Most topiary will need light trimming a few times a year to keep it looking neat and tidy. The plants most commonly used for topiary are yew (*Taxus baccata*) and box (*Buxus sempervirens*). However, if you live in an area susceptible to box blight, you should consider an alternative evergreen small-leaved shrub such as *Ilex crenata* or *Lonicera nitida* (poor man's box).

Hard pruning

If necessary, many evergreens will tolerate hard pruning. An example is camellia – mature stems can be cut back hard after flowering to about 70cm (2ft) above ground level to establish new fresh shoots. Other evergreen shrubs that tolerate hard pruning include *Aucuba japonica*, *Choisya ternata*, *Ligustrum japonicum*, *Sarcococca humilis*, *Taxus baccata* and *Viburnum tinus*.

◀ *Prune lavender once after flowering and once in spring to ensure it stays compact and looking good.*

▲ *Regular clipping of topiary will help to ensure it retains its shape and density and that its foliage looks healthy.*

PRUNING DECIDUOUS SHRUBS AND TREES

There are numerous reasons for pruning a tree or shrub, depending on what you are hoping to achieve. The end goal will determine what technique is used to prune them. Sometimes it may be for foliage effect, at other times it may be to showcase winter stem colour, or to encourage more flowers or fruit. Sometimes it is just to reshape the plant or to remove diseased material.

When to prune

Most deciduous trees and shrubs are pruned when they are dormant, from late autumn through until late spring. This is partly because it is easier to see where the branches are when the leaves are no longer on the tree, revealing the bare bones of the tree's or shrub's structure. Pruning when the plant is dormant also makes it less likely that it will 'bleed' sap, which can weaken it. There are exceptions to the general rule though; for example, trees from the *Prunus* family, such as flowering cherries, should only be pruned when in leaf. This avoids infection from bacterial canker and silver leaf in their open pruning cuts, which can't heal over quickly during winter. Some partly tender shrubs, such as hydrangeas or figs, may also suffer if pruned in winter, and it is best to leave their branches to give them protection until they start growing again in spring. One of the main reasons for pruning deciduous shrubs is to encourage more flowers. In order to do this, some deciduous shrubs are pruned just after flowering to give them as much time as possible to build up strength and enable them to go on to produce more flower buds the following year. Finally, for those who don't like pruning, there are a number of shrubs that don't really need any pruning at all.

Forsythia is a popular springtime shrub with lots of young shoots
▼ *covered in bright yellow flowers.*

▲ *Early flowering deciduous shrubs, such as this mock orange* (Philadelphus coronarius) *will benefit from being pruned after they have flowered.*

Early flowering deciduous shrubs

Early flowering shrubs such as *Chaenomeles*, *Forsythia*, *Philadelphus*, *Deutzia*, *Ribes sanguineum*, *Syringa*, *Weigela* and *Kerria* produce most of their flowers on the younger wood grown in previous years. To encourage more flowers on these types of shrubs, it is best to prune them after flowering, as this will encourage many more shoots further down the bush, which will ensure the shrub has an all-over covering of flowers. Without this regular pruning, the shrubs quickly become congested with twiggy growth, with most of the flowers limited to the top tips of the plant. Use a pruning saw and remove some of the older, thicker stems from near the base of the plant. Remove some of the other stems that have previously flowered, using secateurs to cut them back further down the plant. This should encourage new laterals to form, which will eventually produce flowers.

Pruning hydrangeas

• *Hydrangea marcrophylla*
There are two different types of *Hydrangea macrophylla* – lacecaps and mopheads – but both are pruned in exactly the same way. Their flower heads should be left on over winter to give them extra protection from cold weather.

In early spring, just as the buds are starting to swell, prune back last year's stems to a pair of buds about 15cm (6in) below the old flower head. If the plant is starting to get leggy, it can be cut back further to encourage a bushier plant the following year.

• *Hydrangea paniculata*
This plant will produce huge panicles of flower stems in late summer if pruned correctly. It can look very effective at the back of a mixed border, or even used, grouped, to line a path. The flower heads remain impressive throughout the winter. To achieve the best effect, the new growth should be pruned back to the second pair of buds on the stem in early spring. This will encourage the plant to make lots of growth in the year and send out a huge flower spike towards mid to late summer.

Mid- to late-flowering deciduous shrubs

Most shrubs that flower later in the year do so on wood or shoots produced in the same year. These include *Buddleja davidii*, *Ceratostigma willmottianum*, *Cotinus*, hardy fuchsia, *Hydrangea*, *Perovskia* and *Hibiscus syriacus*. These shrubs are best pruned in early spring. Remove some of the older wood with loppers towards the base of the plant to maintain an open habit. Then prune some of the new growth made the previous year, back to two or three buds, towards the older wood. This will encourage the shrub to produce plenty of new laterals with lots of flowers in the current year.

Shrubs that require practically no pruning

There are some shrubs that need hardly any pruning at all. This is mainly due to their growth habit and the fact that they freely produce flowers without much intervention from gardeners. They include *Amelanchier*, *Chimonanthus*, *Clethra*, *Daphne*, *Enkianthus*, *Fothergilla*, *Hamamclis* and deciduous viburnums.

Prune hydrangeas in early spring to maximise the amount of flowers that will be produced later in the season.

Pruning for winter stem colour

Sometimes shrubs aren't pruned for their impressive flowers at all. Instead, they are pruned for their brightly coloured stems. Two of the most popular types of shrubs for this treatment are dogwood (*Cornus*) and willow (*Salix*).

In order to produce the best effect, use a pair of secateurs to cut all the growth down to a few centimetres above the ground. This should be done in March, just as the plants are coming into leaf. This gives you the maximum amount of time to enjoy the colourful stems when they are denuded of their foliage. Plants that repay this treatment include *Salix alba* var. *vitellina*, *Cornus sanguinea* 'Midwinter Fire', *Cornus alba* 'Sibirica' and *Rubus cockburnianus*.

▼ *Some dogwoods (Cornus) produce brightly coloured stems in winter. Prune back hard in early spring.*

Pruning for foliage

It is possible to prune plants to enjoy their foliage rather than their flowers. The technique, known as coppicing, is very similar to pruning for winter stem colour, in which stems are cut right down, near to the ground, but takes place in either autumn or spring. Popular plants to coppice for their foliage effect include *Paulownia tomentosa* and *Catalpa bignonioides*, which produce massive leaves when cut hard, though the payback is that they won't then produce their impressive flowers in the same year. These plants are often used at the back of a wide border to create a striking backdrop and a splash of colour. Other shrubs that can be treated in a similar way include *Cotinus coggygria*, *Sambucus nigra* 'Black Beauty', most eucalyptus species and *Corylus maxima* 'Purpurea'. Shrubs are also coppiced to produce straight stems that can be harvested and used in the garden to make fences or wigwams for training climbing plants and vegetables. Popular shrubs for this are hazel (*Corylus avellana*), willow (*Salix*) and sweet chestnut (*Castanea sativa*), which all respond well to being cut back hard near to ground level.

PRUNING CLIMBERS

A climber is basically any plant that needs support to grow upwards. Some have tendrils to help them scramble up walls, fences and trees; others have more of a sprawling habit and need propping up and tying in to trellis or a system of wires for support. Whichever way they climb, it is important to understand their growth habit when it comes to pruning them.

How to prune and train a grapevine

Grapevines are one of the most popular types of climber in a garden. Choose a wine grape as opposed to a dessert grape if you are growing it outside; the grapes don't need to be completely ripe to use, so if you want to make your own wine, you might manage a few bottles. Grapevines can be trained up and over pergolas or arches, or on a system of wires stretched between two upright posts. Some varieties, such as *Vitis* 'Brandt' and *Vitis coignetiae*, are chosen for their large ornamental leaves and beautiful autumn colour.

To train grapevines over an arch:
- Plant two grapevines, one on each side of the arch, and tie in their stems or trunks.
- Prune the new growth of the laterals (side branches) back to two buds.
- As the plants grow over the summer, prune their new growth back to three or four leaves past any bunches of grapes.
- Harvest the grapes in autumn.
- The following winter, prune the growth made over the previous year back to two buds. Continue to tie the leading shoot up the arch as it grows until it has reached the centre of the arch. Over the years, it may be necessary to thin out some of the spurs built up from cutting back the laterals each year.

◄ Grapevines are often pruned twice a year to keep them in shape and encourage them to produce lots of bunches of grapes.

How to prune a wisteria

Wisterias are another very popular climber. They are vigorous and need pruning twice a year. The first time they should be pruned is immediately after flowering, when the new growth they have made should be cut back to five leaves.

The second prune should happen in winter, when the new growth made the previous year should be cut back to two buds. Any dense clusters of spurs can be thinned out, and any excess growth removed, leaving a tidy framework of central stems with short laterals coming off them.

How to prune clematis

Clematis is divided into three different categories, and which one a plant belongs to will affect how it is pruned.

The first group (pruning Group 1) is the early-flowering clematis (spring and winter), including plants such as *Clematis alpina*, *C. cirrhosa*, *C. macropetala*, *C. napaulensis*, *C. montana* and *C. armandii*, which produce flowers on the previous year's growth. The pruning is quite simple – after flowering, remove any diseased branches and cut the plant back to fit the space in which it grows. These clematis are usually just given a light trim to keep them looking tidy. They can be cut back much harder if necessary, but you may forgo flowers the following year.

The second group (pruning Group 2) consists of the large-flowering, early summer types, which includes *C. florida* and its hybrids and *C. patens* and its hybrids. This group flowers first in early summer, when large blooms emerge on wood produced the previous year. There is often a second flush of flowers later in the year. This group of clematis is pruned twice. Give a first pruning in spring, before flowering, removing any dead or diseased material, and giving the plant a tidy up – but with a light hand, to avoid damaging any potential blooms. Prune for the second time after the plant has flowered. It should be more robust than the first pruning; it is a form of renewal pruning, in which some of the older material is removed to encourage new growth with flower buds on. The remaining growth is tied in and can be trimmed to keep it tidy.

▲ *Prune wisteria twice a year to provide masses of impressive racemes of blue, white or pink flowers. Another important reason to prune wisteria is to keep it within bounds.*

The third group of clematis (pruning Group 3) includes *C. texensis* and hybrids, plants that flower from midsummer through to autumn, blooming on stems produced in the same year. The group covers types such as 'Étoile Violette', *C. viticella*, *C. orientalis* and *C. tangutica*, including 'Bill MacKenzie'. Pruning these clematis couldn't be simpler – you cut them down to near-ground level in late winter or early spring, and leave them to produce new flowering shoots for the new season. Alternatively, you can trim them much more lightly; this results in more foliage and fewer flowers, but it means that the plants offer a bit more interest in winter, particularly when trained up wigwams in borders.

THE FORMATIVE PRUNING OF TREES

Most deciduous trees require some shaping in their formative years to make them into attractive garden features in maturity. Formative pruning is carried out on trees or shrubs in their first few years to ensure they develop into the right shape and are neither too spindly, nor cluttered with lots of weak branches. The ultimate goal is to have a clear trunk and branches that are well spaced. There are three basic shapes to look at when carrying out formative pruning: centre leader, open centre and multi-stemmed. There are also two different types of sapling to consider: a feathered maiden, which is a one-year-old tree with branches coming off the main stem – the feathers – and a maiden whip, a one-year-old tree that has produced no laterals.

A tree with a centre leader will have one dominant trunk (or leader) with well-spaced branches beneath it. There is usually some space between the ground and the first tier of branches (the crown), which makes a tree look visually more appealing and shows off the trunk. This is particularly effective on ornamental trees with attractive trunks, including *Prunus serrula*, *Betula utilis* var. *jacquemontii* and snakebark maples such as *Acer davidii*. However, having a clear stem is also useful for fruit trees – it means that the crop won't be carried on very low branches, so ensures it won't lie on the ground when the tree is carrying a weight of fruit. It also makes mowing and maintenance around the base of the tree easier. Most deciduous trees should be pruned just after planting, unless a tree is planted in summer, in which case it may be better to wait until winter, when it goes dormant, in order to avoid causing it too much stress. If you are pruning an evergreen tree, this is best done in early spring just as it is coming into growth.

▲ *Prune trees from a young age so that their branches form a good shape.*

FORMATIVE PRUNING SHAPES

CENTRE LEADER
To create a tree with a central trunk, also known as a centre leader tree, you should remove any branches coming off the lower section of the main stem – that is, the first 50cm (20in) up from the ground. Then choose four or five healthy branches that are spaced out evenly around the trunk and remove any others. This is to prevent the crown becoming too congested. A crowded canopy not only looks ugly but is prone to a build-up of pests and diseases when it comes into leaf.

If the tree's crown still looks crowded, prune back any laterals coming off the main branches to a couple of buds. Avoid cutting the leader as this will spoil the overall shape of the tree.

OPEN CENTRE
To create an open centre tree, prune as above, but remove the central leader or trunk back to the highest branch or lateral. This will create the desired 'goblet' shape. Cut back the leaders on the laterals by about a third, taking them back to outward-facing buds. Remove any branches that look as though they will start to crowd the centre of the tree.

To create an open centre tree from an unbranched sapling, prune back the central trunk to about 75cm (30in) above the ground to encourage laterals to form.

MULTI-STEMMED
Finally, some trees are grown as multi-stems, which consist of multiple stems coming off the same base. To achieve this, in the first year the trunk is cut closer to the ground to encourage fresh shoots to grow upwards. The following year, the strongest three or four shoots should be selected, and the remaining shoots removed. Popular examples of multi-stemmed trees include *Betula utilis*, *Eucalyptus gunnii* and *Acer griseum*.

RENOVATION PRUNING

Plants sometimes outgrow their space, or simply develop into something unwieldy and unmanageable in the garden. This is when it may be necessary to carry out some renovation pruning to try to correct their shape. Another reason for renovation pruning is when a fruit tree has stopped being productive and you want to get it back into production again.

There is an old garden saying about fruit trees – that their branches should be spaced out enough for a pigeon to fly through the canopy in winter without hitting a branch. This suggests, rightly, that a well-managed tree should have plenty of space between its branches, allowing sunlight and air to circulate around the whole canopy. In trees that haven't been regularly pruned or managed, this is often not the case: instead, there is a congested mass of branches all running into each other.

The restoration of an over-congested tree should take place over two to three years. Don't attempt to bring it back to its former shape and glory in one pruning session – if you prune too hard, the tree may either die from shock or react by sending out even more vigorous growth after pruning, which will only make the congestion problem worse.

The restoration of most trees, particularly apple trees, should be carried out in winter, when the plant is dormant and leafless, and it is easier to see the structure of the tree. Avoid pruning slightly tender trees and species of *Prunus* in winter, however; instead, prune once they are in growth.

The restoration pruning method

- First, look at the canopy and remove any dead, diseased or damaged branches (known in the world of pruning as 'the three Ds'). A really congested canopy may have a lot of diseased and dead material; sterilise your secateurs when you finish removing it and before you start to prune the healthier parts of the tree, to avoid spreading any infection.

- Next, use secateurs to remove water shoots – the wispy shoots that often grow off the main trunk of the tree. Again, these prevent air circulation, ultimately creating a build-up of diseases or pests in the canopy, and take essential nutrients from the tree without providing fruit or flowers.

- Now look into the canopy and remove as many of the crossing branches as you can, so that the remaining branches have plenty of space and air around them. To remove large branches, it may be necessary to do a three-step cut using a pruning saw (see box below).

- Finally, use secateurs to thin out any clusters of spurs. Repeat this process regularly over the next few years to bring the tree back into production and make it look more attractive.

THREE-STEP PRUNING CUT

Using a pruning saw to remove large branches from a tree:

(1) Take the weight off the branch by removing most of it before making the final cut near the trunk. If the weight isn't removed, the branch can tear back into the trunk, which can cause later infection. Make a cut on the top section of the branch, about 20cm (8in) away from the trunk. Cut about a third of the way into the branch.

(2) Make an undercut a few centimetres closer to the trunk. Cut upwards into the branch and as the blade comes near the top cut the branch will fall away, usually with a clear-sounding snap.

(3) Make the final cut near the trunk, removing the stump of the branch. Cut downwards, using your spare hand to support the weight of the rest of the branch. Avoid cutting flush with the trunk – leave a slight collar for the branch to heal over.

Make the first cut a third of the way into the branch.

Make an undercut here.

Cut downwards for the final cut.

HEDGE CARE

Hedges make wonderful boundaries – or barriers, if you want to screen something like a compost heap or an ugly fence in your garden. They also make great habitats for wildlife. And when it comes to pruning, nothing could be simpler: most of the time, you just need to be able to cut in a straight line.

Hedge-pruning tools

There are a few tools that will make the job much easier. These include the following:

Hedge cutter These are usually electric- or petrol-powered, but battery-powered ones that are charged up before use are becoming increasingly popular. Solar-powered battery cutters are the most environmentally friendly. Electric ones weigh the least, because they don't need a battery or a fuel tank, but make sure that the cable is safely out of the way before starting to trim the hedge. The cutting bar on a hedge trimmer helps to get a really straight line when you're pruning.

Ladder or scaffold tower If your hedge is taller than shoulder height, you will need a ladder, or ideally a scaffold tower, to cut the top. Whichever you use, always ensure it is set up on a flat, or at least a level surface, and that it is secure. Never overstretch to an area you can't easily reach; instead, climb down and move the ladder or tower along.

Hedging shears Use these for pruning smaller hedges. Keep them sharp. The central screw may also need tightening regularly to ensure the blades run smoothly against each other.

Secateurs These aren't suitable for trimming the entire hedge, but they can be used for cutting back the occasional stray stem or branch. Some gardeners advise that large-leaved evergreen hedges, such as laurel and *Aucuba*, should only be pruned with secateurs, because shears and hedge cutters slice through the leaves, making them look ragged and untidy. Unless you have a lot of time, or a very small hedge, though, this is unlikely to be realistic.

▲ *The ruddy tints of copper beech make for a colourful hedge.*

Hedges can be used as an attractive standalone feature in a garden or as a natural backdrop to more elaborate planting schemes. ▶

When to trim

Most hedges should have an annual pruning, but faster-growing species or formal hedges and topiary may need at least two. The usual time for annual hedge clipping, in which only the new growth is trimmed back, is spring or late summer, but restoration work that calls for cutting back into older branches is more often done in winter, when the plant is dormant.

Always check a hedge carefully for nesting birds before you cut. Nesting season can run between March and August, and it's important not to disturb an active nest.

The timings for trimming some of the most popular hedge plants are as follows:
Box Late spring, after frost
Beech Late summer
Holly Late summer
Hornbeam Late summer
Leyland cypress Spring and late summer
Privet Spring and late summer
Yew Late summer or early autumn

Hedge-trimming tips

To cut the sides of a hedge, stand at 90 degrees to it, so that you are looking down its length. This helps you to get a straight line and see where you are cutting. Using a hedge cutter, move the cutting bar up and down the hedge, keeping it as flat and straight as possible as you remove the excess young growth.

Getting the top of a hedge straight is a bit of an acquired skill. If you aren't confident, stretch string between two posts as a guideline to ensure that one end of the hedge will be the same height as the other.

Most hedges have a square-cut top, at 90 degrees to the sides, but some gardeners prefer to cut it at an angle with a slope of about 45 degrees as this allows more sunlight to get into the hedge, preventing it from thinning or dying back in the shade. The slope also makes it harder for snow – which can cause branches to snap – to settle on top of the hedge.

ROSE CARE

They're the quintessential flowering plant for the traditional cottage garden, and most roses offer both exquisite blooms and gorgeous scent. Many also repeat-flower throughout the growing season. But despite their popularity, there always seems to be an air of mystery around the pruning and care of roses. Once you have mastered the basic principles, however, it's really quite easy.

Roses should be deadheaded regularly to prolong their flowering season. If the dead flowerheads are left on, the plant thinks it has done enough to set seed and starts to prepare for dormancy, but if they're removed, the plant is triggered into producing more flowers.

They should also be regularly mulched with organic matter such as garden compost or well-rotted manure, spread around their roots to a depth of 5cm (2in). A layer of mulch helps to suppress any competing weeds and also retains moisture round the plant. It will eventually rot down into the soil, improving its quality and nourishing the rose bush with macro- and micronutrients.

Tie in new shoots of climbing roses in October, before the strong winds of autumn and winter have a chance to damage them.

Rose pruning

Roses need pruning once or twice a year. The technique varies depending on which type of rose you are dealing with.

Bush roses

The most popular type of rose is the modern bush type, divided up into hybrid tea roses, which produce huge single blooms, and floribunda, which produce clusters of blooms.

• After planting, both types should be pruned back hard to 10–15cm (4–6in) above the ground. This encourages vigorous growth that will provide the strong, spaced framework for flowers in subsequent years.
• In the following years, cut away all wispy growth, then cut back the remaining healthy stems to between a half and two-thirds of their length.
• Always cut back to outward-facing buds to encourage an open, pruned bush and not a congested, closed one.
• In exposed areas, gardeners often prune twice – lightly in early autumn to reduce the risk of wind rock, then harder in early spring as described above.

Climbers

- New shoots should be trained onto walls, posts or trellis, and held in place with garden twine.
- Some of the shorter side shoots, which may have flowered in the previous year, can be pruned back to a couple of buds.
- If the rose climber is particularly congested, some of the older wood should be removed using loppers or a saw. This will encourage new growth and a larger number of flowers further down the stem, giving better coverage overall.
- Prune in late winter or early spring.

Shrub roses

There are lots of different types of shrub rose, from the very popular and vigorous 'Graham Thomas', which has golden blooms, to the attractive hybrid musk types such as 'Cornelia' and 'Buff Beauty'. Their habits vary enormously, from arching stems to vigorous upright growth, and generally all that is needed each year is to tip-prune the growth on the new stems.

- On older plants, it may also be necessary to remove some of the older wood, or cut it back hard, to encourage new flowering stems.
- If the shrub isn't as vigorous as it should be, the new growth can be cut back harder, to about one-third of its length.
- Always prune back to an outward-facing bud. A good rule of thumb is 'prune hard for quality of flowers, prune light for quantity of flowers'.
- Prune in late winter or early spring.

▲ Almost all roses need to be pruned once,
▲ or in some cases twice, annually.

▲ Roses will benefit from being deadheaded as the flowers fade, to encourage more blooms to develop.

◄ Shrub roses often have an attractive arching habit. Pruning consists of removing some of the older stems in early spring.

LAWN CARE

A beautiful lawn can be a focal point in its own right, as well as an attractive background to borders, trees and shrubs. Often a lawn is the centrepiece of a garden, with beds and other features placed around it, so it's worth spending some time and effort in making sure it looks good.

Not everybody wants a perfectly manicured lawn with visible mown stripes, but if the lawn isn't maintained at all it can quickly turn wild and weedy, threadbare and patchy, so take a bit of time to master lawncare basics. The number one maintenance job is cutting the grass. That dealt with, there a few other things you can do, including scarifying the lawn, aerating it, and adding top dressing, that will help it to look really green and healthy. These jobs are often included as part of an all-round tidying-up programme in autumn but can be carried out at pretty much any time of year, except in a drought or when the weather is extremely cold or very wet.

Cylinder mowers will give a finer finish than rotary mowers but require more maintenance ▼ and are more expensive.

Lawn mowers

There are numerous different mowers available. Most of the bigger machines for larger gardens are driven by petrol, but there are electric or battery-powered versions too.

Rotary mower These have blades underneath the mower that rotate, a bit like a helicopter rotor, cutting as the mower is pushed across the grass. Some rotary mowers have a roller on the back, and you need this if you want stripes on the lawn. Some are self-propelled, while others need to be pushed. Hover mowers are also a type of rotary mower but they 'float' over the grass on a cushion or vacuum of air. This makes mowing much easier, although it won't give you stripes. A ride-on rotary mower may be necessary for really big areas of lawn – again, you'll need a roller for stripes.

Mulch mowers These are similar to rotary mowers, but rather than leaving the clippings directly on the lawn, or collecting them into a box at the back, a mulch mower chops them into tiny pieces before dropping them back on the lawn. Grass clippings are rich in nitrogen, so mulch mowers are replenishing the lawn with a natural fertiliser.

Cylinder mowers Cylinder mowers have both a fixed blade and a set of rotating blades that spin on a horizontal cylinder, and they're at the top of the range of mowers you can buy. They're mainly used for 'fine' lawns, such as bowling greens and cricket wickets, on which the quality of grass – and the mow – is really important. A cylinder mower can get a very low cut, and also has rollers on the back to give stripes. You can buy a traditional push cylinder mower, which is an environmentally friendly choice, but calls for a higher level of fitness if you're covering a large lawn. Ride-on cylinder mowers are also available, but are very expensive.

Strimmers and brushcutters These are used to reach places that a mower can't, and to cut the grass around posts or fence lines and other awkward spots. There are petrol, electric or battery versions. Take care if you are strimming around trees, though – if the string catches the tree bark it can cause serious damage.

Rotary mower

Push cylinder mower

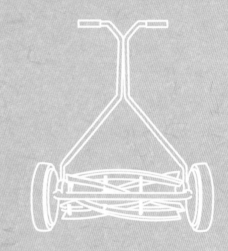

Strimmer

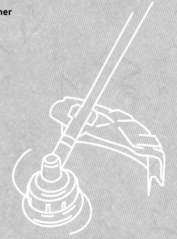

HOW TO MOW

A good-quality lawn, such as a cricket wicket, may be mown as often as two or even three times a week during the growing season, but most gardeners mow just once a week to keep the grass looking neat and tidy.

Here's how to mow a lawn efficiently:

1. Start by mowing the top and the bottom of the lawn, with two stripes at each end.

2. Next, start to mow up one of the longer edges of the lawn, returning back the other way, making sure that the mower cuts just up to the edge of where the previous line was cut. To mow in a straight line, look up and ahead of you at the lines, rather than down at the mower.

3. When you've covered the area, you can either finish in the corner, as shown in the diagram, or, for a professional extra touch, make finishing lines by repeating step one and cutting the tops and bottoms of the lawn again, going across to produce two stripes at each end.

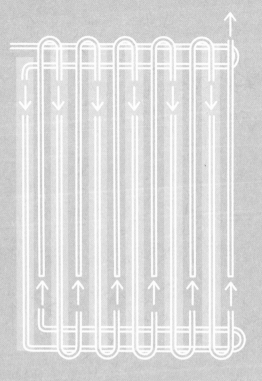

Mowing tips

• Mow the lawn whenever the grass is growing – usually between early spring and late autumn.

• Raise the height of the mower for the first few cuts of the season, then lower it to the height of grass you want for the remainder of the season.

• If there is a drought, then it is best either to avoid cutting the grass altogether, as mowing can cause stress, or to raise the height of the mower so as to leave a slightly longer lawn.

Edging the lawn

Use edging shears to trim the edges of the lawn after it has been cut. Don't edge before mowing, because the roller on the mower will push blades of grass sideways, meaning you'll need to edge again anyway. Edging shears work like a pair of scissors, so keep one arm still while the other moves the cutting blade up and down. Keep the shears as upright as possible. If the edges of the lawn are no longer sharp, use a string line to work out where the edge should be cut, then use a half-moon edger (which, like its name, has a half-moon shaped blade to cut a clean edge) to cut away overgrowing turf and restore the edge. It helps to stand on a plank of wood when you're cutting a straight line, as it gives you a guide to follow. If you need to cut a curve, arrange a length of hosepipe into the shape you want and use it as a guide.

▲ Edging shears can be used to trim the edge of the lawn.

Scarifying

Scarifying is the process that's used to remove thatch – the accumulation of dead pieces of grass, leaf litter and other organic debris – from the surface of the lawn. If thatch isn't removed, it can prevent rain from penetrating down to the grass roots and stop air circulating around them, making the grass susceptible to drought and fungal problems. Professional greenkeepers will remove thatch a few times a year and use a scarifying machine, but most gardeners simply use a spring-tine rake and work over the lawn, scratching the surface vigorously. Work across the lawn first one way and then the other, to remove as much of the thatch as possible. The process does look brutal, but the lawn will quickly recover and look much better for it in the long term.

Scarifiers are used for removing the thatch in the grass,
▼ which will result in a better and healthier lawn.

Aeration and top dressing

Aeration involves pushing spikes into the lawn to break up the compaction, improve drainage and allow the air to circulate around the roots of the grass. It's usually done in autumn. Aeration machines exist but are really only necessary on very large areas of grass – a garden fork repeatedly pushed into the ground to a depth of about 10cm (4in) works just as well. A similar process called hollow tining involves pushing in hollow spikes that, as they are pulled out again, remove cores of soil. Top dressing can then be brushed into the holes, which improves the quality of the soil below the lawn. Top dressing can be bought from garden centres, or made by mixing together 40 per cent sand, 40 per cent loam and 20 per cent organic matter, such as garden compost or well-rotted manure.

Other maintenance jobs

In long periods of drought, lawns may need watering to keep the grass looking green. Some devoted lawn keepers like to verti-cut their lawns, too, which is similar to mowing except that the tillers, or side shoots, of the grass blades are cut instead of the tips, to encourage a thicker sward.

If your grass is looking yellow, it may need feeding. Use a specialised, high-nitrogen lawn fertiliser in spring to help it with its first flush of green growth. Later, in summer and autumn, feed it with something higher in potassium and phosphorus to toughen the grass before the colder winter weather.

CONTAINER CARE AND POTTING

Almost any plant can be grown in a container. The beauty of growing plants in this way is that they take up less space and can be grown even if you don't have any open ground – which is ideal if you only have a small courtyard, balcony or roof garden. It also means that if you move house, you can take your plants with you. However, plants in pots need more care than those growing in the ground.

Watering

The basic essentials for plants in containers are regular watering and feeding. Their roots are restricted, so they aren't able to send out roots in search of extra moisture and are therefore completely dependent on you to keep them hydrated. In dry periods this can mean that they need watering as often as twice a day. Ideally, you should water either in the morning or the evening – in the middle of the day, higher temperatures mean that the water will evaporate much faster, and there is a risk of leaf scorch if the water lands on the leaves. Irrigation systems can help to save time on watering (see page 90), and if you have lots of containers it is worth investing in a water butt or two to harvest rainwater.

To help with drainage, there must be holes in the bottom of the container, and it should also be stood either on container 'feet' or on bricks or blocks, so that water can drain away freely.

Winter care

Tender plants in containers that were brought out onto a patio for summer need to be put away in a greenhouse, shed or porch over winter. Keep an eye on them during the winter months to ensure the compost doesn't dry out completely, but don't water unless necessary because there is a risk the plant will start to rot. Bring containers outside again in summer as soon as the risk of frost is over.

Caring for annuals

Apart from watering, annual flowers and bedding plants need very little maintenance. To maintain their vitality and colour, you can give them a liquid feed once a week. A tomato feed is ideal, as it is rich in potassium, which helps boost a plant's flowering and their colour intensity. Deadhead the flowers as they fade to extend the plant's flowering period.

CARE FOR PERENNIALS

Perennial plants, shrubs and trees grown in containers have the same maintenance needs as annuals, but there are some additional jobs to do to keep them happy and healthy, too. They need repotting every couple of years, because the compost in the container gradually loses its nutrients, and they may have outgrown their pots. Autumn is the best time to repot.

① Gently pull the plant out of its pot and tip away the old compost.

② Remove the drainage crocks and wash out the inside of the pot, using a scrubbing brush to remove any residual pests or their eggs.

③ Herbaceous perennials will often need to be divided. If you do this, discard the centre and replant two or three of the younger sections of the original plant.

④ Trees and shrubs may have become pot-bound, with roots wrapped tightly around the root ball. If this is the case, use a knife to cut away up to a third of the roots to prevent the plant from strangling itself. This will encourage it to put out fresh roots in the new season.

⑤ Fill the container with new potting compost and repot the plant, ensuring that it is firmly settled into the compost.

⑥ Water the plant thoroughly after planting.

⑦ In the years when you're not repotting your plants, they will benefit from a top dressing of compost on the surface of the soil.

OVERWINTERING

Depending on where you live, it's likely that some of the more tender plants in your garden will need protection during the colder months of the year. In colder weather, listen to the weather forecast and if a cold spell or overnight frost is predicted, take action to safeguard any vulnerable plants.

There are numerous slightly tender plants that could need protection if left outside over winter. And it's not always the obvious plants such as bananas, palm trees and tree ferns. Dahlias, for example, are one of the most popular garden plants and yet, depending on where you live in the country, they will probably need protection over the winter months.

Winter protection

Inside: The best option for herbaceous plants like cannas, gladioli or dahlias, or for container-grown specimens that are transportable, is to lift the plant and store it in a frost-free greenhouse or conservatory. As it's unlikely that you'll be able to bring all your plants inside to overwinter them, bear in mind when you're choosing planting that most larger trees and shrubs will need to be hardy enough to survive outside.

Outside: For a tender plant that has to overwinter outside, the most common way to protect it is to cover it with fleece or bubble wrap to help it through the colder months. If you need to protect a tree fern, only the crown, where the fronds are

growing out, needs packing with fleece or bubble wrap. Even if the fronds die back over winter, new ones should sprout once the weather warms up.

Other plants, such as palm trees (including banana plants), hardy gingers, exotic climbers like *Eccremocarpus*, *Bougainvillea* or *Plumbago*, and tender shrubs like *Clianthus puniceus* or *Brugmansia*, should all be protected using a thick protective layer of straw, bracken or horticultural fleece, securely held in place with hessian sacking and thick string, wire or twine. In the case of climbers, a frame can be built against the wall they are growing on and insulated as above. Remove the protection in the spring, when there's no longer a chance of overnight frosts.

To protect plants from frosts or to extend the growing season they can be covered with a fleece or grown under cloches. ▶

OVERWINTERING DAHLIAS

In colder areas, dahlias should be brought indoors over winter to protect them. In milder areas, they can be left in the ground, although you're running the risk of a cold snap, and the tubers may also rot in the ground if you have a very damp winter. *Canna indica* and hybrid tulips should be treated in the same way.

To overwinter dahlias under cover

② The tubers need to drain upside down for about a week to ensure they don't rot while stored. Place them upside down in a tray and leave in a cool place to allow any excess moisture to drain away.

③ After a week, place the dahlias, turned right way up, in a box or tray of sand, vermiculite or coir, and put them somewhere cool, dry and frost-free, such as a greenhouse or shed, for the winter. Check them regularly and remove any rotting tubers immediately.

④ When the risk of frost is over, the tubers can be replanted outside. If you want to bring them on earlier in the season, they can be planted in pots in a greenhouse and then planted out when there's no chance of frost — this will give you flowers a month or so earlier than if you plant tubers into the ground directly from storage.

① As the foliage starts to fade, from mid- to late autumn, dig up the tubers with a fork, taking care not to damage them with the prongs. Cut the foliage back to about 10cm (4in) from the crown.

MAKING COMPOST
AND LEAF MOULD

Compost heaps might not be the prettiest feature of a garden or allotment, but they are certainly one of the most useful. Making your own compost is a great way of recycling both kitchen and garden waste, and the resulting compost adds loads of goodness to enrich your soil.

Even in the smallest of gardens, a small plastic compost container can be tucked away in a corner. If you have more space, the ideal is two or even three compost heaps – one that is filling up with current waste, one in the process of decomposition, and the third full of compost ready for use.

Making compost

The simplest way to make compost in your garden is to have a free-standing compost heap. If you'd prefer to keep the compost tidy and contained, it's easy to make a structure to contain it with some pallets. Place three pallets of equal size on their edges and screw them together in a U-shape to make a back and two sides. Site it in a corner, open front outwards, so that it's easy to add to. Then you can start your compost heap.

Good compost is made with three key ingredients.

• Carbon-rich materials, such as newspaper, wood shavings, old pet bedding, straw, cardboard, or fallen leaves.
• Nitrogen-rich materials, such as grass clippings, annual weeds, stems and fresh leaves, and vegetable trimmings from the kitchen.

The third ingredient is air.

A good ratio of nitrogen to carbon in your compost is three parts nitrogen-rich material to two parts carbon-rich material. Balance is important – too much nitrogen makes the compost damp, soggy and smelly, while too much carbon means your compost heap will be dry and the decomposition process will be very slow.

Ideally, compost heaps should be turned every few weeks, so that the material at the top is moved to the bottom and vice versa. This ensures that plenty of air is reaching all the compost. If you don't have the time or energy to turn it so often, once a year is also fine – your compost materials just won't break down as quickly.

If the compost heap seems dry, add some water (or, if it's covered, leave it open for a while to let any rain get to it) to help with the composting process. Avoid adding perennial weeds, such as nettles, bindweed, ground elder or mare's tail, to the compost heap. Most domestic compost heaps don't get hot enough to kill the seeds, and once put back onto the ground in compost, they'll germinate. It's also best to avoid adding woody twigs or branches, which don't decompose easily, and thick evergreen leaves, like those of laurel, which don't rot down well.

MAKE YOUR OWN LEAF MOULD

Leaf mould is made from leaf litter dropped by trees in autumn. Although it is low in nutrients, it is a great soil conditioner and will help retain moisture within the soil as well as helping to improve drainage. It will also encourage earthworms, which, in their turn, aerate and improve the soil. If your garden has deciduous trees, you'll probably be raking up leaves anyway, and home-made leaf mould will make good use of them.

① In autumn, rake all your fallen leaves up, using a plastic rake.

② If you have one, run a rotary mower over the fallen leaves and then collect them in the mower's collection box. This step isn't essential, but shredding the leaves helps speed up the process of decomposition.

④ If the leaves are dry, add some water to each bag, and poke a few holes in the sides so that air can get in. Fasten the bags at the top and leave them in a corner where they won't be in your way.

⑤ Over the next few months, give the bags a shake or open them and stir the contents around whenever you remember — this isn't a crucial step, but it will speed up decomposition.

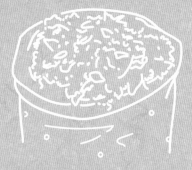

③ Put the leaves in bin liners, old compost bags or gardening bags.

⑥ Within a year — sometimes as little a time as six months — you'll find that the content of the bags has transformed into a dark, earthy-smelling leaf mould. This can be used as a mulch, dug into your borders or mixed into potting mixes when you're planting up containers.

▲ Wood chip or bark is an effective mulch for suppressing weeds and retaining moisture around trees and shrubs.

MULCHING

Bare soil is prone to dry out quickly and can become full of weeds in just a few days. Mulching is one of the ways in which gardeners tackle the problem. There are many different materials that can be used as mulch, but all of them have the same effect: they suppress weeds and help to keep the soil moist.

Organic mulches

The most commonly used mulch is well-rotted animal manure or garden compost. It will eventually rot down into the topsoil, which will enrich the rooting zone for most plants. It encourages worm activity, which aerates the soil, and the organic matter will also add some macro- and micronutrients, although not in the same quantity as fertilisers will. Home-made garden compost is convenient and readily to hand, although it has one disadvantage, which is that a home compost heap rarely gets hot enough to destroy weed seeds.

To mulch around plants, lay the manure or compost around the root area of each plant or shrub to a depth of about 5cm (2in). Arrange the mulch in a doughnut shape, leaving a gap of around 5cm (2in) gap around any tree or shrub trunks or stems. This gap ensures that the mulch won't rot the trunk or stem, and, when you're watering, will help to channel water to the roots around the plants.

The best time to apply organic mulch is in early spring. If you add it too early in the year, it will have washed away before plants start growing. Whether you're using manure or compost, it's important to make sure that it is well-rotted down – fresh manure can burn plant roots, and insufficiently decomposed compost can introduce a lot of weed seeds.

Wood chippings

Wood chippings are a popular mulch, particularly for woodland gardens. If you have your own chipper or shredder, they're also a great way of recycling garden waste. Wood chippings are great for suppressing weeds and for moisture retention, but they have very little nutritional value, and they must be well rotted down before use – too fresh, and they lock up nitrogen in the soil, which will ultimately be harmful to your plants. Sometimes a weed-suppressing membrane is laid on the ground first, to prevent the wood chippings from rotting down into the soil too quickly.

Weed-suppressing membranes

Weed-suppressing membrane is a light fabric that can be laid over the ground to prevent weeds germinating. This is really useful if there is lots of bare ground and it's going to be a while before anything is planted. It's also valuable used around tree bases, but only for a year or so – if it's left longer, it can create problems later when you want to underplant with bulbs or add more plants. If you want to use a weed-suppressing membrane, do buy one manufactured for the purpose. In the past, pieces of old carpet or underlay were often used in the same way as impromptu weed suppressants, but this is now less popular; many carpets contain chemicals that can leach into the ground they're laid on, and both carpet and underlay may start to deteriorate, leaving tiny fragments of rubber, artificial fibres and so on polluting the soil.

Other natural materials that are used by gardeners as a mulch to cover bare ground include gravel, colourful pebbles, shells and sheep's wool. Cardboard and straw are also good options.

Garden shredders and chippers are handy for reducing prunings to wood chip, which can be used as mulch on the beds.

5. GROWING FRUIT AND VEGETABLES

Growing your own fruit and vegetables is, for many people, one of the most rewarding aspects of gardening. With such a short journey from garden to kitchen, your crops have the sort of freshness that you can't buy at the supermarket, and you have the satisfaction of having watched them every step of the way, from seed to harvest. Some vegetables, in particular sweetcorn and peas, taste remarkably different when they've been picked just an hour or two earlier, while longer-lasting crops that can be stored, such as apples or winter squashes, will offer you a taste of home-grown during late autumn and into winter. If you grow your own, you can also be confident that you're getting the maximum nutritional benefit from your food.

There's always room to cultivate some sort of edible crop. Sprouting seeds, herbs, lettuce and microgreens will grow happily on a sunny windowsill, and many of the newer varieties of vegetables and fruit trees, bred especially for those who are short on growing space, can produce excellent crops in pots on a balcony or outside the kitchen door.

If you're lucky enough to have a larger garden, you may opt to have a dedicated vegetable patch or to blur the boundaries and mix crops and ornamentals together. Many modern gardens give decorative vegetables, such as chard, artichokes and runner beans, pride of place among the flower beds or borders. Fruit trees, too, with blossom in spring and a crop to follow, easily earn a place in any garden that has space to grow them.

GROWING YOUR OWN FOOD

If you're enthusiastic about growing your own fruit and vegetables, you'll find that it calls on a range of horticultural skills, which include soil preparation, understanding the needs of many different crops and learning how to care for fruit trees, including pruning.

One of the wonderful aspects of growing fruit and veg is that they can be grown almost anywhere. If you don't have a large garden or an allotment, you can get creative with containers, window boxes, raised beds or even hanging baskets.

With increased knowledge and experience, you'll also find that it's possible to cheat the seasons and produce your own crops a bit earlier or later than usual. Some really skilled fruit and veg growers can produce food all year round if they have the option to raise or grow some crops under cover.

Growing your own produce is a wonderful and rewarding hobby, often resulting in
▽ *beautiful and delicious vegetables.*

New avenues

Growing your own food opens up a raft of different varieties of fruit and vegetables to try, many of which you would never find in a supermarket, because it's not possible to grow them on a commercial scale – round carrots, or purple and red potatoes, or tiny wild strawberries. Plus there are some altogether new foods you might want to grow – cucamelons, which look like olive-sized watermelons but have a fresh, cucumber flavour, perhaps, or scorzonera, a root vegetable with an intriguing earthy taste, or the delicious oca, the New Zealand yam. Some plants more usually grown as ornamentals are edible, too; you probably already know that nasturtium flowers bring a fresh peppery note to a salad, but what about sampling the flowers and buds of day lilies, or the young shoots of hostas or bamboo?

Health benefits

It's increasingly accepted that being outdoors among growing plants and vegetables is good for your mental health and wellbeing as well as your physical fitness. Cultivating the soil gives a gardener as good a workout as a gym can offer, and with rather more tangible results. And you'll always eat everything you grow – you know just how much effort has gone into that crop – so your meals may well begin to feature more, and more varied, fruit and vegetables.

Beautiful produce

Finally, just because you're growing fruit and veg, doesn't mean that your plot can't look great. There are many examples of stunning kitchen gardens and potagers that are as spectacular to look at as the crops are good to eat. An apple tree blossoming in a pot is just as impressive as any ornamental tree, while the textures of the foliage and stems, and the range of colours in the flowers and fruit are as varied and as beautiful as those of any other plants.

▲ *Healthy vegetable plants make your garden attractive as well as productive.*

Growing your own allows you to experiment with varieties that you
◀ *might not see in the shops.*

SOIL PREPARATION

Good soil preparation is key to growing vegetables successfully. Although they are mostly annual crops, they are often demanding, and need lots of nutrients to keep cropping. Fruit trees and perennial vegetables such as asparagus and rhubarb will be in the ground for longer than annuals, so preparing the soil before planting them is even more important.

One of the tricks to growing vegetables successfully is good, thorough soil preparation, including removing all
▼ *weeds before planting.*

Before sowing seeds or planting seedlings and plants, the soil needs to be prepared to give them the best chance of establishing and to enable them to maximise the size of their yield. Sometimes radical clearing may be needed before starting, particularly if you are taking on an abandoned allotment or a back garden full of building rubble.

Clearing weeds

In the case of an overgrown plot, you can first strim and then weed the whole area or, if you're not organic and don't mind using chemicals, you can apply a systemic weedkiller to kill the roots of any perennial weeds.

If you decide to spray perennial weeds, wait until there is maximum leaf cover to ensure the weedkiller is absorbed through the foliage and taken back down into the roots. After spraying, leave the foliage for a couple of weeks to give the weedkiller a chance to take effect. It may be necessary to do a second or even a third spraying with really pernicious weeds. In the unlikely case of knotweed, it may even be necessary to use qualified contractors to eradicate the weed first.

After strimming, it's easier to see what's there and to reach the soil and grub out roots. Ideally, you should do this before annual weeds have had a chance to set seed; once seeded, they quickly spread, so you'll find you have the same problem either later in the season or the following year. Most annual weeds can be easily prised out with a border fork. Perennial weeds, though, need far more work, as some roots can go down as far as a metre (3ft). When you're digging them out, try to remove as much of the root as possible, and don't add them to the compost heap but take them to the local tip, or leave them to dry out in the sun on a rack or fence until completely desiccated and dead, before composting.

If you're lucky enough to take on a well-maintained garden or allotment, it may just need a light hoeing to remove annual weeds before digging.

Digging over

Once the weeds have been removed, dig the soil over to a depth of 30cm (12in), and add some organic matter, such as garden compost or well-rotted manure. Digging over the soil will make it easier to plant, and for young plants' roots to develop and spread. Once the plot has been dug over, it should be raked level and ideally left to settle for a few days before you plant it up or sow seed. If the ground is going to be left for a while before planting, cover it up with a weed-suppressing membrane or another top dressing of organic matter to stop weeds germinating in the bare soil.

Green manure

Green manures are plants sown by gardeners into ground left vacant between vegetable crops. Their roots fix nitrogen from the air, increasing the fertility of the soil they grow in. Green manures are also used as cover for bare soil – a bit like a living mulch, they prevent weeds from germinating. They protect the soil from erosion, and offer additional visual interest; they're nicer to look at than an area of bare earth.

The best time for sowing a green manure crop is in late summer or autumn, and some, such as winter tares and grazing rye, will continue growing all through the winter. Green manures are usually cut down in spring and left on the surface to desiccate. A couple of weeks later, the material on the surface and the remaining plant material in the ground can be dug into the top 25cm (10in) of soil. Allow it to compost in the soil for a further two weeks before planting or sowing.

Green manures can be either annual or perennial. Types worth trying include bitter blue lupin (*Lupinus angustifolius*), buckwheat (*Fagopyrum esculentum*), crimson clover (*Trifolium incarnatum*), red clover (*Trifolium pratense*), fenugreek (*Trigonella foenum-graecum*), grazing rye (*Secale cereale*), white mustard (*Sinapis alba*), phacelia (*Phacelia tanacetifolia*), trefoil (*Medicago lupulina*), winter field bean (*Vicia faba*) and winter tares (*Vicia sativa*).

Fenugreek (Trigonella foenum-graecum) is a fast-growing green manure that is ◄ ready for digging 10 weeks after sowing.

Raised beds offer lots of benefits — they drain well and are less back-breaking to work.

RAISED BEDS

As their name suggests, raised beds are simply beds for growing vegetables or ornamental plants that are raised up from the ground. There are numerous benefits to growing vegetables in this way, and raised beds are becoming increasingly popular in gardens that have poor, or even no soil. They're also helpful for gardeners who have back problems, as they reduce the need to stoop while working.

Raised beds can be any shape and size, though ideally they should be narrow enough to reach across without climbing onto them, which compacts the soil. This means that the centre of the bed shouldn't be over 1.2m (4ft) from the edge, as this is the maximum reach for most gardeners. They can either be built directly onto patios or concrete, or on top of existing beds.

Advantages

• *Added height* Growing plants in a raised bed automatically raises them to a new height, so they are closer for touching, smelling and picking, making gardening a more sensory experience. The extra height can also be useful if you want more seclusion in a specific area of your garden.

• *Style* Raised beds can be made out of almost anything, and can be designed in different ways, whether you want a rustic or a chic effect. By offering a different level, they can give some additional structure to a garden design.

• *Drainage* Because they are above ground level, these beds automatically have better drainage. This is particularly useful on an existing site with poor drainage or soil, or located at the bottom of a slope.

• *Warmth* A raised bed will usually warm up faster in springtime than one at ground level. It is also less likely to be affected by a ground frost.

• *Soil to suit what you want to grow* A raised bed can be filled with customised soil, depending on what you want to grow. For example, if you plan to grow blueberries and cranberries, you can fill the bed with ericaceous compost to suit their requirements for acidic conditions. If you were to add ericaceous compost to a ground level bed, it would be likely to leach away over time.

• *Comfort* Raised beds are at a far more convenient height for planting, sowing, maintaining and harvesting crops. They are also a good choice for gardeners who use wheelchairs, or those with bad backs or other physical limitations.

Keyhole gardening

An increasingly popular type of raised bed is called a keyhole bed. The idea originated in Africa, and is now being adopted all over the world. A keyhole bed is a raised bed, traditionally made out of whatever free materials were available from the surrounding landscape, most commonly rocks. The bed is round, but with a cleft in the side (the 'keyhole') which leads to the centre, where materials to be composted are piled. The compost area is filled with garden waste and, as the material gradually breaks down, it leaches into the surrounding soil in the bed. The theory is that the constant leaching of nutrients and moisture from the compost 'bin' reduces the need to feed and water the plants that grow in the raised bed around it.

Keyhole gardening is a type of raised bed with compost in the centre which leaches into the soil, increasing its fertility.

PLANNING YOUR CROPS

Being able to plan is just as important as having good gardening skills when it comes to working out where and when you are going to grow crops. When it comes to growing fruit and vegetables, there are hundreds of different options, and individual varieties all have different sowing and cropping times, so it's worth making a plan and plotting it out on paper before you start.

Making a plan

Unless you have a huge garden and other people to help you, you'll probably find that you have to narrow down the choice of which crops you plan to grow. Winter is the best time to start planning as most of your growing space will usually be empty. It's also the season when gardeners usually have a little more time on their hands.

If you have a whole kitchen garden or allotment to plan from scratch, look at structure first – where are you going to put paths, beds, cold frame, a compost bin, and even a shed? You may also want to consider if you have room for a small polytunnel or a greenhouse. Next, work out where fruit trees and perennial vegetables such as asparagus, horseradish, globe artichokes, Jerusalem artichokes and rhubarb will go. These perennials will stay growing in the same place for some years, so once they're planted you will be working around them. When all this is planned, you'll be ready to work out which vegetables will go where, and when they'll need to be sown, harvested and removed to make way for other crops. Of course, this is planning on the larger scale – but even if you only have a bed or two, thinking through what you'll grow over the coming year will ensure that you make the most of your space.

Growing your favourites

Start by listing your favourite vegetables – the ones you definitely want in your garden. After all, there is no point in filling growing space with food that you don't particularly like.

Other things to consider include how much space a crop will take up and whether it will earn its place if you have a smaller plot. Vegetables that are either expensive to buy or harder to find – examples include beetroot, French beans, rhubarb, asparagus, Chinese radish, new potatoes, sorrel, Romanesco broccoli and sweetcorn – are always good value to grow. At the other end of the scale, if you have to cross some crops off the list, you might consider those that take up a lot of space on the plot and are always available to buy – for example, cabbages, maincrop potatoes, onions, carrots, swedes and parsnips.

When you've thought through all the options, you should end up with a list of crops that will give good space-for-yield value, and includes your favourites, too.

HOW CROP ROTATION WORKS

Most kitchen gardens use a system called crop rotation, which avoids growing the same plants in the same soil in successional years and reduces the problem of pests and diseases which target specific crops. Most gardeners divide their crops into four categories when they're planning crop rotation, and use four beds to rotate them in.

The rotation pattern works as follows. In the first bed, in the first year, grow potatoes and tomatoes; in the second year, grow root vegetables with onions and garlic; in the third year, grow peas and beans, and finally, in the fourth year, grow members of the cabbage family.

In the second bed, in the first year, grow root vegetables with onions and garlic, in the second year, peas and beans, in the third year, members of the cabbage family, and in the fourth, potatoes and tomatoes. And so on — meaning that each bed will only repeat a crop every fourth year.

Crops which tend to be less problem prone, including pumpkins, squashes, cucumbers, sweetcorn and lettuce, can be slotted into any of the beds, wherever there is space.

BED 1

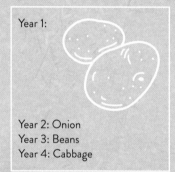

Year 1:

Year 2: Onion
Year 3: Beans
Year 4: Cabbage

BED 4

Year 1:

Year 2: Potatoes
Year 3: Onion
Year 4: Beans

BED 3

Year 1:

Year 2: Cabbage
Year 3: Potatoes
Year 4: Onion

BED 2

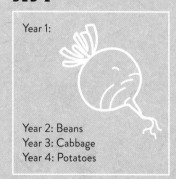

Year 1:

Year 2: Beans
Year 3: Cabbage
Year 4: Potatoes

VEGETABLES FROM SEED

Many of the vegetables to be found in a productive garden are grown from seed. Each crop has its own special cultivation needs but the basic guidelines for successful sowing are similar in almost all cases.

Buying seed

Good-quality vegetable seed is available from many reputable suppliers. Buying fresh, well-stored, vacuum-packed seeds will certainly help with successful germination once sown. The variety of seeds on offer can be bewildering, as suppliers compete to breed bigger, better, more disease-resistant varieties, although there is a growing trend for reverting to the old heritage crops. When you're choosing your seeds, read catalogue and online descriptions carefully, and concentrate on choosing cultivars for taste, reliability in a specific set of conditions, and pest or disease resistance.

▼ *Broad beans are one of the hardiest vegetables and can be sown directly into the soil even in cooler temperatures.*

The majority of seeds are sold by the packet, either just as they are or sometimes with a coating to make them easier to handle or to improve germination rates. Certain seeds are also available as 'seed tape' which means they're embedded into tape to ensure ideal spacing as you sow. Once bought, seeds should be stored in a cool, dry place, well away from pests such as mice and rats (both love eating seed packets and their contents). Difficult seeds, such as parsnips, can be pre-germinated indoors on a piece of damp kitchen paper a week or two before sowing.

Sowing seed outside

There are several ways to sow seeds outside. You can sow them directly in the bed where they will grow till they crop, or start them off in trays or pots, or in a dedicated seedbed, from which they can be transplanted into their final positions.

There are some, mostly root crops, that should not be transplanted, because the process will disrupt the straight growth of their tap root, and others, such as many salad crops, that grow so quickly that they will be harvested before there is any need to transplant. Others, though, can be started elsewhere until space becomes available to move them on. In a rotation system, this is very helpful. Seeds, whatever their size and shape, should only be sown in properly prepared ground. Well-dug soil should be raked to remove large stones and debris until a fine 'tilth' is achieved. This is soil that is made up of evenly sized crumbs, neither too dusty nor too full of heavy clods. If the soil is wet, it is best to stand on a board while you work, to avoid damaging the nearby soil structure. Most seeds need a soil temperature of above 7°C (45°F) to germinate successfully, and also have to be kept moist during the germination process, so covering the sown area with protective fleece can be useful.

Sowing seeds inside

Sowing seeds in pots or trays in a greenhouse or on a windowsill is necessary for most summer crops, such as tomatoes, that need to germinate early and to have a long, warm growing season. It can also be used to grow earlier crops if the spring weather is unusually cold, and if the ground outside is slow in warming up.

Drilling seeds

The most common way to sow seeds is to take out a 'drill'. Using a string line as a guide, make a small, straight channel with a hoe or trowel at the right depth for the seed you're sowing. As a rule of thumb, the bigger the seed, the deeper you need to plant it. With larger seeds, it is often recommended that they are sown at a depth of two or three times their size; seed packets usually offer advice on seed depth. Sprinkle or space seeds evenly along the drill, making sure not to sow too thickly. Cover and firm the soil gently before watering.

Crops that will be harvested young, or those that can tolerate growing close together, can be sown in wider drills or broadcast-sown. In broadcast sowing, a square of soil is raked to a fine tilth and the seed is scattered evenly over the whole area before being raked over lightly once more and gently watered. Larger seeds, such as beans, can simply be pushed into the soil by hand individually at the correct depth and spacing.

Thinning out

Even small seedlings need a certain amount of room to flourish, so you should thin them out before overcrowding causes a problem. If seedlings are delicate and closely spaced, use a pair of scissors to cut the weaker ones off just above ground level, or gently pull them out by hand, leaving evenly spaced, stronger plants to grow to maturity. Thinnings don't necessarily need to go to waste – some, such as those of carrots or beets, can be eaten as a nutritious gardener's perk.

SALADS AND LEAFY CROPS

Most salads and leafy crops are easy and fast to grow. They generally don't take up much space, either, so they can be grown in window boxes and containers. If you live in a flat or have a small garden, they're ideal. They'll even tolerate a bit of shade, so can be sited in a porch or used to brighten up a dappled, shady area of the garden where other sun-loving vegetables might not be so happy.

Not only do salad leaves offer a crunchy, flavoursome addition to sandwiches and salads, but the range of colours and textures can also look spectacular in the garden. In potagers, you often see a deliberate tapestry of leaf colours and patterns, making a feature that is just as good to look at as it is to taste.

The key to growing leafy crops is to sow and harvest little and often. This helps to avoid gluts, because salad leaves don't keep long once they're picked and can quickly run to seed if left in the ground for too long. They are quick to germinate, so it is better to sow every couple of weeks and to harvest regularly than to sow a single large crop. Small sowings ensure that you always have plenty of fresh leaves. The other beauty of salad leaves is that they can be grown as catch crops – that is, you can sow them in between slower-growing vegetables and harvest them before their neighbours have matured.

Lettuce varieties

There are a few different types of lettuce to try:
- Crisphead types include the most popular lettuce: iceberg. Crispheads are ball-shaped, producing tightly packed, big, crisp leaves with a large central heart.
- Romaine (or Cos) types have a looser arrangement of leaves than the crispheads, with a more elongated shape. The leaves are crisp.
- Butterheads generally have a loose head of softer leaves with a buttery, mild but sweet flavour. Butterhead lettuces usually last longer than the other types if kept in the fridge.

Some lettuces and other salad leaves are 'cut and come again', meaning that you can harvest the fresh new growth with scissors, and the plants will keep sending out new leaves to be harvested again a week or two later.

◀ *Rocket is a fast-growing salad leaf with a peppery flavour.*

Other salad leaves

Other popular salad crops include spinach, which has varieties suitable for either autumn or spring sowings, and rocket, which has a strong, hot flavour and is grown in a similar way to spinach. The leaves can be picked as and when they are required for salad.

Chicory is usually grown for its bitter flavour, which adds a 'bite' to salads. Endive is similar to chicory in flavour, but is usually grown as a 'cut and come again' crop. Chinese cabbage, also known as 'Chinese leaves', has heads that can either be steamed like cabbage or eaten fresh like a lettuce. Oriental vegetables such as Japanese mustard spinach, mibuna, mizuna, Chinese mustard greens and pak choi are all becoming increasingly popular to grow, and most are very versatile to cook with: they can be added raw to salads, steamed, or added to flavour stir fries, soups, stews and many other dishes.

Sowing lettuce seed

Salad leaves don't need deep soil. As little as 10 to 15cm (4–6in) is usually enough, but they must have drainage. They prefer to be in sun or dappled light, but they can often struggle with heat in the middle of summer, so may need shade in the middle of the day. Rake the soil to a fine tilth and then take out a thin drill using a cane or your finger. Lightly sprinkle seeds into the drill, cover over with the soil, and water. If you're growing a 'cut and come again' crop, the seedlings won't need thinning out, but if you want fully grown, hearting lettuces, they will need thinning out when they're about 2.5cm (1in) high to an eventual spacing of 30cm (12in) apart (smaller types such as semi-cos can be spaced more closely).

Iceberg lettuce forms a round ball of tightly packed, crunchy foliage.

Mizuna is a Japanese leafy vegetable with attractive dissected leaves and a peppery flavour.

Romaine (or Cos) lettuce has an elongated shape and loosely packed leaves.

Pick spinach when young or leave to mature for a stronger flavour.

TOMATOES AND OTHER 'FRUIT'

Botanists would refer to most of these crops as fruits because they contain their seeds inside the flesh, but in the gardening world they are considered very much part of the vegetable patch and are mainly used in savoury dishes in the kitchen.

Crops in this group include tomatoes, aubergines, cucumbers, peppers, chillies, courgettes, marrows, pumpkins and sweetcorn. Fruiting vegetables need some protection from the cold, ideally in a greenhouse or a polytunnel, until they are fairly mature plants. Some, such as indoor cucumbers and aubergines, may need to be grown completely under cover for them to ripen.

Tomatoes

Tomatoes should be sown in a heated greenhouse from mid- to late winter for indoor cultivation, or about eight weeks before the last frosts are predicted if they're going to be grown outdoors. They should be pricked out when they are about 8 to 10cm (3–4in) tall and potted on. When they're about 20cm (8in) tall they can be planted into growing bags, pots or directly into beds. Most tomatoes are grown as cordons (sometimes called 'indeterminate' types), which need supports for their rangy growth. As the plant grows, sublateral shoots need to be pinched out so that all its energy is concentrated into the production of flowers and fruit. However, some tomatoes have a bush habit (called 'determinate') and need little or no support. The 'tumbling' types of tomatoes can even be grown in hanging baskets.

Watch out for tomato blight, which causes plants to suddenly brown and wither, and choose varieties with resistance if it is an annual problem. Plants will need a weekly feed rich in potassium (such as a specific tomato feed) once they have started to form trusses of fruit.

Cucurbits

The cucurbits (pumpkins, cucumbers, courgettes and marrows) should be sown in pots undercover from mid- to late spring and planted out only after the risk of frost is over. The cucurbits have large seeds which are often sown on their sides to prevent water sitting on the flat surface and rotting the seed. When the seedlings are planted out, give them lots of space and add plenty of organic matter into the planting holes and surrounding soil – cucurbits require plenty of nutrients and moisture to develop to their full size and produce lots of fruit. They may also need feeding with a tomato feed every couple of weeks once they start to flower.

Tomatoes are easy to grow but need a long growing season, so should be sown ▼ early in the year under cover.

Cucumbers

There are two different types of cucumbers: ridge cucumbers, which are better suited for growing outside once the risk of frost is over, and the smoother, indoor types, which crop more reliably. Outdoor cucumbers should be sown in late spring, but the indoor types can be sown in a heated greenhouse from late winter. In a greenhouse, plants should be grown up a support, usually a cane or wire, and the tips of side shoots off the main stem pinched out two leaves past a female flower. Outdoor types can either be left to sprawl on the ground or trained up netting or a trellis.

Peppers and chillies

Peppers and chillies should be treated in the same way. Sow them in a heated greenhouse in late winter. When they are between 8 and 10cm (3–4in) tall, thin them out and pot them on into large containers or growbags if growing inside, or plant them outside once the risk of frost is over.

Aubergines

Except in really warm summers, aubergines rarely do well when grown outside, but if you decide to try, do pick as warm and sheltered a site as possible. Sow seed from mid- to late winter in a heated greenhouse. The plants will need supporting with sturdy stakes when the fruits start to develop.

Sweetcorn

Sweetcorn is sown indoors in mid-spring or directly outdoors after the risk of frost is over. The plants are wind-pollinated (that is, they depend on pollen from the flower of one plant blowing onto another, and vice versa) and should therefore be planted in a grid shape to maximise their pollination chances, with plants spaced about 40cm (16in) apart. The grid should contain at least 16 plants in a 4 x 4 formation for it to be effective; more plants in a bigger grid are even better.

▲ *Cucumbers grown outdoors can be trained up supporting canes.*

▲ *Bird's eye chillies grow well in pots, with clusters of chillies pointing upwards.*

▲ *Warmth is essential for growing aubergines so choose a sunny spot if growing them outside.*

◀ *Plant sweetcorn in a block rather than a row to help pollination.*

THE CABBAGE FAMILY

The cabbage family, or brassicas, includes Brussels sprouts, kale, cauliflower, broccoli and, as you'd expect, cabbage. Turnips and swedes are members of the same family but tend to be grouped with other root crops, as is the less well-known kohlrabi. They are all easy to grow and collectively one of the most nutritious of all the different vegetable groups.

The brassicas can provide vegetables almost year-round, but they are particularly useful from winter through to spring, when there is not much left to harvest in the kitchen garden. All brassicas like similar conditions and tend to suffer from the same pests and diseases. They are best grown in a different place each year to avoid too many problems. Brassicas are usually sown in a seed bed before transplanting them out later, and this method can also help pest control. They generally need firm, fertile soil with plenty of nitrogen and regular watering to do well. Lime can be added to the soil in the autumn before planting – this helps to prevent club root, which is one of the worst diseases to which brassicas are prone. The soil must also be firmed properly before planting: this prevents wind rock which can result in loose heads forming.

Kale and Brussels sprouts

The hardiest of the brassicas is kale, followed by Brussels sprouts; both overwinter well. Brussels should be both planted firmly and staked, to prevent individual sprouts from opening up, or 'blowing'. Kale is a little more easy-going, and red and black kale cultivars are available.

Kale is a flavoursome winter crop. ▶

Broccoli and calabrese

Broccoli and calabrese are both useful and productive plants to grow. Broccoli, including purple sprouting broccoli, is planted in spring and allowed to grow at its own pace before the spears are harvested early the following spring, while summer calabrese is considerably faster to crop. Calabrese is best sown directly into the ground, as its otherwise rapid growth may be checked by transplanting.

Cauliflower

The fussiest of the flower-head brassica crops is the cauliflower. It needs plenty of water and food and may perform badly if conditions are not exactly right for it, but when treated well the results are worth it. As well as the traditional summer varieties, new cauliflower cultivars have extended the season, cropping in autumn and winter too.

Cabbage

Similarly, cabbages can be grown successfully pretty much all year round. The cabbage season begins with 'spring greens', sown the previous autumn and encouraged to grow loosely. These are then followed by spring-sown summer cabbages and, later, by cabbages that can be harvested through autumn well into winter. Many winter cabbages, including the dark, crinkle-leaved Savoy, can withstand frost and can stay in the ground until required.

Brassicas are a favourite food source for pigeons, caterpillars, root flies and whitefly, and, as a result, all family members will need protection, including collars round the roots and netting or mesh, to keep out unwelcome diners.

▲ Calabrese is one of the faster growing members of the brassica family and is often sown directly into the ground.

▲ Cauliflower is one of the trickier members of the brassica family to grow.

◄ Cabbages can be grown practically all year round. Watch out for pests such as cabbage white caterpillars.

▲ *Rhubarb is a vigorous perennial plant producing lots of juicy and succulent stems from spring to midsummer.*

THE PERENNIALS: RHUBARB, ASPARAGUS AND ARTICHOKES

Perennial vegetables need space and a suitable site as, once established, they will remain in situ for many years. They can sometimes be slow to get started but will eventually produce a regular crop for anything up to 20 years without the annual preparations called for with most other fruit or vegetables.

Rhubarb

This is an invaluable crop in the veg garden, offering deliciously tart fruit in the early part of the year when nothing similar is available.

Rhubarb is normally planted as a bare root during the dormant season, at intervals of 1m (3ft) or so. It needs well-drained soil with plenty of rich organic matter dug in before planting. A sunny site is best, but rhubarb will tolerate a slightly shadier spot that may not be so good for other crops.

Rhubarb should not be harvested in its first year, and only a few stems should be picked in the second. Once fully established, it can be picked regularly from March to July, leaving it time to recover. Only the stems are edible; the leaves are mildly poisonous. At the end of each season, remove all the old leaves before mulching the crowns with manure or compost. It's a relatively trouble-free crop but should be protected from slugs and snails.

Forced rhubarb is something of a speciality, with its pale pink colour and mild flavour. To produce it, you need to cover the plant's crown with a container that blocks out light for a few weeks before the season begins, and the result will be a crop of skinny, sweet stems.

Asparagus

A short but prolific season makes asparagus a luxurious joy if you can find space for it. It needs a very well prepared bed in a sheltered, sunny position. Weed the bed very thoroughly before digging out a trench and adding plenty of organic matter. Asparagus is usually planted as bare root crowns, which are spread out on individual mounds at least 30cm (12in) apart before being covered with soil and watered.

Allow the plants to build up strength over the first two years, and resist the temptation to harvest until the third. The spears should be cut off just below ground level as soon as they are of eating size; the more you harvest, the more will grow. After midsummer, the ferny foliage can be allowed to develop. Maintenance is easy. Cut down dying foliage stems in winter, mulch and apply fertiliser in spring. Asparagus especially enjoys a seaweed mulch. All-male varieties are the most productive.

Artichokes

Two types of artichoke are commonly grown but, despite the shared name, they are not related.

Globe artichokes dislike the cold and benefit from a winter mulch. They grow large, silver, prickly leaves and flower buds that are harvested around midsummer. Like asparagus, they are usually grown from root cuttings or offsets planted in the dormant season in a sunny, sheltered site enriched with organic matter. They are large plants and can easily shade out other crops, so site them appropriately.

Jerusalem artichokes have edible tubers and are much less fussy about their growing conditions. As long as they are in a sunny spot they will grow happily in poor soil, producing a mass of tall sunflower heads in late summer. They have a tendency to spread, so you do need to control them – it's best to dig up the patch annually. Harvest plenty of the nut-tasting tubers in late autumn and replant just a few for the following year.

Globe artichokes can provide a focal point among flower or vegetable plants.

PEAS AND BEANS

Collectively known as legumes, these are staples of the vegetable garden, producing heavy crops from late spring to late summer, full of useful protein and relatively easy to grow. Some legumes are able to tolerate cooler conditions while others originate from warmer climates and will need a little help at the start.

All the legumes are usually planted in a sunny site in very enriched soil, preferably newly manured or composted, although they can produce their own nitrogen in nodules on their roots. They need regular watering; feeding is less essential. The climbing varieties also need something to wrap their tendrils around as they climb. This can be either a wigwam of canes, a frame of sticks or some sort of supported netting.

Broad beans

Broad beans are delicious when they are young and freshly picked but the plants are tough enough to survive through winter. Sowing in late November is standard practice and will produce a much earlier crop the following spring, but later sowings can be equally successful and will extend the season right through summer. Broad beans don't need any additional care. Dwarf cultivars are available, but taller varieties may need some support. In spring, the tops should be pinched out once enough pods have begun to form. This encourages a better crop and helps to prevent blackfly attack.

Peas

Peas are also relatively hardy and early sowings in trenches are often possible under cloches or fleece. The sweet flavour of a young pea fresh from the pod is unsurpassed and can become quite addictive. Twiggy brush and sticks work well for growing most peas on, but taller varieties may call for a firmer support.

Peas should be harvested regularly and, unless you prefer the older, floury crop, they're best taken young, before their sugars turn into starch. When cropping is finished, cut the stems off at ground level but leave the plants' nitrogen-fixing roots in the ground to feed the next crop.

As well as standard peas, varieties such as mangetout and sugarsnap, where you eat the whole pod, are also available.

Runner beans

A classic sight in a traditional summer vegetable patch, the runner bean is both beautiful and highly productive – the more the beans are picked, the more new pods will grow. Support for runner beans needs to be strong and tall. They are energetic climbers and can be very heavy when laden with pods.

Runner beans originate from South America and are best started off inside, warm and protected, before being transplanted, although later sowings can be made outside in late spring. They thrive in rich, moisture-retaining soil, preferably in a previously prepared trench filled with uncomposted kitchen waste, provided they are watered regularly, especially when flowering. Blackfly is the most common problem and should be dealt with early, as soon as the first pests are spotted.

French beans

This group includes both climbing beans, such as borlotti, and dwarf varieties that rarely reach more than half a metre (18in) high, making them perfect for pots. They are all tender and, like runner beans, are best started off with protection, but their basic requirements are the same as other peas and beans. You can find purple and yellow varieties, as well as the standard green.

▲ *Young peas eaten raw from the pod are one of the most delicious gardener's perks.*

▲ *Exotic looking purple-podded mangetout peas can be used raw to give a crunch to salads, or lightly boiled or steamed (though they do turn green when cooked).*

◀ *Runner beans should be picked every few days to keep the plant cropping regularly throughout the season.*

▲ *Onions are more easily grown from 'sets', although they can also be grown from seed.*

THE ONION FAMILY

Food would be much blander without this group of vegetables, which bring taste and savour to a huge variety of dishes in the kitchen. They have a reputation stretching back centuries for boosting good health and vitality but, whatever their status medicinally, they are easy and rewarding to grow.

Both onions and shallots like a sunny spot, with rich, well-drained soil. Good airflow will help prevent rust, the most common of the onion diseases, which can weaken the plant, though it rarely kills it. Other members of the onion family include spring onions, fast-growing small onions for salads, perennial Welsh onions and chives.

Onions

Onions can be grown from seed or from sets, which are baby onions planted out to grow to maturity. Seeds are sown inside in late winter or early spring before being transplanted out in spring. Separate into individual plants if you want the largest onions, or, for smaller bulbs, leave in little clumps to grow on. Onion sets can be planted out later in spring as they need less time to grow on. They are usually planted in drills, pushed gently into the ground until only the tips show. Newly planted sets are sometimes pulled up by birds, so protect them straight after planting.

Onions are available in both brown and red varieties; of the two, red are considered the sweeter. Water the crop when dry and weed carefully around the shallow-rooted bulbs until the leaves begin to bend over in summer, at which point your onions are ready for harvesting. Lift them carefully and dry for several days, preferably in the sun, before storing them.

Shallots need a longer season than onions and are normally grown from sets. They are usually planted in late winter (Christmas day was the traditional planting date). Each set will gradually form a clump of new shallot bulbs, which are harvested in the same way as onions, but just a little earlier than onions. French shallots, with their elongated torpedo shape, are considered to have a finer flavour than the round varieties.

Leeks

Another classic staple of the vegetable garden, leeks are one of the few vegetables that enjoy heavy, more acidic soil, but they will thrive anywhere as long as they are given rich, moist conditions. Leeks are sown under cover in late winter before being transplanted out into deep holes to ensure a good length of white stem. Later in the year, the seeds can be sown directly into drills, especially if they are to be harvested young as mini-veg. Left to grow on to full size, leeks can be harvested from autumn through to the following spring.

A popular winter crop, leek seedlings are planted in deeply to blanch the stem and therefore make it more tender. ▶

Garlic

For maximum flavour, nothing beats garlic, an onion family member associated with the Mediterranean. Choose the right variety and garlic will grow perfectly happily in the UK. It is always best to buy specialist garlic bulbs from a horticultural supplier; if you plant cloves from ordinary supermarket-bought garlic they are unlikely to thrive.

Garlic needs a cold period followed by a long season of sunshine to do really well. Plant individual cloves, tip upwards, in late autumn in rich, moist soil on a well-drained and sunny site, and water in dry spells. Garlic can be eaten fresh while still green, when the taste is milder, or left until the leaves yellow before being lifted and dried for storage.

POTATOES, BEETROOT AND OTHER ROOT CROPS

Root vegetables are a mixed bunch. They come from a variety of families but have some things in common. Nearly all dislike fresh manure in the soil they grow in, which can result in distorted and divided roots. Stony ground that hasn't been carefully enough prepared can also mean split roots. Root crops need both space and time to mature, so are perhaps best suited to the larger plot.

Potatoes

Potatoes are not technically a true root crop, because we harvest and eat the tubers, not the roots. They are grown from 'seed' potatoes, egg-sized tubers that are usually encouraged to start producing shoots before planting in spring, a technique known as 'chitting', which speeds up growth and encourages earlier cropping. Planted in rich soil, potatoes are traditionally earthed up over the growing season before being harvested when their flowers open (early potatoes), or left to the end of summer (late croppers).

Parsnips

A light, stone-free soil that has been deeply dug suits parsnips best, along with plenty of sun. Parsnip seeds can be annoyingly erratic in their germination, especially if the soil temperature is not right, so it is worth pre-germinating them on a piece of damp kitchen roll before sowing. Once germinated, thin out the seedlings carefully, and do not overwater. They can be harvested from late summer onwards, although they are frost-hardy, so you can also leave them in the ground for longer. Traditionally it is claimed that their flavour improves with a touch of frost.

Carrots

Carrots are at the top of most people's list of tasty roots. They can also almost be treated as a salad crop: regular sowing will ensure repeated yields of baby carrots all through the summer, and you can leave some to grow on and grow bigger until winter. For carrots to produce long, straight roots they prefer light, sandy soil, cleared of any stones, and with reasonable fertility. If you have a heavier soil, choose one of the ball-shaped varieties which will be less affected.

The seeds are very fine, so thinning is usually necessary. You can either cut through unwanted thinnings with a pair of scissors to avoid any root disturbance, or gently pull them out – these tiny infant carrots make very tasty eating. Water carrots regularly; if they're left to dry out, the roots are prone to splitting.

Carrots are very susceptible to attack by the carrot fly, which lays its eggs in the roots. The larvae then burrow through the carrot, causing substantial damage. Any disturbance to the seedlings releases a scent that attracts the flies to lay. The easiest way to deal with them is to fence the carrot bed with a fine mesh at least a metre (3ft) high; the adults can't fly above 60cm (2ft), so this makes an effective barrier.

Beetroot

The beet family is usually included in this group; while a few beetroot types are grown for their leaves only, most are cropped for their roots. They taste earthily sweet and are full of nutrients. Beetroot can be sown from spring through to early summer and are best harvested around six weeks later, when the beets are around the size of a golf ball, for the most tender crop. Bigger roots can tend towards woodiness. A wide range of varieties is available, in a number of colours, including yellow and pink-striped types as well as the more familiar deep purple.

▲ *You may be surprised at how generous a crop a few chitted seed potatoes will yield.*

◀ *Once parsnips have grown to size, they can be left in the ground until they're needed.*

Turnips and swedes

Both are members of the cabbage family and can cope with slightly richer soil than some other root crops. Turnips, especially young ones, are enjoying something of a revival in popularity after years out of the vegetable spotlight. Grown in rich, moist soil, baby turnips can be harvested after only six weeks. If you prefer them slightly larger, harvest them within three months; left in the soil too long, they can become woody and unpleasant. They prefer cooler springs so are usually sown under cover early before being planted out with as little root disturbance as possible. Swedes take much longer to grow; the seeds are sown directly into the ground in spring to mature in the winter months. As with all root crops, thin out carefully to avoid unnecessary disturbance.

Beetroots can be sown successionally every few weeks to provide a regular supply of
▼ *tasty roots throughout the season.*

HERBS

Even if you are not planning to grow fruit or vegetables in your garden, herbs are such a garden mainstay that you will probably find them working their way on to your planting lists. Who, after all, could plant a garden without at least considering lavender, rosemary, sage, thyme, fennel and mint?

You can have a lot of fun with herbs. Fantastic results can be achieved with very little effort in almost any growing space, from beds and borders to containers on windowsills. All you need is well-drained soil (dig in lots of horticultural grit if you are not sure) and plenty of sun. Herbs tend to be grown together in gardens as most call for similar growing conditions, but feel free to try them out mixed into ornamental beds or borders, too.

If you have the space, a formal herb garden can look very good. Traditionally these are arranged in defined compartments, edged with low shrubs, clipped to shape, to create interesting patterns. The edging plants play an important role, maintaining the structure and interest of the beds in winter, when most of the herbs are dormant. In a small or less formal garden, you can plant herbs through gravel or into the tight spaces between paving stones on a sunny patio.

If you like cooking with herbs it's helpful to have them growing next to the house, ideally near the back door in a trough, container, raised bed or even a window box. It needs to be placed in a spot that gets at least six hours of sun daily in midsummer; any less, and your herbs will struggle to thrive and may lose their flavour.

Thyme can be planted in light, well-drained soil but can just as easily be grown in a container for easy harvesting.

Making a herb bed

To set up a new herb bed, dig in 5kg (11lb) of well-rotted organic matter per square metre to raise fertility levels. This gives the new plants a great start, after which your herbs will rarely if ever need feeding. After an initial few weeks of watering to help the new plants take root, watering should no longer be necessary either. Regular picking and trimming, along with the occasional check through to remove any dead material, will keep your herbs in good shape.

Herb	Sun/Shade	Soil	Moisture	Hardiness	Height	Spread (cm)	Plant (cm)	Flower
Chives (*Allium schoenoprasum*)	●	●● ●●	●	H6	40	30	Mar–May	Jun–Nov
Coriander (*Coriandrum sativum*)	●▶	●● ●	●	H5	40	25	Mar–Sept	May–Oct
Dill (*Anethum graveolens*)	●	●●	◡	H4	90	30	Mar–Jul	Jun–Sept
Fennel (*Foeniculum vulgare*)	●▶	●● ●●	●	H6	200	50	Apr–Jun	Sept–Nov
Mint (*Mentha suaveolens*)	●▶	●	●	H5	100	150	Feb–Sept	May–Oct
Oregano (*Origanum amanum*)	●	●	◡	H3	10	50	Mar–Apr	Jun–Sept
Parsley (*Petroselinum crispum*)	●▶	●	●	H4	45	45	Mar–Jul	May–Nov
Rosemary (*Rosmarinus officinalis*)	●	●● ●●	●	H4	150	100	Mar–May	Jul–Oct
Sage (*Salvia officinalis*)	●▶	● ●	●	H4	100	100	Mar–May	Jun–Oct
Sweet basil (*Ocimum basilicum*)	●	● ●	◡	H1C	45	40	Feb–Apr	May–Oct
Thyme (*Thymus vulgaris*)	●	●●	●	H6	45	45	Mar–Apr	Jun–Oct

Situation

● Full sun preferred

▶ Partial shade preferred

Soil Type

● Loam

● Sand

● Chalk

● Clay

Watering

● Moist but well-drained

◡ Well-drained

Hardiness

On a scale of 1 to 6

▲ Most herbs can be grown in containers outdoors.

PLANTING A HERB TROUGH

Before you start, choose a selection of herbs that complement each other well. For a Mediterranean mix, for example, try a mix of chives, sage, thyme, tarragon and rosemary.

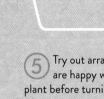

① Check that the trough has holes in its base for drainage.

⑤ Try out arrangements of the plants until you are happy with the overall look. Water each plant before turning it upside down and easing it out of its pot.

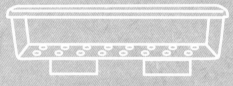

② Position the trough where you want it to go, raising it off the ground slightly using bricks or flat stones.

⑥ Dig a hole in the compost large enough for the root ball and place the plant in it.

③ Line the base of the trough with a layer of grit or gravel.

⑦ Firm the compost around the plant using your fingers. Plant up the rest of the trough in the same way, then level the compost and water in well, giving it a good soaking.

④ Fill the trough with soil-based compost, leaving a 1cm (½in) space between the top of the compost and the rim of the trough.

⑧ Top off the compost with a layer of gravel or grit. The purpose of the grit is to keep the leaves clean from compost, but it is also a nice ornamental touch.

▲ If you're short of space in the garden, a
range of herbs can be grown in vertical herb
troughs attached to a wall or fence.

Growing herbs

Herbs prefer a sandy, free-draining loam. They may
struggle in very heavy clay soils or highly acidic
ones. In such cases, the best solution is to grow
your herbs in a container or raised bed filled with
a well-drained soil-based compost.

Harvesting herbs

The best time to harvest herbs is on a warm, sunny
day, just before they start to flower. Use a sharp
knife or scissors and try to take material from all
over the plant to keep the shape balanced. Do not
worry about frequent harvesting; provided that you
don't cut back into the older woody growth, herbs
will happily cope with such treatment.

RASPBERRIES, STRAWBERRIES AND OTHER SOFT FRUIT

Many different soft fruits are grown in kitchen gardens and allotments, and there's something to suit most tastes. Soft fruit also doesn't take up too much space, and a lot of varieties can be grown in pots; strawberries can even be grown in hanging baskets.

Raspberries

Raspberries prefer slightly moist and acidic soil in full sun. There are two different types and their cultivation and pruning are different, so when you're buying canes (or if you've inherited some in an existing garden) you need to establish which type you're looking at. First, there are the autumn-fruiting raspberries, which bear fruit from late summer through to early winter. Then there are the summer-fruiting types, which produce fruit from early to late summer, depending on the variety.

The autumn-fruiting types produce all their fruit on canes formed in the same year. They are very easy to care for. Simply cut the entire plant down to ground level in late winter or early spring, which will encourage new, vigorous, fruit-bearing canes the following autumn.

Summer-fruiting raspberries bear their fruit on canes produced the previous year. To prune them, the old fruiting canes should be cut down to ground level after they have finished fruiting. The new canes, produced the same year, can then be tied in, leaving a spacing of about a hand's width between each one. Any surplus canes can also be cut back to ground level.

▲ *Raspberries are either summer or autumn types: the type determines how they should be pruned.*

Gooseberries and redcurrants

Gooseberries are less commonly grown than they once were, but if the fruits are thinned out when young and the remaining crop is left for slightly longer on the bush to allow the flavour to develop and deepen, the taste can be a delicious revelation. Redcurrants look beautiful when they are in fruit, the bush looking as though it is dripping with red translucent berries. Both gooseberry and redcurrant bushes have a very similar growth habit, and they are often trained and pruned in the same way. They can be grown as open-centre bushes, stepovers or upright vertical cordons, standards or fans. Both will tolerate shade, so are useful plants for growing as fans on north- or east-facing fences and walls.

Both gooseberries and redcurrants fruit on older wood, at the base of the previous year's growth. To prune a gooseberry or redcurrant as a bush, clear any suckers or growth coming off the short central leg the bush sits on. Select five or six branches that are facing outwards, then remove growth coming up through the middle of the bush, leaving it open-centred, shaped like a goblet on a short stem. In subsequent years, the new growth on the branches should be pruned back to a couple of buds between late autumn and late winter, except for the leaders of each branch, which should be cut back by a third. Keep the centre of the bush free from other shoots.

Blackcurrants

Although the two are closely related, blackcurrants have a different growth habit from redcurrants. They fruit on young shoots produced the previous year. They are grown as stool bushes; this means that they are deeply planted, with the top of the root ball several centimetres below the surface of the soil, and this encourages a multi-stemmed habit from the base. Their growth habit means that blackcurrants are not suited to growing as cordons, fans or open-centred bushes.

Blackcurrant pruning is easy. Simply use a pair of loppers to remove about a third of the thicker, more mature wood at the base of the plant between late autumn and late winter. Always remove any wayward shoots that are low enough to rest on the ground when they are laden with fruit.

Strawberries

There are two types of strawberries grown in the kitchen garden. The most popular are the summer-bearing types, which carry large fruits from late spring through to midsummer. There are also ever-bearing or perpetual types, which fruit for most of summer and early autumn, but don't produce such large fruits. Both sorts are traditionally grown in strawberry beds, the plants spaced about 30cm (12in) apart, in rows 70cm (28in) apart. As the fruit develops, straw is usually laid around the plant, under the foliage, to stop the berries rotting on the ground. Strawberries can also be grown in hanging baskets, planters and growing bags, ideally raised above ground level to deter slugs and snails. Birds sometimes also take the fruit, but can be deterred by netting laid over the plants.

Strawberries produce runners on the main plants. These should be removed while the plant is growing, so that it channels its energy into the production of fruit, but can be potted up and planted out as new plants the following year. Strawberry plants are usually grown for two or three years before being dug up and replaced with new stock. If space allows, the replacement plants should go in a new bed to reduce the chance of pests and diseases.

Strawberries are mainly summer-bearing types that crop in midsummer or ever-bearing types
▼ *that fruit throughout the season.*

APPLES AND PEARS

Apple and pear trees offer at least two seasons of interest every year, with glorious blossom in spring and attractive fruit in late summer or autumn. Even in winter, their bare trunks and branches can bring an attractive architectural element to a garden.

Both apples and pears have similar growth habits and can therefore be given the same treatment. Both exist in forms that can be grown in containers, meaning that you don't need a large garden to grow them. For your trees to bear fruit, they need pollinating from another fruit tree nearby, which must be of a different variety but in flower at the same time.

Garden centres and nurseries have devised a system of categorising fruit trees into pollination groups to ensure that trees will have adequate pollination when planted. If there is an apple or pear tree in a nearby garden this may be enough to ensure that your tree is pollinated; if not, you may need to buy a pair of trees in the same group, rather than just one. It is best to get expert advice from a specialist nursery regarding pollination groupings, to avoid disappointment later, when a tree fails to crop.

A healthy, heavily cropping apple tree looks as appealing in the autumn garden as one full of blossom does in the spring. ▷

ROOTSTOCKS

Apple and pear trees are grafted or budded onto rootstocks, and it is these rootstocks which determine their eventual height. Rootstocks are identified by letters and numbers, which tell you how tall the tree will grow.

APPLE ROOTSTOCKS

The most commonly found apple rootstocks are as follows:

M27 Extremely dwarfing – suitable for stepovers, growing in containers and as a free-standing tree. Grows to 1.2–1.8m x 1.5m (4–6ft x 5ft).

M9 Moderately dwarfing – suitable for stepovers, cordons, growing in containers and as a free-standing tree. Grows to 1.8–2.4m x 2.7m (6–8ft x 9ft).

M26 Dwarfing – suitable for fans, cordons, espaliers, growing in containers and as a free-standing tree. Grows to 2.4–3m x 3.6m (8–10ft x 12ft).

MM106 Semi-dwarfing, the most popular rootstock – suitable for fans, cordons, espaliers, growing in containers and as a free-standing tree. Grows to 3–4m x 4m (10–13ft x 13ft).

M111 Vigorous – best grown as a free-standing tree. Grows to 4–4.5m x 4.5m (13–15ft x 15ft).

M25 Very vigorous – best grown as a free-standing tree, but may be too large for many gardens. Grows to at least 4.5m x 6m (20ft x 15ft).

PEAR ROOTSTOCKS

Quince C Dwarfing – suitable for cordons, espaliers and as a free-standing tree. Grows to 2.5–3m (6–10ft).

Quince A Semi-vigorous – suitable for fans, cordons, espaliers and as a free-standing tree. Grows to 3–4.5m (10–15ft).

Tree shapes

Apples and pears are particularly versatile and can be trained into many different shapes. The most common shapes are shown in the box on page 158 but some gardeners, with a bit of imagination and pruning knowledge, can create even more elaborate and impressive shapes. These deliberately trained shapes are known as 'restricted forms', indicating that the trees are regularly pruned to a desired ornamental shape, as opposed to being left to grow into a free-standing, though pruned and shaped, tree.

Pruning apple and pear trees

Free-standing trees are pruned mainly in winter. Pruning includes removing crossing branches and thinning out laterals to ensure that the canopy isn't too dense, and sunlight is able to reach most of the tree. On open-centre trees, any branches growing into the centre should be removed.

Restricted forms of fruit trees are pruned in late summer after they have finished growing. A method called the Modified Lorette system is used, which involves pruning back the new growth to one or two buds. In winter, any dense clusters of spurs can be pruned out.

TREE SHAPES

OBLIQUE CORDON

One of the most commonly seen shapes in the garden. It consists of a central trunk with a system of short spurs, and laterals coming off them. It is grown at an angle of about 45 degrees to slow down the vigour of the plant and encourage better flower and fruit distribution along its trunk.

FAN

A very attractive method of training fruit trees onto a wall or fence. Trees are grown on a short trunk and then branches are spread out in a fan shape and tied on wires attached to the fence or wall.

CENTRAL-LEADER/SPINDLE TREES

Grown with a central leader and a 'Christmas tree' shape, with tiers of branches narrowing towards the top of the tree. This shape ensures that the higher sections of the tree cast minimal shade on the lower branches.

ESPALIER

Probably the most ornate method of pruning an apple tree. It is suitable for training a tree against a wall or fence, or on a system of wires stretched between two upright posts. It has a central stem or trunk, with numerous tiers of horizontal branches trained out on either side of it. Along these horizontal branches are short fruiting spurs and laterals. There is usually about 25cm (10in) between each tier. There are usually three or four tiers, although there can be more — as many as the vigour of the tree can cope with.

STEPOVERS

Simply a single-tiered espalier. Stepovers are a popular and ornate method of edging pathways or vegetable beds. They're usually grown on M27 or M9 rootstocks, as other rootstocks are too vigorous. The first tier is about 40cm (16in) off the ground – low enough to be stepped over, hence the name.

FREE-STANDING TREES

Bush tree, grown on a single trunk with a goblet or open-shaped structure above.

STONE FRUITS

▲ Apricots are traditionally grown under cover.

All stone fruits that can be grown in the garden belong to the genus *Prunus*. The trees are generally easy to grow and look just as good covered in spring blossom as they do later in the year, laden with fruit.

One of the key things to remember about stone fruit is that the trees should not be pruned in winter, as this leaves them susceptible to disease. Instead they are usually pruned in spring or midsummer. For the same reason, avoid pruning trees in this group when it is raining, or in a prolonged damp spell.

Plums

One of the most popular of all the stone fruits – with the variety 'Victoria' being particularly favoured. Plums are mostly grown as free-standing trees, but also sometimes trained as fans on warm south- or south-west-facing fences or walls. Plums are prone to over-cropping; to avoid the risk of branches snapping under the weight of the fruit, the crop must be thinned – to a spacing of every 5–8cm (2–3in) or a pair every 15cm (6in) – as the young plums start to swell.

Plums don't respond as well to pruning as apple and pear trees, and therefore it should be kept to a minimum, and used only to help shape the tree, remove crossing, dead or diseased wood, or to thin out a dense canopy.

Peaches and nectarines

These two are very closely related, and are grown in the same way. They both need a warm, sheltered site to ripen well, and are usually trained as fans on south- or south-west-facing walls. In early spring, the swelling buds may need protection with a plastic cover from the rain, which can cause peach leaf curl, a fungal disease. The trees fruit on wood produced the previous year, so pruning should involve removing some of the older wood and tying in newer shoots. It is important to thin the fruit to ensure that the crop ripens fully. When fruits are the size of a hazelnut, they should be thinned to 10cm (4in) apart, and when the size of a walnut to 20cm (8in) apart.

Apricots

These have a similar growth habit to plums. Their fruit should be thinned out to 5–8cm (2–3in) apart when hazelnut-sized. Like peach trees, they bear their fruit on growth made the previous year, but also – like plums – on short spurs from the older wood. Pruning is therefore best done as a combination of some replacement pruning and some spur pruning.

Cherries

There are two different types of cherries, sweet and acidic (sour) ones. They have different cropping habits, and therefore the pruning and training for the two is also different. Sour cherries (such as morello) bear fruit on wood produced the previous year, so pruning entails removing some of the older wood to give new shoots room to grow. Sweet cherries produce fruit on an older system of spurs, so pruning should entail shortening some of the branches to encourage fruiting spurs. Pruning should take place from early to midsummer.

Cherries are best grown as fans. Sweet cherries need more sunlight and should be grown on a south- or south-west-facing wall, but acidic cherries will tolerate some shade. They can also be grown as free-standing trees.

159

OTHER POPULAR FRUITS

There are many, many different fruits that you can grow in the garden or allotment. Some of the more popular ones are described below, but other exciting and unusual options are constantly being introduced, so look out for them in plant catalogues or nurseries. After all, one of the pleasures of growing your own fruit is being able to eat something you might not readily find in a shop.

Hybrid berries

Blackberries are the most popular type of hybrid berry, but there are many others worth trying too, including tayberry, tummelberry, loganberry, Japanese wineberry, boysenberry and dewberry. They are related to brambles and are generally vigorous plants, and many are thorny, so must be pruned with care. However, most of them produce delicious fruit.

They mostly have a similar fruiting habit to summer raspberries, producing fruit mainly on growth produced the previous year. They should be pruned after fruiting, removing the older fruiting canes by cutting them at the base, and tying the new growth onto a system of wire or trellis. These new canes will produce fruit the following year.

A few blackberry varieties, such as 'Reuben', are the exceptions, in that they fruit on canes produced in the same year. These should be pruned like autumn raspberries, cutting all growth back to ground level in late winter. If you're buying new blackberry plants, check which type you have.

Blueberries

Blueberries are a delicious soft fruit, but need an acidic soil of 5.5pH or lower in order to thrive. If your garden can't offer this, they can be grown in containers or raised beds filled with ericaceous compost. If you're planting in the ground, plants should be sited 1.2m (4ft) apart, in full sun and in moist but well-drained soil. If you are growing blueberries in a container, they should be watered with rainwater to avoid increasing the pH levels of the soil.

Plants should be pruned by removing about a third of the older wood towards the base. This is to encourage younger shoots, which will produce the berries. The best time to prune is early spring just as the buds are beginning to swell. This will help you to identify any dead branches so that they can be removed as you prune.

Kiwi

This is a climbing, sprawling plant and needs some support. Most kiwis need both male and female plants to produce fruit – although one male plant will pollinate up to eight females. Plants should be planted about 4m (13ft) from each other. However, self-fertile varieties, such as 'Jenny' are available, which will crop on a single plant, and are more suitable for smaller gardens. Kiwis need a warm, sunny site, and may need to be wrapped in fleece to protect them from frosts in early spring.

They should be pruned in winter, by cutting laterals back to about three or four buds beyond the final fruited shoot. In addition, about one-third of the oldest laterals should be cut back to about 5cm (2in) from the main trunk – this will encourage new shoots the following year. Kiwis grow extremely vigorously, and may need a summer prune as well, to keep them in check.

Fig

With its luxuriant, glossy foliage, the fig can conjure up a Mediterranean ambience in a garden like no other plant. Left to its own devices, it will develop into a large sprawling bush or a small tree, but may not produce much fruit. The key to getting a good crop is to restrict the fig's roots – this will discourage it from producing lots of leafy, non-fruiting shoots, and instead channel its energy into fruit production. The best way to restrict its roots is to grow the fig in a pot, but this means it will need daily watering during dry spells and feeding once a week. Alternatively, you can plant it in a 'fig pit'. This is made by digging a hole about 50cm (20in) wide and 50cm (20in) deep, and lining the bottom with hardcore and the sides with patio slabs.

Figs should be pruned in spring or late summer. Remove some of the older wood and tie in new shoots. Because figs produce fruit in the tips, some of the new shoots can be cut back to encourage more tips to form, which will in turn produce more fruit. Although fig plants are fairly hardy, they may lose overwintering figs during winter, so will benefit from being wrapped in fleece in colder parts of the country, or over particularly chilly spells of winter weather.

6. GROWING UNDER COVER

You can control many aspects of what happens in your garden –
you can improve your soil, recycle garden waste into nutritious
compost, organise windbreaks to make growing easier in gusty
corners, feed and water plants, and place them appropriately
according to whether they prefer sun or shade. But not even the
best gardener has any say in the weather.

How to grow plants that need more sheltered conditions or
germinate seeds and bring on seedlings or cuttings in weather
that stubbornly stays unseasonably cold, has been a question that
gardeners have been trying to answer for centuries. The answer is
to grow under cover, offering plants protection when they need it,
whether in a greenhouse or, if that's beyond your means and space,
using a cold frame or cloche.

PROTECTING YOUR PLANTS

Growing under cover is all about protecting your plants from extremes of weather, and today's gardeners have a large range of greenhouses, cold frames and cloches to choose from. All of these have been used extensively in the past, and are likely to become even more important in the future as we learn to cope with changes in weather patterns that are likely as a result of climate change.

Greenhouses

In ordinary gardens the greenhouse, whether heated or not, is probably the best-known and most common form of protection for plants. The earliest greenhouses are believed to date back to the Romans; in Britain, orangeries, as a means of growing fashionable citrus trees, arrived in the sixteenth century, although growing under glass remained the preserve of the very rich until the early 1900s, when small greenhouses began to feature in much more modest gardens.

Greenhouses are invaluable for protecting tender plants from frost or damp in winter, as well as housing collections of plants that would not survive in a temperate climate. They can also play a useful role in plant propagation.

Cold frames and cloches

There are other, cheaper, forms of protection available. Cold frames, holding trays of newly germinated and pricked-out crops; cloches, protecting newly planted seedlings, or polythene tunnels covering crops that need a little extra warmth, are all common sights in most vegetable gardens. These simple protections can be surprisingly effective in influencing growing conditions and sheltering vulnerable plants.

Inexpensive square or rectangular plastic cloches are useful for early salad crops, protecting them from chilly nights and slug and snail damage.

Greenhouses give you the opportunity to grow crops that need warmer conditions than outside, and can protect your favourite tender potted plants from the worst of the winter weather.

COLD FRAMES, CLOCHES AND TUNNELS

Cold frames and cloches are most often used to protect germinating seeds and seedlings, while tunnels provide shelter, warmth or sometimes shade when plants are growing.

Cold frames

A cold frame has lots of different uses. If space is limited, it can be treated as an unheated greenhouse to overwinter half-hardy plants and autumn-sown seeds, or to shelter plants, such as alpines, that dislike the damp. Most commonly, though, it is a useful halfway house – for plants that were started off indoors, on a warm windowsill, or a heated greenhouse or propagator – to give them the chance to get used to outside conditions. This is a gradual process known as 'hardening off'.

A standard cold frame is made up of clear sides, either glass or plastic, with one or more top frames known as 'lights'. The cheapest versions have lightweight aluminium frames, which means that they're easy to move into different spots around the garden. This sort of cold frame gives plants the maximum amount of light but isn't as sturdy as frames that have wood or brick sides, and may have to be pegged down in very windy weather. It also offers less insulation than the wood or brick versions, although you can fix this to some extent by adding layers of insulation, such as bubble wrap or old carpet, overnight, removing them during the day to let light and air in.

Frames that have brick or wood walls, with clear, liftable lights over the top, are sturdier and retain warmth better. They can be made at home if you have some DIY skills – old windows can make good lights – although obviously the brick versions can't be moved around. There are plenty of ready-made wooden cold frames available, too, but they are more expensive than the plastic versions.

The top of a cold frame, the lights, should be either sliding or hinged, so they can be propped or partially opened to allow for different degrees of ventilation. Whether you choose glass or plastic will depend on your circumstances; if small children or pets are often in the garden, you may want to take the plastic option (although it doesn't transmit light quite so well as glass) to avoid the risk of accidents.

Cold frames are useful, especially in springtime, to harden off young seedlings before planting them out in the ground. ▶

← Cloches

The word 'cloche' covers a number of different shapes and styles of protective cover. While they're generally useful all over the garden, they're most usually seen in the vegetable patch.

You can make the most basic kind of cloche for a (smallish) individual plant by cutting off the end of a plastic bottle and sinking the raw edge into the earth around the plant. Many of the bought alternatives, such as the bell cloche, which is often made of glass, are considerably more attractive. For larger groups of plants, or taller plants, you will need a tent or barn cloche. These are made of flat panes of either glass or plastic, which are clipped together. Plastic is less effective at keeping the cold off than glass. Tent cloches can be placed over groups of plants either to give them extra protection and warmth in winter or to speed up the start of the growing season in spring.

← Tunnels

Tunnels, like cloches, protect and warm both the plants and the soil underneath them, and are often used to encourage earlier cropping. They can be rigid or flexible, and are made from a series of hoops which support a length of either plastic or fleece. Alternatively, the hoops can be covered with shade netting, in which case they're used to protect plants, like lettuce, that are prone to bolting under direct sun. A polytunnel works along exactly the same lines as these smaller tunnels, but on a much larger scale.

CHOOSING A GREENHOUSE

A greenhouse is invariably a useful addition to any garden, although you have to remember that the plants grown in it are completely dependent on the gardener for their needs – they can't be left to their own devices. There are two basic types: heated and unheated.

Used to the maximum your greenhouse can greatly increase the range of plants you can grow by keeping out the extremes of cold, wind and rain. Even an unheated greenhouse will warm up quite quickly in spring and, in autumn, will lengthen the growing season of many plants.

Choosing a greenhouse

There are many, many styles and sizes of greenhouse on offer, from the most common 'span' type, which has a roof with two sloping sides in an inverted V, to the 'mansard' type, which has a curved roof and tends to be both rather more expensive and more difficult to construct. Choose one that works with your overall garden design and is suitable for the space available. Even in a very small garden or yard, a lean-to (which, as the name implies, is built leaning against an existing wall) or a mini-greenhouse may be a possibility. Specialist styles, such as alpine houses, are also available but are designed for specific purposes rather than general use.

There are styles of greenhouse available to suit every garden: they can be bought 'off the peg', or, more expensively, customised to your specific requirements.

Siting a greenhouse

Check which orientation will suit your needs best. If you're planning to use the greenhouse mainly to overwinter tender plants or to raise new plants in spring, orient it east to west to make the most of winter sunshine. If you're planning to use it mostly during the summer months, orient it north to south.

If possible, choose a site close to services. You may not need access to electricity or water when you're just starting to garden under cover, but equally you might want to make some additions further down the line.

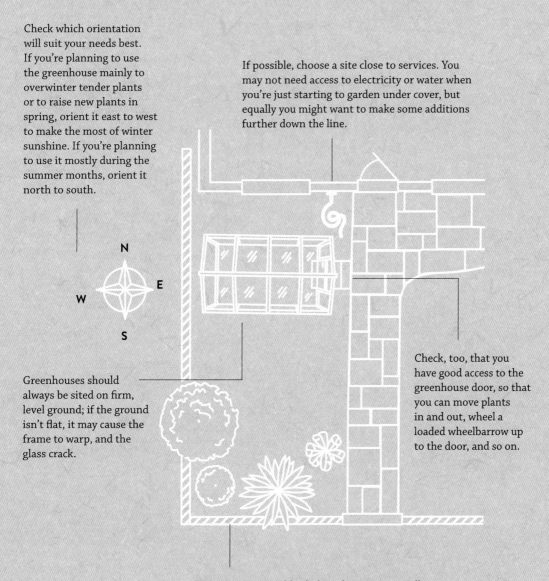

Greenhouses should always be sited on firm, level ground; if the ground isn't flat, it may cause the frame to warp, and the glass crack.

Check, too, that you have good access to the greenhouse door, so that you can move plants in and out, wheel a loaded wheelbarrow up to the door, and so on.

Aim for a reasonably sheltered site, near a wall or windbreak, and avoid siting in a wind tunnel or a frost pocket. Don't site near a large tree, which will cast shade – a free-standing greenhouse shouldn't be in the shade for more than a few hours a day (a lean-to greenhouse, on the other hand, should be positioned in slightly more shade than a free-standing one, to avoid overheating).

GREENHOUSE GARDENING

Successful greenhouse gardening may mean some juggling to get the environment and conditions just right to suit the plants inside. An unheated greenhouse is economical and suitable for growing summer crops such as tomatoes but won't protect plants from the worst winter weather. Adding heating allows you to grow a larger range of plants and will give you more chances at propagating plants that need warmth to get started. If you want to grow tropical plants, though, bear in mind that they'll only thrive in a minimum temperature of 13°C (55°F).

Heat is a key factor, especially for growing plants that are not suited to the outside climate, but shading through the hottest days of the summer is equally important, however much plants like the sun. As you get used to gardening under cover, you'll learn to balance plants' needs for ventilation, humidity and heat retention.

Shading

Shading helps control the temperature in the greenhouse and protects vulnerable young plants from too much sunlight, which can lead to dehydration and leaf scorch. On average, shading should reduce light levels in the greenhouse by around 50 per cent, and this can be achieved either by applying a specialist shading paint directly onto the glass or by installing greenhouse blinds, which are adjustable and can be automated for convenience. Plastic netting and mesh can also be used to act as impromptu shading if needed.

Ventilation

Even over the winter months, ventilation is essential in the greenhouse. It avoids a build-up of damp, stale air, which encourages disease. If your greenhouse is heated, it may also need to be ventilated to allow fumes to escape. In summer, it is also vital to control temperature. The sunshine that enters a greenhouse cannot escape back out through the glass so the heat must be dissipated through open windows, doors and even extractor fans if necessary. If you can't be constantly around to open windows when the greenhouse is getting too hot, window systems that will open automatically when a specific temperature is reached are available.

Heating

Any greenhouse heating needs to be powerful enough to maintain the required minimum temperature for the plants inside. If you have a power source nearby, electric heating is the cheapest and most reliable. Mains gas is also a possibility. Stand-alone heating, using bottled gas or paraffin, is available for greenhouses that are too far away from a mains supply, or that need heat on a less regular basis. Although stand-alone systems are less controllable, relatively expensive and will need regular checking and ventilation, they still may be useful on a small scale. You can also use in-house insulation such as bubble wrap in particularly cold conditions; this will help to keep heating costs down.

▲ With extra heating a wider variety of plants can be grown, including more tropical specimens.

Watering

Whether or not you need a watering system depends on how much time you have available, and what kind of plants you are growing. In many greenhouses, a watering can does the job as well as anything else, as each plant's needs will be slightly different. Automatic systems such as seep hoses and capillary watering, which uses an overhead reservoir, are practical if you need to go away, but still need to be checked regularly to ensure the plants are getting the right amount of water, as this varies not only from plant to plant, but also from season to season.

For tropical plants that need extra humidity, the greenhouse should be 'damped down' when watering, with extra water left on the paths or benches. Alternatively, you can install a spray mist system, which is especially useful for propagating cuttings. In hot weather, damping down will also cool the temperature in the greenhouse and increase humidity – which, in turn, helps fruit growth and pollination, and will control spider mites. The best time to damp the greenhouse down is early in the morning; this will allow evaporation gradually over the course of the day, as the sun heats up.

Automatic watering systems will ensure that plants receive a regular supply of water and help to keep ◄ cuttings healthy.

GROWING UNDER GLASS

Managing space in the greenhouse is a constant issue for many gardeners. While specialist greenhouses for groups of plants, such as ferns or orchids, have just one job, the average home greenhouse is used for quite a wide variety of different things at different seasons. The more organised you are, the easier you will find it to maximise your greenhouse space.

Most greenhouses have space at ground level for plants growing directly in the soil or growing bags, space to display and store specimen plants or those that need overwintering, and space for seed trays and cuttings. There will also be a place for the equipment you need for propagation and potting up. Usually this means the greenhouse will have a central path with beds or staging, either permanent or removable, on either side and at the far end.

← Staging

Staging usually takes the form of a wide, shelf-like surface at worktop level. It's useful for raising plants to a height which makes caring for them much easier and also doubles as a work surface when you need one. Quite often greenhouses have shelves for extra storage below the staging, which are useful for storing dormant plants, equipment and anything that needs shadier conditions. For maximum efficiency, stand-alone staging can be used in winter and removed in summer to allow bigger plants to grow in the bed below, while permanent shelves are best used for display and propagation.

← Propagation

In a small greenhouse, a separate heated propagator will be helpful without taking up too much space. In a bigger, warmer greenhouse, you will increase propagation possibilities if you fit soil-warming cables and misting units on some of your staging. Investing in automated systems can reduce your workload considerably while ensuring continuous care for your plants, especially if it isn't feasible for you to check them daily.

→ Ventilation

Adjustable windows that can be held open at different degrees are a useful feature in a greenhouse, enabling you to vary the amount of ventilation.

CONDITIONS NEEDED FOR DIFFERENT TYPES OF PLANTS

Plant type	Minimum temperature	Ventilation	Shading
Seeds	7°C–24°C (44°F–75°F)	Low	Shade until germinated
Cuttings	7°C–24°C (44°F–75°F)	Low, extra humidity required	Shade until rooted
Overwintering alpine plants	No heat	High	No shading required
Overwintering tender plants	2°C (35°F)	Low	No shading required
Subtropical and tropical plants	13°C (55°F)	Low, extra humidity required	Shading required in summer
Bedding plants, flowering pot plants and summer crops	2°C (35°F)	Low	Shading required in the summer
Cacti and succulents	2°C (35°F)	Low	No shading required

GREENHOUSE CARE AND HYGIENE

Having invested in a greenhouse, it makes sense to ensure it remains in good condition for as long as possible. If you make regular routine checks and to maintain it well, it will help you to avoid larger outlay in the future.

Routine maintenance

The best time to carry out routine greenhouse maintenance is in autumn, before it becomes too cold to leave tender plants outside for a few hours.

Outside, dirt and moss can be gently scraped away from the exterior glass using a plastic spatula before it is washed with water and, if necessary, a specialist greenhouse cleaning product. Don't place too much pressure on glass panes; any small cracks can be taped temporarily but broken panes should be replaced.

Gutters and downpipes should be cleared of debris and repaired, and any rotten wood or rusty fittings repaired or replaced. Aluminium greenhouse frames don't usually need much attention, but wooden ones should be painted regularly to prevent the wood rotting.

Inside, take all the plants out before cleaning the glass, the structure and the floor. Brush or vacuum away dirt and debris before applying diluted garden disinfectant to the structure, staging and floors. Wash the glass and if algae build-up is a problem, clean it with a specialist algae remover while the plants are out of the greenhouse. A thorough clean will help to reduce future problems with pests or diseases. Finally, check any fixtures and fittings such as ventilation windows, and repair or replace if necessary. As soon as the cleaning and repairs are finished, return the plants to the greenhouse.

Keeping the greenhouse tidy, clean and orderly will go a long way to reducing the possibility of pests and diseases.

Greenhouse hygiene

Good hygiene is essential in a greenhouse, where the specialist conditions suit some pests and diseases, as well as your plants. Spider mite, whitefly and a variety of fungal diseases can spread rapidly through plant stock unless they're checked. As a rule, prevention is better than cure, and clearing away any debris and dealing with any early signs of disease on a regular basis will certainly help. Ensuring the greenhouse has enough ventilation is also important.

Pest populations can build up extremely quickly unless they're caught early on – be vigilant. Although chemical controls and fumigants are available, if you prefer to avoid chemicals, biological pest control is also an option. Natural predators should be introduced as your pest population is starting to grow; this is a question of balance, as they need to have enough food to survive and multiply. Once in place, they should keep the pest problem in check. Sticky yellow traps which hang from the greenhouse roof are also a cheap and effective anti-pest measure.

Fungus attacks are best avoided by good greenhouse habits – keep the greenhouse well ventilated and dispose of any plant debris promptly.

◀ Keep a regular check on plants in the greenhouse to ensure that diseases, such as (from top) damping off and powdery mildew, and pests, such as glasshouse whitefly and red spider mite, don't take over and damage your crops.

7. PROPAGATING PLANTS

New plants for free sounds like one of those statements that's rather too good to be true, but if you learn a bit about the various ways in which plants propagate, from seeds and roots to divisions and cuttings, you'll also discover that you can easily grow your own stock without extra outlay.

This section looks at a range of simple techniques that should see you raising your own plants; once learned, you'll find that not only can you refresh your beds and borders with home-grown, but you should also have plenty of plants left over to make swaps with fellow gardeners.

PROPAGATION BASICS

Raising new plants from scratch is both economical and satisfying. With a basic grasp of the methods on the following pages and some simple equipment, you can add considerably to the range and number of plants in your garden without spending a fortune on ready-grown nursery stock, swap anything that's surplus to requirements and even try your hand at breeding new varieties.

Plant reproduction

Plants reproduce either by vegetatively replicating their own tissue (see page 33) or by producing seed, which, in its turn, germinates and grows into new plants. Runners from parent plants, bulblets that grow around the edges of bulbs, and tree branches setting roots where they touch the ground are just a few examples of vegetative reproduction – that is, the natural ways by which plants multiply.

◄ *This pelargonium cutting is already on the way to being well rooted and should quickly establish when potted on.*

Propagation methods

Many plants can be propagated in more than one way, but most have one method which will be more effective than the others, and in some cases there will only be one possible means of propagation. Rare, unusual plants may simply not be available in anything other than seed form, while certain hybrids have to be propagated vegetatively to ensure the offspring breed true. The most common way to propagate is to remove small pieces of tissue from the parent plant and use them to grow young plants. Given the right conditions even small pieces of stem, leaf or root can grow into independent plants.

Outside, hardy vegetables and annual flowers are often directly sown into the ground to germinate in the soil. Most sowing takes place in the spring after the risk of frost has passed and the soil has warmed a little, but autumn sowing is sometimes recommended for an earlier show the following year.

Indoors, the range of plants that you can propagate, whatever the method, is wider. Seeds and cuttings often respond better to warmth, and you'll get faster results. Windowsills, cold frames and greenhouses are all useful aids when it comes to propagation.

TOOLS, EQUIPMENT AND COMPOST

Propagation calls only for a number of very simple tools and
materials – pots, compost, labels – many of which you probably
already have and all of which are easily obtainable if not.
The processes of propagation, too, are very strightforward.

A basic propagation toolkit

• *Pots and trays* A selection in plenty of different
sizes. Trays are usually used for seed sowing,
while pots are better for taking small quantities
of cuttings, or for bigger seeds, such as squash,
which are best grown individually. Trays
consisting of individual modules can be used for
both seeds and cuttings, leaving each individual
baby plant with its own space to grow. Module-
grown plants are also much easier to pot on,
because you don't have to disentangle the fine
roots of multiple seedlings.

• *Compost* Despite its name, all-purpose compost
is not ideal for seed sowing and cuttings; it tends
to be rather coarse and contains nutrients better
suited to mature plants. Proprietary seed and
cutting compost, on the other hand, is blended
specifically for propagating. It contains much
smaller amounts of nutrients, so that seeds
and cuttings don't put on too much top growth
too quickly, and is much finer in texture. It also
contains a higher proportion of fine drainage
material, such as sand, to allow free drainage –
rot and mould are the big enemies of successful
propagation. Other forms of growing medium are
also available. Perlite, vermiculite or even sand
can be used to cover seeds gently, or for rooting
some cuttings.

• *Labels and a pencil or waterproof pen* These are
essential to keep track of the plants you grow.
If you are growing several varieties, it's easier
than you might think to forget which seeds or
cuttings are which.

A wide variety of containers and pots
are available for propagation purposes,
depending on the technique being used.

- *Secateurs, a sharp knife, and a watering can with a fine rose* The first two will be needed when you're taking cuttings, and the fine rose on the watering can means that you can water cuttings or seeds in gently.

- *Dibber* This is a small pointed stick which is useful for pricking out seedlings and making holes in compost so that you can insert cuttings easily.

- *Hormone rooting powder* This is used to speed up the rooting process, and may help with more difficult plants.

- *Clear plastic bags and elastic bands* Plastic bags, fastened with an elastic band, are useful for enclosing small containers or pots of cuttings, and giving them useful humidity. On a slightly larger scale, a propagator tray with a lid, whether heated or unheated, does the same job for a modest extra outlay.

- *Additional outdoor space* These won't be options for every gardener, but some dedicated outdoor space for growing hardwood cuttings, which need a minimum of attention but a year or so to 'take', is useful, as is a seed bed for raising plants from seed that can then be planted out elsewhere.

Professional equipment

If you become a propagation enthusiast, you may want to invest in some professional equipment. Options include misting units, which help keep the air humid, preventing too much water loss in the early stages of propagation, and a variety of heating systems, including units, mats or even buried soil-warming cables, which go under the plants and encourage faster rooting.

▲ Small tools useful for propagation include secateurs for cutting plant material, dibbers for making holes and trowels for compost.

WATERING AND HYGIENE

Plants are more vulnerable during propagation than at any other time and need to be looked after carefully. Tiny seedlings are prone either to drying out or rotting in unfavourable conditions, while cuttings need to be monitored regularly to ensure they have the best chance to 'strike' and thrive.

▼ *The plastic bag over these dahlia cuttings will keep moisture in but can also cause rotting if left too long.*

Moisture management

Whichever method you are using, propagated plants usually need to be kept moist but not waterlogged, kept out of direct sunlight and given adequate fresh air. A damp atmosphere with poor ventilation will encourage fungal diseases, and waterlogged soil will deprive young roots of essential oxygen.

Seedlings, for example, are prone to 'damping off', which results from overcrowding and damp, ill-ventilated conditions, and can cause the whole tray or pot of seedlings to keel over and die off.

Cuttings, too, have their issues. Softer cuttings and those with more leaves are most at risk. Straight after the cutting is taken it lacks roots and is unable to take up water from the medium it is planted in, so it needs to be prevented from transpiring too heavily and drying out. It's best to cover it with a clear plastic bag or a lid, trapping moisture around it to keep it turgid. The downside of this is that you need to remove the bag and air the cutting regularly, or the stale air inside can encourage mould and cause the cutting to rot. Turn plastic bags inside out at least daily, to allow fresh air in and prevent any build-up of algae or mould.

The best propagating environment of all is created by a misting unit, which generates a fine mist of water over the top of cuttings, ensuring that the leaves are covered with a layer of water which prevents transpiration. Mister units supply a gently humid atmosphere but maintain the free flow of air as, if you're using one, plants do not need to be covered. Combined with some sort of bottom-heating system, often buried soil-warming cables, misting units are the professional choice for successful propagating.

Good hygiene practices

Along with the right conditions for propagating plants, it's also important to maintain good hygiene practices. In greenhouses, tools, equipment and surfaces should all be regularly disinfected and cleaned, and plant debris, dead or infected tissue should all be removed promptly. Sometimes fungicides may be useful to prevent fungal problems, which are common in propagation.

As many plant diseases are carried in soil or water, be careful to minimise the chance of cross-contamination from boots, other plants, and equipment. Tap water and bottled water are less likely to carry diseases and should be your preferred option unless you're dealing with a plant that is particularly sensitive to chemicals, as is the case with carnivorous plants, for example.

Never try to propagate from material that is carrying diseases, such as viruses or other pathogens, as this will simply magnify the problem. Any diseased plants that have been unwittingly propagated should be disposed of carefully straight away.

▲ These cuttings of rosemary will benefit from careful moisture control to prevent rot.

PROPAGATION FROM SEED

The result of plant sexual reproduction, seeds are the most common way in which you can reproduce a wide variety of plants. Seeds to grow new trees, shrubs, perennials, annuals and vegetables are all readily and cheaply available.

Collecting seed from plants yourself, usually in the autumn, is even more cost-effective, and can give you a fresh supply of a favourite plant. Not only that but, since variation in plant life is mostly the result of different combinations of genetics when the seed is created, you may find that you've grown something excitingly different when the seeds germinate.

Seeds can be sown individually into pots before being placed into a propagation tray to give them the right conditions.

It is easy to forget what you have sown, so clear, informative labelling is always a good idea.

A lid placed over seedlings in a propagation tray will help to keep essential moisture in during the germination period.

Collecting seed

Fresh seed should be collected as soon as it's ripe, which is usually the point at which the seed capsule begins to split. Apart from a few that need to be sown straight away – including hazelnuts, walnuts and acorns – most seeds can be stored in a cool, dark, dry place in paper bags, or placed in a refrigerator until the following spring. In all other respects, they can be treated in the same way as shop-bought seeds.

Germination

Several factors are involved in successful seed germination: water, air, warmth and dark conditions, with the exception of a few plants whose seeds germinate in light.

- Under cover, it is important to sow seeds thinly in order to discourage damping off, so choose an appropriately sized pot or tray for the quantity of seeds you are sowing. Ensure that all equipment is thoroughly clean.

- Seeds should be sown on good-quality seed compost that has been gently firmed, rather than compacted. Delicate roots need to be able to push through and to access air and water easily.

- Unless they need light to germinate, seeds should be covered lightly with compost or vermiculite. Seed packets will usually recommend a planting depth but if you are unsure, the rule is that seeds should be covered to a depth of once or twice their diameter. If in doubt, shallow sowing is usually preferable to sowing more deeply.

- Water gently with a fine rose to avoid dislodging seeds and leave the pot or tray in a warm place. Germination can take anything from a few days to several weeks, depending on the plant, but the average is around seven to ten days.

- Make sure that germinated seedlings stay moist and get plenty of light. Turn the pot or tray regularly to stop them from stretching out towards the light and becoming leggy, and pot them up individually when they produce their first true leaves.

- Plants destined for outside planting need to be hardened off – introduced gently to outside conditions. This is usually managed by placing them in a cold frame, for example, for limited periods, and gradually increasing their exposure.

- Seeds sown outside are usually sown into finely raked soil in rows or scattered thinly ('broadcast'). They need to be kept moist until well established.

Germination problems

There are a number of reasons why germination may not be successful, even if all the environmental conditions are suitable.

- Unviable seed. Seed that is old, or that has been exposed to extremes of temperature, is far less likely to germinate successfully. This is why seeds are sold with a use-by date and must be stored appropriately.

- Seed dormancy. Seeds sometimes have an inbuilt dormancy mechanism to prevent germination in unsuitable conditions. This may need to be broken in order to induce seedlings to grow. Hard coatings, which protect the seed through unfavourable seasons in the wild, can be gently filed down or nicked to allow water to enter and germination to begin. Other seeds may need stratification – that is, a recreation of the sequence of hot and/or cold conditions that will trigger germination.

F1 and F2 hybrids

F1 hybrids are seeds resulting from the selective crossing and recrossing of two parent plants with specific desirable features to achieve a uniform quality. They are more expensive to buy because of the amount of effort required on the breeders' part, but produce better-quality, more vigorous plants. The seeds of F1 hybrids, commercially known as F2 hybrids, will not grow true to type, which is potentially disappointing for the gardener. Where uniformity is not an issue, F2 hybrid seeds are sometimes available, and are less expensive to buy.

PROPAGATION FROM ROOTS

BASIC STEPS OF ROOT PROPAGATION

Ideally root cuttings should be taken between late autumn and early winter. Plants suitable for root propagation include *Anemone japonica, Papaver orientale, Primula denticulata, Acanthus, Verbascum* and *Phlox,* as well as *Chaenomeles, Syringa* and *Robinia.*

A variety of plants can be propagated successfully in this way, including trees and shrubs that sucker naturally, and, in the case of a few herbaceous plants, most notably oriental poppies, it is the only method which will succeed.

① Choose healthy, vigorous plants, lift them when dormant and wash the roots clean. Ideally, choose roots that are as thick as a pencil, although herbaceous root cuttings can be a little thinner.

③ The minimum length for root cuttings should be around 2.5cm (1in), although they will need to be larger if they are not being grown in a heated, protected environment. Normally 5–10cm (2–4in) cuttings will work well.

② Cut the roots close to the crown of the plant, removing no more than a third at any one time before replanting the parent as soon as possible.

④ It is important to distinguish which end is which when planting, so always cut the top horizontally and the bottom at an angle so that you can tell by looking at them. New roots will only form on the end that was furthest from the parent plant.

5) Insert the cuttings, angled end down, in a pot filled with very free-draining compost to which gritty sand or perlite has been added. Place the cuttings vertically, so that the flat tops are level with the surface of the compost, about 4cm (1½in) apart.

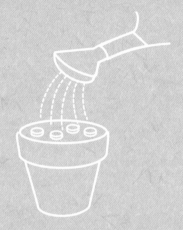

6) Add a thin layer of gritty sand or perlite, water gently and place the pots somewhere warm or, if this is not possible, in a cold frame.

8) For plants that are too large to lift, dig down on one side to find a suitable section of root to cut away, then follow the steps above.

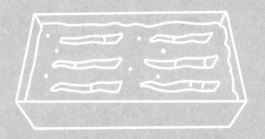

7) The cuttings should be growing well by the following spring and can be potted up when they have clearly rooted sufficiently. Grow them on before planting them out.

9) Plants with roots that are too thin to be inserted vertically, such as phlox, need longer root sections to survive, so lengths of 7.5cm to 12.5cm (3–5in) will work best. These thinner cuttings are placed horizontally on the compost before being covered with a mix of compost and gritty sand.

PROPAGATION FROM DIVISIONS

Of all the forms of propagation, division is probably the easiest, taking advantage of herbaceous plants' natural tendency to spread. It has other benefits, too; dividing plants that are congested will refresh the look of beds and borders, and keep plants heathy and vigorous for much longer.

Suitable plants that respond well to division are hostas (below), asters, ornamental grasses, bergenias and iris, but almost all clump-forming perennials, as long as they have fibrous roots, can be treated this way.

▼

DIVIDING RHIZOMES AND CORMS

Plants such as *Crocosmia* and *Iris*, which have storage organs as well as root systems, can also be divided successfully with a little extra care.

Crocosmia needs to be carefully dug out before you gently separate the chains of corms. These can either be separated individually, if you want a large number of new plants, or split into smaller clumps with the chains intact, something that the plants themselves tend to prefer.

Irises with rhizomes benefit enormously from being lifted regularly and split, as the central rhizomes, left to themselves, become increasingly congested and weak. Simply lift the clump and cut away the outer, healthiest-looking fans, each with a portion of rooted rhizome attached. Trim if necessary, and replant the new plants as soon as possible, making sure that the rhizome protrudes just above the soil or compost level. Discard any rhizomes that are weak or withered.

HOW TO PROPAGATE
BY DIVISION

Division can be done at any time as long as the divisions are watered well afterwards, but ideally you should do it when the plants are not actively growing. As a rule, summer-flowering perennials are divided in early autumn or the following spring, just before the new season begins, while spring-flowering plants are divided in summer, as they begin to produce new roots.

④ Larger, tougher plants may require more effort to separate. Two forks inserted back to back through the centre of the root mass can be used as levers to pull it apart before smaller sections are separated out.

⑤ In the most difficult cases, a knife, edging iron or spade may be needed to chop through very tough, woody, or fibrous crowns and root balls. The divisions in this case should be a little larger to compensate for the extra damage caused to the plant.

⑥ Discard any old or unhealthy-looking pieces. These will often be at the centre of the original plant – the youngest, most vigorous growth tends to be on the outside of a clump.

① Lift suitable, healthy plants with a garden fork, gently, to avoid damaging the root ball. Shake off excess soil.

② Smaller clumps can be gently pulled apart by hand to make a number of smaller plants, each with its own roots.

③ If suitable, individual plantlets can be pulled away gently from around the edges to be replanted separately.

⑦ All divided plants should be planted up or potted up as soon as possible, and watered well.

PROPAGATION FROM STEM CUTTINGS

Stem cuttings are a popular and effective way of increasing plant stock and in some cases can produce large quantities of new plants in a relatively small space. Pelargoniums, argyranthemums and other favourites are popular choices for this method of propagation – cuttings being taken in case of winter loss – as are many ornamental shrubs. In some cases, where plants have been highly bred or are variegated, stem cuttings are the only way to ensure that the characteristics of the parent plant are maintained.

Stem cuttings are identified by a range of names that mainly refer to the maturity of the material used, but in all cases, the technique is similar. Early in the growing season plant tissue is softer and greener, so early cuttings are called softwood or greenwood cuttings. The softest cuttings are taken from the growing tips of tender and herbaceous perennials as they wake from winter dormancy. Semi-ripe cuttings are those taken a bit later in the season and, finally, those cuttings taken when the plant tissue has fully ripened and become woody are known as hardwood cuttings. The earlier in the season cuttings are taken, the quicker they will tend to root, although very soft plant material is at increased risk of rotting.

While some unfussy plants are easy to propagate at almost any time of year, others may be a little choosier. If in doubt, research the method recommended for the specific plant, or experiment with trial and error, trying out cuttings at different times of the year to determine which works best.

Some shrubs are best propagated when semi-ripe or fully ripe. Many prefer to be taken with a 'heel', which will come away from the main stem if a side shoot is pulled off gently. Evergreens and conifers are also often taken more successfully in this way. Others respond to wounding, which involves making a clean, shallow cut at the base of the cutting to expose more of the pith inside the stem before you plant it.

If you are rooting succulents and cacti, cuttings must be dried out for a few days to callus over before being pushed into a medium such as sand or perlite, that ensures very sharp drainage. Although the cuttings need some moisture, they will quickly rot if the atmosphere is too humid.

Taking cuttings from pelargoniums means that fresh new flowering plants can be produced each year for seasonal displays.

HOW TO PROPAGATE FROM STEM CUTTINGS

① Choose healthy, preferably non-flowering, shoots and cut early in the morning, if possible, when the plant tissue contains more water. If there is an unavoidable delay in potting up the cuttings, store them in a plastic bag in the fridge until ready.

② Individual cuttings are usually prepared by first making a cut just below a leaf joint, or node. This is where the plant's growth hormones are most concentrated, and the point where new roots will form.

③ The length of a cutting depends on the size and attributes of the parent plant but should usually be five to six nodes long, or around 5-10cm (2-4in). Cut to size just above a node, making a slanting cut away from the node. Hardwood cuttings are usually cut a little longer as, being taken at the end of the growing season and taking much longer to root, they need larger reserves of food.

④ Strip off the lower leaves of the cutting, and trim by half any large upper leaves to ensure that it does not suffer from too much transpiration loss before rooting can take place. Leafy cuttings still need to photosynthesise, but this must be balanced with water loss while the plant is still rooting.

⑤ Dip the cut end into hormone rooting powder and insert it into free-draining seed compost in a pot or tray. Ensure that cuttings are not touching each other.

⑥ Water well and place somewhere light and warm, but not in direct sunlight. Leafy cuttings benefit from a humid atmosphere so should be placed under mist or covered with a clear lid or plastic bag. Keep the plastic away from the cuttings with sticks or a frame. Hardwood cuttings are inserted more deeply into the medium and need very sharp drainage. They are normally left outside in pots or trenched into the ground directly, to allow for a longer, slower period of rooting.

Internodal cut

Make a cut just above a node (between nodes).

Nodal cut

Make a cut just below a leaf joint.

8. PROBLEM SOLVING

Making a garden takes a fair amount of time and energy. Whether you're starting from scratch or creating something that's perfect for you in a garden that was begun by someone else, there are a lot of decisions to be taken – from making a plan and considering any hard landscaping that needs doing, to improving the soil and collecting the plants that will turn your original idea into reality.

After all that hard work, you certainly don't want your precious plants to succumb to pests and diseases. The good news is that by catering to plants' needs, whether for water, nutrients or light, you can greatly reduce potential problems. Regular checking will help you to keep on top of any pests that sneak in under the radar, while early intervention can prevent them from spreading. And if you do find yourself tackling an outbreak, there are tools at your disposal, including biological control, physical barriers and, in a last resort, pesticides. Finally, make space for birds and other wildlife in your garden – not only are they enjoyable to watch, but many of them will also feed on the pests you're less pleased to see.

PESTS AND DISEASES

Garden plants are susceptible to a range of pests and diseases which have the potential both to harm your ornamentals and reduce crop yields. So it's worth taking a regular wander around your garden, looking carefully at your plants. It's much easier to deal with any problems if you spot them early.

The organisms that cause problems for plants are many and varied. The largest are hungry herbivores, such as deer and rabbits, while at the other end of the scale are the microscopic bacteria and viruses which can cause just as much damage. The term 'pest' refers to animals that feed on plants, including mammals, birds, and insects and other invertebrates like slugs and mites. Some eat plants wholesale, others pierce the stems and leaves to extract sap, or concentrate their attacks on particular plant organs, such as roots or seeds. Diseases, on the other hand, are usually the result of attack by fungi (and their relatives), bacteria or viruses. To combat both pests and diseases, you need to identify what's causing the problem. If you find any sickly specimens among your plants, note any damage caused and check them over carefully to see if you can spot symptoms that will narrow down the possibilities of what it is that's harming them.

What to look for

Pests and diseases can affect all parts of a plant, so check a sickly plant all over for specific indicators of trouble.

Whole plant General collapse is usually a symptom of drought, but if the plant has been well watered, it might indicate a disease such as wilt.

Roots Often targeted by vine weevil larvae. As they're below ground, you may only notice when the whole plant keels over, so regularly lift pot plants to check the roots. Root mealy bug and the larvae of chafer beetles and crane flies can also cause problems.

Stems Fruit trees can harbour diseases like canker and scab, while woolly aphids and some other sap-sucking pests also cause stem damage.

Leaves Foliage problems are usually the easiest to spot, though some pests hide on the lower surface of the leaf, so check on both sides. Check what sort of damage – it may identify the pest. Holes or distorted leaves and powdery or sticky deposits are all common symptoms.

Flowers Many leaf pests can also affect flowers. Specific flower pests such as earwigs and thrips can damage petals – they eat them, or cause distortions or discoloration, or reduce flower density overall.

Fruits Many edible crops are targeted by insect pests, which cause holes in the ripening fruit. Once the fruit has been breached, hungry birds and further fungal ailments may exacerbate the damage. Hungry animals may also target fruit and seed crops, leaving little evidence behind.

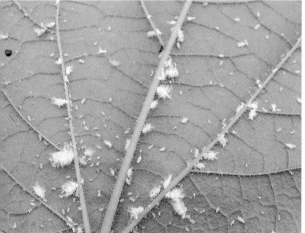

Control methods

There are various ways to protect plants and help them after a pest or disease attack has started. Integrated pest management (see pages 208–9), chemical controls (see page 210) and harnessing beneficial creatures (see pages 206–7) are discussed later in the chapter. Before you look at these methods, it's worth considering a handful of quick and easy physical controls.

- Quarantine any new plants, both those you have bought and any that have been given to you. Inspect them thoroughly for pests and diseases, remembering to check the roots, then keep them in a sheltered spot or cold frame away from the main garden. If they still look healthy after a few weeks, plant them out.
- Barriers keep many problems at bay; plastic sheeting put up in autumn will keep peaches and nectarines free of peach leaf curl fungus, for example, while horticultural fleece will keep carrot flies away from carrots and parsnips. Slugs and snails may be kept off plants with rings of crushed shells, bran or copper tape. Slug and snail traps can also be successful and are easily made from sunken pots filled with beer, or scooped-out melon and grapefruit halves.
- Finally, the easiest way to deal with pests that you can see is to remove them from the infected tissues by hand. Strip aphids from tender shoots with your fingers and collect snails or slugs into a bucket for disposal. Prune out diseased leaves and stems from plants (clean the blades of your secateurs between one plant and the next to avoid spreading any problems between them). Gather fallen leaves and flowers from ailing plants and put them in the bin – don't compost them; you don't want to pass any problems on.

With a little practice you'll quickly learn to spot different pests and diseases and the problems they cause. From top: flower buds and young fruit have been pecked and damaged by birds, while the undersides of leaves may be shielding colonies of white mealy bugs or sap-sucking aphids. Finally, every gardener is familiar with the glistening trails and holey leaves left by slugs and snails.

IDENTIFYING PESTS

Given how many garden pests there are, you may wonder how easy it will be for you to nail down the one responsible for your plant's problem. The chart here highlights ten of the commonest pests to steer you in the right direction – if you don't find your culprit here, take pictures or collect some of the plant's affected material, then visit the website of the Royal Horticultural Society, which is a good one-stop shop to identify a huge range of pests and offer advice on their control.

Pests	Plants Affected
Aphids	Most plants.
Capsid bugs	Many species, including apples, roses, clematis and dahlias.
Caterpillars	Many plants can be affected. Brassicas can be severely damaged.
Deer	Many woody plants, including roses, fruit trees. Also herbaceous plants like hostas, tulips, etc.
Leaf miners	Many plants including holly, alliums, beetroot and chrysanthemums.
Mealy bugs	Many greenhouse and houseplants, including cacti and succulents, orchids, citrus, New Zealand flax, grapevines, etc.
Scale insects	Many plants, both indoors and out, including citrus, orchids, camellias, fruit trees and wisteria.
Slugs and snails	All plants.
Greenhouse red spider mite	Many indoor or greenhouse plants, including peppers, tomatoes, citrus, orchids.
Vine weevil	Leaves of rhododendron, bergenia, hydrangea. Roots of heucheras, sedums, strawberries, especially container plants.

Main Symptoms	Physical Control	Chemical Control	Biological Control
Pests clustered at shoot tips, sticky deposits, poor or distorted growth.	Remove by hand or flush with a hose.	Apply sprays containing pyrethrum, fatty acids or systemic pesticides such as lambda cyhalothrin.	Encourage ladybirds, lacewings, hoverflies and birds outside. Release parasitic wasp (*Aphidius*) or midge (*Aphidoletes*) in greenhouses.
Young growth distorted, peppered with tiny holes. Flower buds open irregularly. Flowers may be distorted or absent. Apple skins covered in small, raised bumps.	Keep weeds in check as they can act as hosts. Choose apple varieties that are less prone to attack.	Spray with systemic pesticide such as deltamethrin, but don't spray flowers.	None available. Most plants survive capsid attack and the damage is unsightly but superficial.
Holes in leaves with frass (fine powdery refuse produced by insects and their larvae).	Remove caterpillars and eggs by hand. Use fleece or netting to exclude adult butterflies.	Apply pyrethrum or deltamethrin, though carefully follow package limits when using on edible crops.	Predatory nematodes can control caterpillars on brassicas.
Shoot tips and flowers eaten, tree bark eaten or scraped.	Employ robust fencing at least 1.5m (5ft) tall, or electrified fence. Use plastic sleeves to protect young tree stems. Choose plants that deer dislike, such as barberry and daffodils.	Repellent sprays can deter deer, but must be reapplied regularly.	Deer avoid predators, so employ your pet dog to patrol the perimeter.
Larvae excavate tunnels within the thickness of the leaf, leaving pale areas that later turn brown.	Remove damaged leaves or crush the pest inside. Cover crop plants with fleece. Gather fallen leaves from larger plants and destroy.	Leaf miners are protected within the leaf and so are hard to treat with chemicals. Systemic acetamiprid may give some control.	There are no biological controls, though birds may eat leaf miners.
White waxy secretions, sticky deposits and sooty moulds.	Remove bugs using a cotton bud. Dispose of heavily infested plants.	Apply systemic acetamiprid on houseplants. Use a winter wash on deciduous trees and vines.	A predatory ladybird (*Cryptolaemus*) and several parasitic wasps can be released in greenhouses.
Brown, helmet-shaped bug, usually immobile. Sticky deposits and sooty mould are common side effects.	Remove bugs using a cotton bud. Dispose of heavily infested plants. Use a winter wash on deciduous trees and vines.	Apply deltamethrin, lambdacyhalothrin or cypermethrin or acetamiprid.	Several parasitic wasps can be released in greenhouses.
Irregular holes in leaves, often with slime trail. Holes in potato tubers.	Collect molluscs at night. Use barriers and traps. Choose more resistant potato varieties.	Apply slug pellets containing ferric phosphate or metaldehyde.	Predatory nematodes can control slugs and snails in warm weather.
Yellow mottling on leaves, which fall early, webbing between leaves and stems, tiny red mites active.	Keep greenhouses clean and remove fallen leaves and badly infested plants. Increase humidity.	Use frequent applications of plant oils or fatty acids, or the systemic pesticide acetamiprid.	Predatory mites can be released in greenhouses.
Irregular notches in leaf margins caused by adults. Wilting and death of plants caused by larvae.	Collect adult weevils at night. Lift pot plants and remove larvae.	Drench compost with acetamiprid (only suitable for container plants, not for use on soil or edible plants).	Predatory nematodes can control this pest on both edible and decorative crops. Effective both in pots and open soil.

IDENTIFYING DISEASES

Diseases can sneak up surreptitiously, so always keep a watchful eye for changes in the appearance of your plants. Look for altered colour and texture, or for any evidence of toadstools or unusual growths on or near the plant. The onset of symptoms can be sudden, as with clematis wilt, or may be visible in a much more gradual decline. Remove infected material rapidly to prevent spread, but keep samples in sealed bags as evidence, to help you to identify the problem.

Diseases	Plants Affected
Club root	Brassicas, including swede, radishes, cabbages, sprouts, wallflowers.
Damping off	Seedlings of most species.
Downy mildew	Many plants including brassicas, peas, onions, pansies, busy lizzies.
Honey fungus	Many plants including roses, apples, pears, privet, lilac, rhododendron.
Potato blight	Potatoes, tomatoes.
Powdery mildew	Many plants including roses, peas, courgettes, honeysuckle, bergamot.
Rust	Many plants including hollyhocks, fuchsias, leeks, pelargoniums, mint, broad beans and pears.
Scab	Apples, pears, olives, poplars, willows, rowans and cotoneaster.
Viruses	Many plants including cucumbers, tulips, sweet peas, daffodils, tomatoes and strawberries.
Wilt	Many plants including clematis, peony, roses, maples, barberries.

Main Symptoms	Physical Control	Chemical Control	Biological Control
Stunted growth, sometimes wilting. Roots grossly swollen.	Control weeds and choose resistant varieties. Practise crop rotation.	None available. Adding lime to increase soil pH can help.	None available.
Seedlings collapse and die. White mould sometimes present.	Only use commercially produced seed compost and new or sterilised pots and trays. Reduce watering and improve ventilation.	None available. Only use mains water as collected rainwater and grey water are not sterile.	None available.
Discoloured patches on upper sides of leaves, with mould on lower sides. Leaves may fall, some plants die.	Control weeds, avoid dense planting and choose resistant varieties. Practise crop rotation. Remove and destroy infected leaves and plants. Avoid overhead watering and watering in the evening.	None available. Downy mildews are especially common in wet summers.	None available.
Premature death, often preceded by heavy flowering, fruiting or early autumn colour. Dead roots with white fungal growth beneath bark.	Remove and destroy infected plants and install plastic root barriers to prevent spread.	None available.	None available.
Foliage turns brown and collapses. Tubers begin to rot.	Destroy infected material. Earth up potatoes. Employ crop rotation. Grow tomatoes in a greenhouse.	None available. Choose resistant varieties, though changes in the fungus can make these less effective.	None available.
White powdery deposits often visible on leaves, flowers and fruits.	Remove and destroy infected material. Reduce susceptibility by watering to prevent water stress, then mulch.	The fungicide tebuconazole can be used on ornamentals, and plant invigorators can be used on all plants.	None available.
Pustules form, usually on the lower sides of the leaves, releasing spores. Infected leaves yellow and fall.	If spotted early, remove infected leaves and destroy. Avoid excess fertiliser applications.	The fungicide tebuconazole can be used on ornamental plants but not edibles.	None available.
Dark lesions on leaves, yellowing and leaf drop. Black, aborted flower buds. Dark lesions (scabs) on fruits.	Destroy infected material. Prune trees to improve airflow through canopy. Choose resistant cultivars.	The fungicide tebuconazole can be used on ornamental plants but not edibles.	None available.
Streaking or discoloration of leaves and flowers, distortion.	Destroy infected material and plants, disinfect pruning tools. Choose resistant varieties.	None available. Viruses are often transmitted by aphids and other pests, so control these too.	None available.
Sudden wilting of whole plant. Death of whole branches. Brown patches on leaves, flowers fail to open.	Destroy infected material, improve plant health by mulching, disinfect tools, avoid moving contaminated soil.	None available.	None available.

DIAGNOSING SICK PLANTS

Sometimes an ailing plant is not under attack; instead, it's suffering from an absence of the things it needs – light, water and nutrients. The answer in these cases is, where possible, to give it care that fits its needs better, or, if that's not possible, to replace the plant with something better suited to the growing conditions you can offer.

When a plant is unhappy with its living situation, it is often because it originates in a very different habitat from the one you've provided. Plants from the Mediterranean Basin, such as rosemary and lavender, will not thrive in shade or on wet soils, as they are used to full sun and dry roots. In some less extreme cases, it will be possible to perk up your plants by altering the amounts of light, water and nutrients they are getting, or the soil they are growing in.

Light

Sunlight gives the energy that plants need to make their food by means of photosynthesis, but species differ widely in the amounts of light they need or tolerate. Plants from shady habitats, such as ferns, hostas and Japanese maples, will not thrive in full sun, and their leaves may scorch and wither when overexposed. In contrast, plants from sunny climates – most herbs, vegetables and many conifers – will produce sparse, elongated growth when grown in the shade. Many garden plants sit between the two extremes; check a plant's preferences before you buy, and don't forget that trees and buildings may cast shade at certain times of the day on an otherwise sunny garden.

Heat

Plants exposed to extremes of heat or cold can suffer. Bedding plants and tender veg, such as tomatoes, may have a lack of vitality and show purple mottling on their leaves if planted out too early in the season. Winter frosts will turn some exotics to mush and defoliate others, so be ready with protection for them before temperatures drop. At the other end of the temperature scale, British summers are rarely hot enough to cause physical damage, but in enclosed greenhouses and conservatories, overheating can retard growth and damage crops and flowers, so ensure they have plenty of ventilation throughout the warmer months.

Water

Gardeners have no control over rainfall, but you can augment soil moisture when there's a prolonged dry period. By adding organic matter or grit, you can improve the drainage or moisture-holding capacity of the soil, and hoses or sprinklers will help if rain doesn't arrive when it's needed. But while most plants will tell you if they're thirsty by wilting, the signs of too much water can be tricky

to spot. Plants from dry climates generally suffer first, so watch lavender and other herbs. Too much water becomes a real problem if it is combined with freezing winter temperatures, and this can kill sensitive plants such as succulents and yuccas, which might have survived if kept dry.

Container culture

With their roots confined, container plants are dependent on gardeners. They cannot spread their roots into the soil to seek additional moisture and nutrients, so they may be the first casualties of a hot summer. Even when it's pouring with rain, not much of it will find its way into the compost of a container.

Careful preparation when you're planting a container can reduce the risks of it drying out. Choose the largest container you can accommodate, as it will hold more moisture, then add slow-release fertiliser and moisture-retaining gel to the compost, so that it can make the most of any water it is given. Choose container plants that will tolerate some drought – avoid trees, climbers and plants with large leaves, as all three are very thirsty. Where possible, install drip irrigation on an automatic timer in your containers, as this is the most efficient use of water, and will save you the work of daily, or even twice-daily, watering during dry spells.

▲▲▲ Greenhouse crops can suffer in the heat if not well ventilated.

▲▲ Regular watering should prevent plants from wilting in dry weather.

▲ Mediterranean lavender needs full sun and a well-drained soil to thrive.

◀ The leaves of some plants will scorch if given too much exposure to direct sunlight.

WEEDS

If weeds are simply plants growing in the wrong place, why do gardeners worry so much about them? First, because the rapid growth of most weeds often outcompetes that of the plants we've actually chosen, smothering them and setting them back. Second, weeds not only take up their share of nutrients and water you intended for planned planting, but may also introduce pests and diseases to the other plants.

Annual or perennial?

Just as with other plants, garden weeds are classified as annuals or perennials. Annuals complete their life cycles in a single year, often within just a few months, and include hairy bittercress (*Cardamine hirsuta*), meadow grass (*Poa annua*) and groundsel (*Senecio vulgaris*). Perennial weeds live for many years and can be herbaceous, like ground elder (*Aegopodium podagraria*), bindweed (*Calystegia sepium*) and horsetail (*Equisetum arvense*), or grow as woody vines and shrubs, like bramble (*Rubus*) or ivy

(*Hedera helix*). Annuals are generally easier to eradicate than perennials, and different strategies are needed to control them. Whether annual or perennial, though, all weeds are fast-growing and reproduce readily, often by both seed and other methods, such as deep root systems that travel far and wide, which are hard to eradicate. Seeds can float into your garden on the wind, or be delivered in bird droppings.

Brambles are some of the most persistent perennial weeds, and need to be dug out
▼ *thoroughly if they are not to reappear.*

WEEDING

- Annual weeds are best pulled by hand, ideally before they produce seeds. Regular hand weeding deals with them very effectively, and a thick mulch will prevent any remaining seeds from sprouting. You can put the debris of annual weeds onto your compost heap, unless it includes plants in flower, which may carry seeds with them.

- Perennial herbaceous weeds are much more challenging to control by hand weeding, as any roots left in the soil will re-sprout. Avoid using rotavators as they cut up the weed roots and spread them throughout the soil, which may actually make the problem worse. If you're digging, carefully remove as many roots as you can find and be prepared to return for additional sessions. Never compost any perennial weeds, as they can survive in the compost and reinfest the garden.

- Woody perennials are best removed completely, roots and all. Larger woody weeds, including trees, may need to be removed by a professional. Take woody weeds to the tip, rather than composting them at home. As a final resort, convert weedy patches to lawn; after several years of mowing, even the most vigorous weeds will be gone.

Physical barriers

The easiest way to control weeds is to stop them from entering your garden in the first place. Check all new plants, both those you've bought yourself and any you've been given by other gardeners, and remove any weeds you find in the soil. If weeds are invading under a garden fence from next door, use a plastic barrier, such as those designed to control bamboo, to keep them out. Weed membranes control perennial weeds because they exclude light, though the weeds may still pop up in the holes you've cut in the membrane as spaces for your chosen plants.

Chemical control

Weedkillers, or herbicides, can be an effective method of weed control provided that you follow the instructions on the pack meticulously. Contact herbicides kill only the parts of the plant they touch and are most effective on annual weeds and seedlings. Systemic herbicides are absorbed by the plant and transported around its body, killing the roots as well as the stems and leaves. These are the most effective chemicals for use on perennial weeds. If you are spraying a herbicide, choose a dry, still day – rain will wash away the chemical, while wind can cause it to drift from its intended target. Keep children and pets away from the sprayed area for 24 hours after application. Where perennial weeds are growing through your garden plants, choose a systemic herbicide that can be painted onto the leaves, as this reduces the risk of damaging valued plants. For woody perennials, cut plants down to the ground, then apply systemic herbicide to the stumps, to kill the roots.

CHOOSING HEALTHY PLANTS

While designing your garden and choosing the plants to grow, it's important to consider their future health; that way, you can avoid problems rather than trying to tackle them when they arise. At the nursery or garden centre, only pick those in fine fettle and, where possible, opt for disease-resistant varieties. When you're planning your garden, include species that you know will thrive in your area; plants that aren't suited to their location are more prone to ill health.

Right plant, right place

Selecting the right plant begins not at the nursery, but at home. If you choose a plant that is not happy in the environment you can provide, you'll have to cope with a whole suite of potential problems. Carefully assess your garden, looking in particular for the basic plant needs: light, water and soil. Once you're familiar with your own plot, visit neighbouring gardens and local parks, to see which plants thrive near you. With your own garden in mind, begin to look for plants in gardening books and online, taking note especially of their native habitats. Plants from woodlands will likely do well in a shady area with rich soil, for example, while those from arid scrub are well suited to a sunny location with sandy soil. Put together a list of possible picks, then head to the garden centre or find a good mail order or online retailer.

Only purchase plants with healthy root systems, avoiding poorly rooted or pot-bound specimens. ▶

Checking plants' health

If shopping in person, look for plants that are free of pests and diseases, show no signs of wilting and have well-established root systems. Don't be afraid to carefully remove the pot to check your plant has a well-developed crop of roots. Avoid any with more compost than root, or so many roots that you can barely see the compost. If something catches your eye but you're uncertain of its requirements, check the label or ask the staff – it's always best to avoid impulse purchases, however tempting.

In some plant groups in which diseases are especially common, such as roses and fruit trees, breeders have developed a number of disease-resistant cultivars. Research these to see if there's anything that will match what you want. Finding a plant with built-in disease resistance can potentially save you a lot of problems in future.

Be climate aware

There are, of course, many popular plants that are not really suited to the British climate. Bedding plants are a good example: many originate from tropical areas and must be protected from frost. They also need large amounts of water and fertiliser to keep them looking their best, but the hard work is short lived, as most end up on the compost heap in autumn. If you are tempted by larger exotics, such as bananas, tree ferns and olive trees, be prepared to give them the extra care they'll need to survive the winter. A possible silver lining to the dark cloud of climate change is that these plants may become easier to care for in the future.

Crop rotation

In the vegetable garden, you choose plants based on what food they'll produce, rather than what conditions they need. Most vegetables want full sun and rich, well-drained soils to crop well, but planning an annual crop rotation can improve your results. Crop rotation involves growing different groups of vegetables in different areas each year (see page 133).

If you stick to the same patch for your potatoes over several years, for example, then potato pests and diseases may build up in the soil and mean that future harvests won't do so well. If, though, you plant a crop from a different group, such as beans or onions, in the previous year's potato bed, the new plants won't be susceptible to most potato problems. Take another example: beans and peas – legumes – bind nitrogen from the atmosphere into the soil, so plant hungry veg such as brassicas into last year's bean bed and they'll happily absorb the fixed nitrogen that the bean crop left for them. This should result in healthy plants which may also have less need for pest control.

▼ *With such great diversity readily available, there's a plant suited to every situation.*

BENEFICIAL WILDLIFE

While it may sometimes seem as though there's no end to the parade of pests ready to attack your plants, there are also many species that will actively help to control them. Many garden birds are indefatigable insect predators; hedgehogs and toads, if you're lucky enough to have them, help keep slug numbers down. Some less noticeable species also play invaluable roles in the garden – spiders, beetles and wasps are all effective hunters of other bugs, and flowers and crops are pollinated not only by bees, but also by a huge number of other pollinators, from wasps and hoverflies to beetles.

For many years organic gardeners have relied on this natural hit squad of hungry, busy creatures both to control garden pests and to pollinate their plants. With a little encouragement, birds, mammals, reptiles, amphibians, insects and other invertebrates will make a home in your garden and reduce the need for using potentially harmful chemicals. Welcome them into your outdoor space by offering food, shelter and nesting materials, and don't forget access – a hole cut in the bottom of your fence makes a welcome doorway for Britain's critically endangered hedgehogs. Once in your garden, keep them safe by eliminating the use of pesticides, offering safe shelters and controlling inquisitive household pets.

- Many gardeners actively feed wild birds, purely for the pleasure of watching them, but once attracted into your garden, they will often forage for bugs to feed their young. Hanging nest boxes and providing nesting materials, such as feathers and pet fur, will also draw them in.
- Nesting boxes for bats will encourage these hungry aerial predators to visit your property and they'll scoop up numerous night-flying insects, including moths and mosquitoes.
- A compost heap is the perfect home for hedgehogs, amphibians or grass snakes. Always be slow and careful when turning compost to avoid damaging any unexpected inhabitants. Hedgehogs can be fed special hedgehog food (available online or from pet stores) or small amounts of non-fish-based cat food – if you're lucky enough to have a visiting hog or hogs, never offer milk, as it causes stomach upsets – and they will return to your garden regularly, snacking on snails and slugs as well.

Build a pond

Providing a reliable water source year-round is the best way to attract a wide range of beneficial wildlife. Frogs, toads and newts feed on snails, slugs and many insects, too, and the ideal way to attract them is to build a pond. As well as amphibians, birds, hedgehogs, grass snakes, dragonflies and many other predatory insects will take advantage. The best wildlife ponds are at ground level – raised edges exclude many creatures – and are lushly planted, both with marginal perennials and those with floating leaves, such as waterlilies. Ornamental fish eat many beneficial insects and amphibian larvae, so a wildlife pond is best without them. Ensure the water is topped up over summer if necessary, ideally using collected rainwater; in winter, float a ball on the pond – this will leave a hole if ice forms over the surface, so any creatures living in the water aren't cut off from air.

Caterpillars are usually considered pests, but some species will eat weeds for you, such as this Red Admiral caterpillar munching on a nettle. ▼

Plant protectors

Grow plenty of flowers in your garden and many pollinating insects will follow, including the bees that fertilise the flowers of crops such as apples and tomatoes.

- Many pollinators are multi-taskers – hoverflies are valuable pollinators, for example, but their larvae also feed on pests such as aphids.
- The caterpillars of nectar-eating Red Admiral and Tortoiseshell butterflies feed on weedy stinging nettles.
- Some companion plants actively prevent garden pests. The scents of some herbs can repel bugs: summer savory (*Satureja hortensis*) can protect broad beans from aphids, for example, while hyssop (*Hyssopus officinalis*) deters cabbage white butterflies from eating brassicas.
- In the greenhouse, grow French marigolds (*Tagetes*) or basil to protect tomatoes and cucumbers from whitefly.
- Some easy-to-grow annuals can act as sacrificial lambs in the vegetable plot – lettuces readily draw in slugs and snails, thus sparing more important or slow-to-grow crops, while nasturtiums (*Tropaeolum majus*) – are often chosen over brassicas by hungry caterpillars.
- The vigorous herbs mint and tansy (*Tanacetum vulgare*) can take over the herb patch if they're not regularly trimmed, but their cut leaves, scattered around the greenhouse, are said to deter ants.

▲ *Attract beneficial creatures into your garden by providing a reliable water source.*

INTEGRATED PEST MANAGEMENT

Originating in agricultural practice, integrated pest management (IPM) aims to reduce our reliance on chemical pesticides. Rather than looking to eradicate pests entirely, IPM aims to manage pest populations, keeping them at acceptable levels using a variety of methods. Gardeners who incorporate IPM principles into their own landscapes benefit: using fewer chemicals not only protects the natural environment but also saves money.

Horticulture is not the only discipline to incorporate IPM; it's also proved successful in agriculture, forestry, museum specimen care and domestic pest control. This success comes as a result of taking a scientific approach. Pests are identified, their populations evaluated, and the damage they're causing is monitored. Any control measures taken are proportionate to the damage caused. And IPM, rather than reacting to individual outbreaks, focuses on the entire ecosystem.

Set up slug traps baited with beer around vulnerable crops such as lettuce.

Standing guard

A key tenet of IPM is to monitor pest populations. This can involve hanging sticky traps in the greenhouse, placing pheromone traps in fruit trees, or simply wandering round your garden on a regular basis checking for pests. In many cases, if you catch a pest or disease early enough, you can remove the offending bugs or infected leaves by hand without needing to resort to chemicals. It's worth keeping notes on what you discover and regularly reviewing the success of your efforts, as with especially troublesome pests you may need to up the ante.

'Prevention is better than cure' is an important aspect of IPM. Seal up cracks in greenhouse glazing and net open windows to stop bugs getting inside.

- When buying new plants, check for hitch-hiking pests and weeds or quarantine new acquisitions in a cold frame prior to planting.
- Regularly remove weeds that may shelter pests, and dispose of dead and diseased material promptly to keep the garden 'clean'.
- Clean shears and pruners regularly, to avoid passing any problems from sickly plants to healthy ones.
- Finally, ensure you give your plants the right amount of both water and fertiliser. Too little or too much can both cause stress, making plants susceptible to disease. For example, excess fertiliser causes plants to produce soft growth that is especially attractive to pests, so learn to recognise when your plants have had enough.

Biological control

Encouraging beneficial wildlife (see pages 206–7) will help in the fight against pests, but sometimes you'll need a bit more assistance. Biological control is the use of specific predatory or parasitic organisms to target pests. It's especially effective in enclosed greenhouses and conservatories where whitefly, scale, mealy bug and mites can all be controlled. Outside, minute worm-like nematodes can be applied to the soil to help to control vine weevils, slugs and carrot fly. Biological control will not eradicate all pests but it can reduce their populations.

A last resort

If you've exhausted all other methods, IPM does allow for the carefully controlled use of chemicals (see page 210). Avoid spraying widely and frequently, as this can have unexpected consequences – those pests that survive are more likely to be immune, and future populations will grow from these hardy bugs, so future infestations will be even more difficult to control with chemicals. Even when this is not the case, you should always choose the mildest chemical that will do the job, and apply it over the smallest possible area, as any chemical control may adversely affect any predators introduced for biological control, not to mention bees and other wildlife.

When controlling slugs and snails, start by collecting them by hand. Check popular snail hideouts, under rocks and at the foot of walls. Employ barriers like crushed shells or copper rings around especially vulnerable plants. If they're still causing major problems, try using traps baited with beer or bran, or upturned melon or grapefruit halves. Resort to a chemical control, such as slug pellets, only as a last resort, and check and follow the manufacturer's instructions. If you do choose to use them, do so very sparingly, as often just a few pellets are enough to do the job.

Hang sticky traps near susceptible plants to monitor pest levels; if they become excessive you may need to employ suitable controls. Check them regularly in case bats or small birds get stuck on them.

USING CHEMICALS

A range of chemicals is available to control weeds, pests and diseases. Using them is safe, providing all package instructions are followed meticulously, but some can negatively affect the environment and many gardeners choose not to use them at all, or only when they consider it absolutely essential.

If you're using chemicals in your garden, it's important that you read and follow any instructions closely (it's also a legal requirement). The package generally includes a use-by date and safety instructions. Never dispose of unwanted or expired chemicals by pouring them down the drain – contact your local council to find an approved disposal site. Store chemicals in a safe location, away from children and pets, and wear protective clothing when applying them. Most garden chemicals can be bought in concentrated form, requiring dilution in water, or as ready-to-use packs. Ready-to-use packs are best for small applications; if you want to treat a larger area, use concentrates.

Spray a winter wash over fruit trees to kill pests and their eggs.

Pest and disease control

Chemicals are available to control insects (insecticides), slugs and snails (molluscicides) and fungi (fungicides). Most are sprayed directly onto the plant, except for slug and snail products which usually come as pellets. As with weedkillers, they are best applied on dry, still days, and you should avoid spraying flowers directly, as the chemicals can affect pollinating insects. Keep children and pets away from sprayed areas for 24 hours after application, or as recommended in the instructions, and avoid spraying around ponds and other water sources.

Insecticides work in several different ways, combating pests directly or in a systemic fashion, whereby they're absorbed by the plant and transported throughout its body, damaging any insect that feeds on the plant. Plant invigorators discourage sap-sucking insects.

Recent legislation has greatly reduced the number of chemicals available to home gardeners, and organic pesticides are becoming more readily available, though they may require more frequent applications. You'll find plenty of recommended home-made solutions for pests and diseases on online forums, including the use of washing-up liquid, baking powder and vinegar; generally, they're best avoided – they may simply be ineffective, or their effects may be unpredictable.

LAWN REPAIR

A neatly clipped, vividly green lawn is the perfect foil for blooming borders, but it can be hard to achieve. Lawns are susceptible to a variety of problems, from brown patches to fungal infestations or large areas of moss, that can leave them looking less than perfect. Many of these problems can be solved with better overall lawn care, but direct action is often needed to control weeds and diseases.

Perhaps the most common lawn problem is discoloured patches, and these have a wide range of causes – pests and diseases, drought, excessive chemical application or even the acid effects of dog urine. Mower blades may scrape the turf, too, especially in humps or hollows, or along edges. Weeds, including moss, are another common lawn problem, though they may have some benefits: clover typically stays green even through dry periods, and the flowers of dandelions, clover and others are popular with pollinating insects.

▼ *A verdant lawn sets off your blooming borders, as long as it's healthy.*

211

Patch up

You need to identify the cause of bare or discoloured patches in your lawn before you can find the solution.

Possible causes include
- Insect larvae, such as leatherjackets and chafer grubs, cause dead patches to appear. The larvae often attract hungry birds; if you see birds regularly pecking at the lawn in particular spots, it may be a sign of their presence. They can be controlled using predatory nematodes watered onto the grass.

- Fungal diseases of grass include red thread, rust, fusarium and take-all patches. These commonly begin as red or yellow patches that turn brown as the grass dies. There are limited options for the chemical control of lawn fungi, but regular mowing and improving turf aeration will help prevent infestations. Remove clippings after you mow to avoid a build-up of thatch which can encourage fungal growth.

- Circular clusters of toadstools, known as fairy rings, often cause the grass nearby to die. The only way to get rid of them is to excavate the ring to a depth of 30cm (12in), which is quite heavy work. Alternatively, you can simply fork the dead areas and reseed, an approach that will also help repair damage caused by other fungi and insect larvae.

- Yellow patches due to dog urine can be cured by watering the grass immediately after the dog does, though any spots you miss may ultimately need to be reseeded.

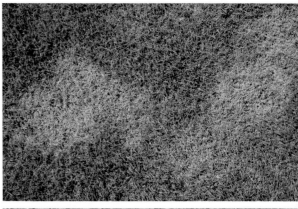

Rust fungi commonly affect longer grass in late summer or early autumn.

Fairy rings are circles of mushrooms. They can cause adjacent grass to die.

Dog urine kills grass, leaving irregular brown patches on the lawn.

Summer drought can leave your lawn looking brown and faded.

▲ *Heavy growths of moss can indicate poor soil drainage and insufficient light.*

- Chemical damage is easily avoided by following package instructions. Spilled mower fuel and oil can also harm the grass, so take care when topping up.

- Physical damage to the turf happens when a mower runs over a hump or slips off an edge, scalping the grass. Even out humps and hollows by carefully lifting the turf with a spade, then remove or add soil until the surface is level before putting the turf back. Damaged lawn edges can be repaired in the same way; cut a square around the damaged section, then lift and turn the turf so the outer edge faces inward. You'll be left with a clean, straight outer edge, and the damaged section can be repaired by seeding.

- Summer drought can lead to the entire lawn turning brown. Most healthy lawns will recover once the rains return and watering your lawn in high summer is to be avoided because it's very wasteful of water. You can help, though, by raising the cutting height on the mower and leaving the clippings on the soil to act as a mulch.

Weeds and moss

Some gardeners love a patchwork lawn with daisies, clover and buttercups mixed in (and it's certainly the most environmentally friendly choice) while for others only a uniform carpet of grass will do. If you prefer to remove the weeds, there are several ways to do it:

- Keep the grass healthy by feeding, forking and raking – this ensures it is vigorous and able to outcompete the weeds in the first place.

- Raise your mower blades for a slightly longer cut; this can encourage grass at the expense of weeds.

- Hand-remove weeds with a trowel.

- Specialist lawn weedkillers can be applied in spring and summer, and a few of these include a moss-killing chemical. Some lawn fertilisers also contain a chemical weed and moss killer.

- Moss is often symptomatic of damp, shady lawns with poor drainage. Improve the health of the grass by feeding, forking and raking up the moss.

- Consider clearing overhanging tree branches to allow more light onto the lawn.

- Top-dress with a sandy mix in autumn and apply lime in areas with acidic soils.

213

9. PLANTING DESIGN

Design has become a critical feature of all aspects of daily life, and information about styles and trends in horticulture is as easily available as it is for other areas of life. Before thinking about the look and design of your garden, though, or even paying your first trip to the garden centre, there are two key questions to ask yourself: 'What will the garden be used for?' and 'How much time do I have to look after it?'

To end up with a good-looking garden that works, you need to answer both honestly. If children and dogs will be sharing your garden space, for instance, you need to allow for them and their activities, while if you want a vegetable garden, you need to be sure that you'll have the time to look after it, too. Even the loveliest planting scheme needs maintenance, as well as the design flair to put it together in the first place. Take into account the amount of time you'll able to spend looking after your garden when you plan and plant it, and you'll be much more likely to create something that, as well as being beautiful, is realistic to maintain.

PLANNING

A brand new garden is the easiest sort to plan, because it's a blank slate for any kind of scheme, without the distraction of pre-existing features. It does, however, call for a bigger element of creativity and it may cost more in plants and materials if you want to create an established look in the first year.

Commonly, a garden that is new to you is already established, inherited from a previous owner, and you may want to make changes. As a rule, it is always worth biding your time and simply observing the garden for a full year to see how it looks through all four seasons before choosing which parts, if any, you want to incorporate into your future plans.

While it's not essential to make written and drawn plans for your garden, they are useful to help you keep track of your overall aims, and to avoid possible digressions and mistakes.

How to plan

The first step is to make a rough sketch of the individual elements you want in the garden, including any existing features. Sketching over a photo, using basic shapes, is an easy way to begin the design process. Don't worry about colour or form at this stage, but include necessary practical elements, such as space for rubbish bins, washing line, parking, compost heap and shed, and think about how these may be hidden or disguised. Think about existing paths and any new ones you would like, too, and what route they should follow.

This early stage is a good time to check whether there are any conditions that could interfere with your future plans. For example, the garden may be subject to site-specific restrictions, or a tree or trees may have Tree Preservation Orders. It's also worth being aware of the positioning of services on the site, and know where the drains – and, if there is one, the septic tank – are located. Check the condition and characteristics of the garden's soil at this point, too.

Adding detail

Following your first rough sketch, make a more detailed site plan with accurate measurements and schematics – especially important if you are planning hard landscaping features which need to be installed before any planting takes place. Include details from any existing site surveys, and note any factors such as frost pockets, prevailing winds, microclimate, soil type and pH. In short, add anything useful that will affect the final scheme.

Finally, decide on a particular style, and make some notes of plants that will work within it. You could make a mood board to help with ideas, and drawings of the look you want to achieve. Research similar looks in magazines or online for inspiration. Think about seasonal interest and the times when you will use the garden most. Eventually, all these elements will come together and help you with more detailed planting plans further down the line.

It's a good idea to make a detailed site plan with accurate measurements of a garden prior to starting a design or planting scheme. ▶

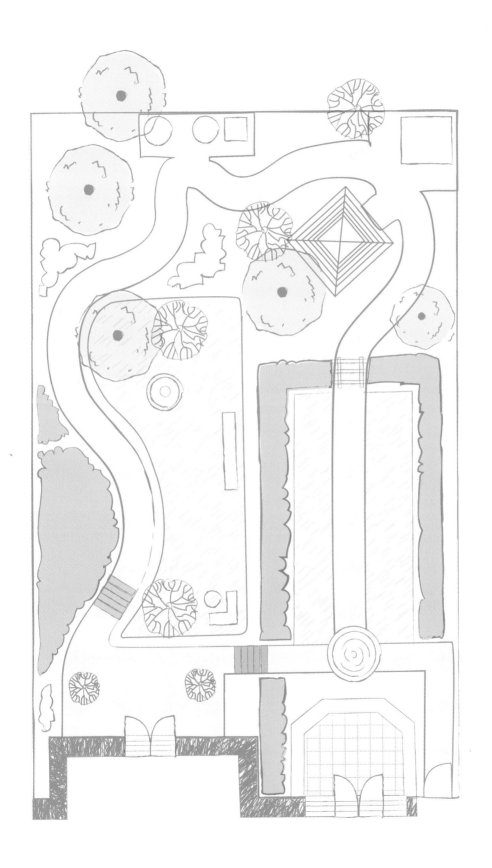

BASIC DESIGN PRINCIPLES

Good design need not necessarily be complicated, as long as you follow a few basic principles. There are no hard and fast rules, and the only limit to what you can create in your garden is your imagination.

A sense of place

Well-designed gardens and planting schemes always look as if they belong exactly where they are – almost as if they have designed themselves. They should pick up the horticultural and social environment around them appropriately, whether they fit into the wider landscape around them or shut it out, creating instead the atmosphere of an exclusive and secret place. A sense of place is a difficult concept to define, but it's the ultimate goal of good design, and you'll know it when you see it in a successful garden.

Style

Style is very much a combination of personal preference and practical considerations. It may be formal or informal, low-maintenance to relax in or high-maintenance for the plant lover who has plenty of time for their garden, contemporary or historical, wildlife-friendly, child-friendly, wheelchair-friendly – it's a list that can go on. The crucial factor is unity and cohesion – if random style choices end up jumbled together, they will be jarring to the eye and give an unfocused feeling to the whole.

An old water pump in a courtyard provides a focal point for the area and gives a sense of place to the design.

Scale

Gardens come in all shapes and sizes, but a design that takes account of scale both overall and in individual features will look better than one where scale has been ignored. Each element of a garden should be in proportion to its surroundings. One small pot on a patio or a large lawn surrounded only by narrow borders will look empty and barren, but at the other end of the scale, too much planting may feel fussy and claustrophobic, especially if it grows too high. Vertical and horizontal elements should balance.

Shape and space

Combinations of straight lines, squares and rectangles can be very effective at making a garden seem larger by leading the eye along them, and they are easy to design if you balance proportions between the different elements. A simple rule is to divide areas into three, then combining thirds to make larger spaces.

Using circles and curves in a design, on the other hand, gives a more natural, organic feeling, and helps to create a sense of intimacy and informality.

All gardens need an element of space, a resting point for the eye, and good designs take account of this, using plants and features to frame and define areas of space, rather than crowding every corner of the garden with plants or features.

Borrowed landscape

'Borrowing' the landscape around a garden is originally a concept from Japan. It can sometimes be used to make a garden seem much bigger. The idea is that the gardener integrates features outside the garden's boundaries into its design to make them seem connected. A tree-topped hill in the distance, for example, might be glimpsed and framed by a gap in the garden's planting, drawing the eye beyond its boundary.

Focal points

Focal points are useful features that add purpose to garden design. A path that leads straight to a dead end is a frustration for the garden visitor. Far better to provide some sort of reward – a piece of statuary, perhaps, or a specimen plant – to draw the eye forward and create a deeper sense of perspective.

Navigation

Routes round the garden and accessibility are key features of design. Gentle meandering paths are informal and friendly, often introducing elements of surprise, whereas straight pathways tend to indicate a definite direction and may add to a sense of formality.

Straight paths add a touch of formality to a design, while also ▼ *leading the eye to focal points such as this bench.*

PLANT FORMS AND HOW TO USE THEM

Choosing your plants is often the most enjoyable part of garden design, in which your tastes and preferences find their fullest expression. Even so, unless you want your garden to have a single theme, you will need a variety of plants to create the most pleasing outlook. The juxtaposition of different elements makes for a cohesive design, and different plant forms have an important part to play.

Key plants

Choose some specific plants which can be considered as key to a scheme, and which will be repeated through different areas to give a sense of continuity. Designs that don't have this element, instead consisting of lots and lots of different plants, can look fussy.

➔ Planting for structure

Plants such as trees and larger shrubs give structure to a garden, adding vertical elements and height, a backdrop for smaller plants. They can also be used as hedges and screens to mask unwanted features or views. Tall, columnar trees provide the strongest vertical accents, while more spreading trees soften the line between ground and sky. They may also offer welcome shade.

↑ Architectural plants

Bold plants make a strong statement in a design, drawing the eye towards them, breaking up softer lines and adding excitement and drama. They should be used sparingly, too many and their impact will be lost.

↑ Sensory plants

Try to include something for all the senses in a garden plan. Scented plants, textured plants that invite you to touch them, and plants that move and rustle in the wind should all be considered as important aspects of your planting scheme.

↑ Ground cover plants

Used to cover bare patches and around other plants, ground cover plants help to keep weeds down and, like taller filler plants, work quietly away, complementing more noticeable 'feature' planting. In difficult areas, such as under trees, they may also be your only realistic option.

↑ Seasonal plants

Seasonal plants include far more than the bedding plants and annuals that bring extra colour to the summer months. Many types of plant can ring seasonal changes in the garden. Don't neglect any of your options. Trees and shrubs flower early in spring or put on a glorious autumn display of colour and berries. Bulbs signal the arrival of spring; coloured winter stems light up cold, dark days and perennials offer long seasons of interest.

USING COLOUR AND TEXTURE

More than any other facet of a planting scheme, colour influences the mood and atmosphere of a garden. Our brains respond subconsciously to the visual stimulus provided by different hues. Red is exciting, while yellows, oranges and bright pinks are also stimulatingly hot. They have the illusory effect of bringing the garden towards you. Blue, white, green and purple, on the other hand, have a calming influence and bring a cooler feel to the garden.

Texture

Texture can help to bring a planting scheme together. It also allows for the combination of harmony and contrast that makes all the difference. Prickly upright stems, rough tree bark, flat flower heads, silver felted leaves and the shine of berries each bring depth and an extra dimension to a planting scheme.

Experiment with textural contrasts. Grasses, with their feathery plumes, add lightness to a planting scheme, while larger-leaved hostas or rodgersias bring solid structure at a lower level. Contrast them with ferns for a stylish shady area. Spiky plants alongside flattish clumps of daisy-type flowers are also a wonderful combination.

▼ *Planting schemes can either use contrasting colours, complementary colours or, as in this case, a single colour.*

The colour wheel

This is a device that helps you to determine colour combinations which fit well together. The wheel consists of the three primary colours, red, yellow and blue; the secondary colours made by combining the primaries – purple, orange and green – and the tertiaries, made by combining adjacent primary and secondary colours.

Colours directly opposite each other make for dramatic but pleasing contrasts that bring out the best in each colour

Combining colours adjacent to one another will give you subtle tonal arrangements

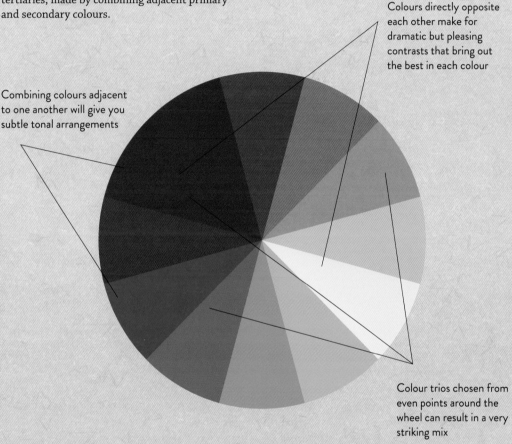

Colour trios chosen from even points around the wheel can result in a very striking mix

Simple colour combinations

- Variations on a theme. Plants with similar tones make for easy, harmonious combinations that please the eye with a subtle block of graduated colour that can sweep across a border.

- Using pairs. Opposing colours create a sense of excitement, bringing out the best features in each.

- Working trios. Trios from colours that are evenly spaced around the wheel can work wonderfully well. An effective way to use three colours together is to plant two of them in balanced quantities, and to use the third slightly less, to accent the other two.

- Single-colour gardens. Although single-colour gardens take a lot of planning, and are actually a mix of subtle tones (since few plants are purely one colour) they can look wonderfully elegant.

ARRANGING PLANTS

The art of arranging plants successfully in a planting scheme takes account of all the design factors already discussed. With a clear idea of what the final look should be, and a few simple rules to follow, it should be an enjoyable experience.

Informal style

Style will play a huge part in how you choose to arrange your plants. An informal look is best achieved by organising plants for as natural an effect as possible. The traditional herbaceous or mixed border, for example, is usually laid out to look spontaneous and flowing, although plenty of care will have gone into achieving the look.

Both cottage gardens and gravel gardens are made up of flatter plantings in fluid, lozenge shapes, while the modern style usually referred to as 'prairie planting' takes this fluidity one step further, with larger drifts of grasses and flowers, making a bold display with plenty of movement.

Using plants by height

Following simple rules will help you to avoid messy, random-feeling borders and beds. In beds, taller plants are usually positioned in the centre, smaller ones around the edge, while in borders, larger shrubs, trees and plants are arranged towards the back, medium-sized plants in the middle and smaller plants towards the front, although you may opt to break this up with individual plants out of 'height order' so the overall impression isn't too regimented. Repeated plants provide a sort of rhythm that links a bed or a border. Unless you specifically want to create a symmetrical impression, it is standard practice to plant only in odd numbers.

Formal style

By their nature, formal gardens look more
controlled. Symmetry is far more important in
this approach, so planting in even numbers is the
order of the day. Clipped hedges often define areas
of planting, and although planting may be looser
within the hedges, it tends to be arranged in a
relatively subdued way, evenly spaced, with fewer
varieties of plants, many of them sharing similar
characteristics. This may also be true of bedding
arrangements, although as with all bedding, the
planting is dense, without visible spaces between
the plants.

Modernist garden design, especially in
sophisticated urban settings, also tends to be
formal, with plant arrangements that are sparse
and architectural, but often asymmetric. Blocks
of plants and a limited palette are appropriate for
this kind of look.

◀ *Traditionally, beds are structured with taller plants at the
back and lower ones at the front.*

▲ *Following symmetrical patterns and
shapes will often create a sense of
formality and structure in a design.*

*In a very favourable climate you may
even be able to grow exotic-looking
plants such as this bird of paradise
(Strelitzia reginae).* ▶

Creating sustained interest

Plants should always be arranged to provide the
greatest possible length of interest and seasonal
variation, spread throughout the planting scheme.
Maturity should also be taken into account in your
plans. It may take several years in a new garden
design to achieve the final planned look, so spread
out plants, mixing quick and slow growers, to give
the garden a balanced appearance in the meantime.

PLANTING STYLE – FORMAL

Formal garden styles focus heavily on symmetry and geometry. They give a feeling of proportion and balance, and are usually rather restrained in terms of plant numbers and types. All in all, they should look as if nature is utterly under control.

Historically, formal gardens are associated with grand houses. Their grandeur and manicured looks were markers of culture and wealth. Influenced by classical culture and kept in perfect condition by an army of gardeners, they remained largely the preserve of the upper classes for centuries. Today, this formal style still exists, although in most gardens in a somewhat reduced form.

Some gardens emphasise their formal layouts with integrated combinations of planting and hard landscaping; ▼ here, shaped walls surround low, clipped hedges.

Order of layout

Formal gardens have a distinct order and pattern, defined by hedges, walls and screens. These are arranged symmetrically or geometrically to give a consistent feeling of balance. The most extreme example of formal pattern is the knot garden or parterre, created from low hedges, heavily clipped and planted in intricate patterns, which are designed to be seen from above, usually from the upper windows of the house nearby. It is possible to create designs for a modern garden which, while much less complex, follow the same principles.

Topiary

Topiary is an important feature in formal gardens, used to enliven the expanses of clipped green. Clipped topiary can introduce a note of fun and whimsy, too, relieving the austerity of a highly formal style.

Water

Water features tend to be still, reflecting the sky and garden around them, and are used to emphasise the balance and mirror symmetry of the overall design.

Statuary

In keeping with its classical origins, a formal garden design often includes statues. They make excellent focal points for the long, straight lines characteristic of this style. On a smaller scale, pots, urns or even plain stone blocks will fulfil a similar function.

▲ Clipped box hedges in stylised geometric shapes add structure and interest in a formal front garden.

Avenues

The formal gardens of great estates often had long, tree-lined avenues radiating away from the main house. In today's gardens, the feature can be recreated on a smaller scale with straight paths marked at intervals by smaller shrubs – topiary balls or lollipops.

Subdued planting

A relatively small range of plants is used in most formal gardens, although a breakout area of looser planting in one part of the garden may help to lighten the overall effect. Looser planting should still be contained by the more formal elements to maintain proportional contrast overall.

PLANTING STYLE – INFORMAL

Where formal gardens give the impression of the gardener controlling nature, informal gardens are usually designed to give an appealing feeling of controlled chaos. Despite the relaxed, easygoing style, an informal garden takes work to be successful. Even those who find themselves the owner of a wild space, such as a wood, will still need to carry out regular maintenance – keeping paths clear, and removing deadwood – to prevent the wildness from taking over completely. An informal style is also a much easier and more realistic aim for a family garden, where any outdoor space will be used for recreation, too.

Relaxed maintenance regimes

Grass left long, annuals allowed to seed and spread, and shrubs that are only pruned for health all reduce the demands on the gardener and help to give a more natural feel to the garden. They also tend to be better for wildlife. Birds singing, pollinators busy among the flowers, and the snuffle and shuffle of a hedgehog in the dusk will all contribute greatly to the atmosphere.

← Curves and contours

Gentle shapes, curves and contours are essential to an informal look. Unlike a formal garden, where lines purposely direct you in a clear direction, informal gardens are meant for meandering, for stopping at any or all points to admire. Curves are naturally restful and are not visually demanding in the way straight lines are.

↑ Softening with plants

In an informal garden, unwanted hard lines and unsightly features can be disguised easily using plants. Climbers can be left to smother walls, plants can spill out over paths, and ponds can be surrounded by marginal plants. Generally, planting should flow from one area to another.

↑ Rustic landscaping features

Features of an informal garden should be in keeping with the overall theme, using materials that blend with and reflect the wider landscape. Natural stone and wood, as well as reclaimed and recycled items, will add to a relaxed atmosphere.

← Exuberant planting

Swathes of plants help to encourage a more casual feeling. The great art of creating an informal garden is to make it look as if no-one has been involved in its creation. Colours are often deliberately mixed up and unsubtle, especially in cottage gardens. Growing vegetables and flowers together, potager-style, is possible even in a small garden. Colour combinations, whether muted or vivid, should look as natural as possible.

PLANTING STYLE – CONTEMPORARY

Contemporary designs are based on the idea of the garden as an additional living space, reflecting modern lifestyle choices. Today's gardeners have a wide variety of uses for their gardens, from entertaining and dining al fresco to exercising, playing with children and growing their own food. The spaces they make must work for all these and also look good – worlds away from the traditional display of horticultural prowess that characterised most gardens of the last century.

Distinct areas

Contemporary designs tend to split gardens into a series of discrete areas – a place to eat and entertain, usually near the house; a place to relax; a place to grow food and herbs; a play area for the children, and so on. Even in a smaller garden, clever screening and planting can break the garden up into sections while still keeping the overall sense of place.

Even in small gardens, it is possible to define specific or distinct
▼ *areas that make the space more structured and interesting.*

230

Garden furniture is an important aspect of design, as are unusual features such as the impressive wall planter in this contemporary garden. ▶

Garden furniture and structures

Contemporary gardens tend to have more furniture integrated into the initial design, and often include structures, such as shelters or garden rooms, that can be used all year round or offer inspirational spaces for creativity. Lighting and heating are also increasingly important in a contemporary garden.

Hard landscaping

Contemporary designs often emphasise the textures and forms of features such as walls and paving, bringing them to the fore. In very contemporary gardens, the plants complement the hard features, not the other way around. Walls painted in strong colours, a variety of different building materials used together, and the juxtaposition of new and old elements are all common themes in contemporary hard landscaping.

Contemporary planting style

In keeping with modern, pared-down design,
planting colours may be unified in tone. Fewer
plants with more impact seems to be the trend.
Shapes are architectural and dramatic, with colour
a secondary factor. Colour tends, too, to come in
blocks of planting, like a modernist painting, rather
than in the combinations and contrasts of a more
traditional garden.

▲ Less can be more,
as in this contemporary
design using a simple
palette of colours and
limited planting for
dramatic effect.

◀ Sometimes the plants
take a back step and
just provide a foil to a
an architectural feature,
such as this beautiful
contemporary wall.

DESIGNING FOR A SMALL GARDEN

More people than ever before are living an urban lifestyle in which space is at a premium. Small gardens, balconies and shared communal spaces are often the only access city dwellers have to the outside. Despite, or possibly because of this, there is a trend for using what space there is for lots of different purposes.

Multiple uses can present a real problem in small spaces, which can easily become cluttered and fussy without plenty of forethought. Planning an overall look and style and sticking to it, in even the tiniest plot, will make a garden feel less cramped, but there are also many design tricks that will make the most of what space there is.

A 'ladder' of containers that draws the eye upward gives an impression of lavish planting without occupying much ground space.

233

Use height

Most gardens have walls, fences or the sides of buildings enclosing them, and all of these can be pressed into use either to store essential equipment, or to host plants, or both. Climbers and wall-trained shrubs, planters fixed up high, and vertical planting schemes will all help. Cupboards and shelves can be fixed outside as easily as indoors, keeping clutter away from the precious ground space. Mirrors placed on walls bring extra light into dark corners and will also make the garden seem bigger.

Plant size

Don't be tempted to miniaturise the planting because the space is small. Used well, bigger plants can be expansive, drawing attention away from the size of the garden itself. Consider whether the space will fit a tree, too, which can give shade in a small, exposed space, as well as drawing the eye upward.

◄ The neat, geometric design of this small garden extends to the planting: broad paved paths surround a central 'bed' which combines textures – a slate floor planted with loosely shaped topiary balls.

Colour

To make the most of the eye-cheating aspects of colour, plant hot hues nearest the house and cooler blue-green ones further away.

Furniture

Any tables, chairs and so on should be models that can be folded and stored away when they're not in use, so as to maximise the available space.

Paths

A pathway leading away from the house at a right angle will emphasise how close the end of the garden is, while a meandering path is likely to look too fussy to be successful. In a small space, a diagonal pathway is likely to be the best option.

Pots

A surprising number of plants can be grown in pots, including many vegetables. Rather than using lots of small pots, which will look and feel cluttered, use several large ones and make them a feature of the garden in their own right.

▲ *This tiny walled yard uses comparatively large plants to joyous effect; the hollyhocks and hydrangeas, and the overflowing planter on the wall all add to the impression of generosity and colour.*

MAKING A PLANTING PLAN

For individual planting schemes, a detailed plan will be useful to help you to work out the right placings for plants, and the quantities you'll need. This is the final step of planning, which can be followed by the pleasures of real-life planting, and of watching your scheme develop.

If you haven't had a site survey, start by measuring out the space and making an accurate drawing of it on paper, or use drawing software on a computer. Double-check the conditions – soil, aspect, sun – and check that the plants are suitable for the space.

Try to visualise what the plants will look like in place. If sketching an elevation plan or a 3D view seems a step too far, use physical props to mark where plants are to be placed, keeping the proportions as accurate as possible. It is easier to move things around now, before you have bought any plants. Estimate the mature size of the plants in your plan, and allow for this in your final spacings – the 'Find a Plant' service on the RHS

website gives the ultimate height and spread of the mature plant, along with the ages at which plants mature. When everything seems to work, begin to mark the plants on the plan, remembering that what you're making is simply a 2D view from above.

Plot trees and large shrubs on the plan before filling in with perennials and smaller plants. Label everything; you may not remember the finer details later on. As the plan is to scale, once it's complete, it should be possible to estimate quantities easily. Bulbs, annuals and perennials can be spread out or brought together during planting, as required. All that is left now is to obtain the plants and plant them.

GARDEN DESIGN SYMBOLS

There are common symbols used in garden design; using them will make your final plan easier to 'read' and interpret.

Shrubs are represented by proportionally smaller circles.

Wall shrubs and climbers are represented by a lozenge or triangle.

Trees are shown as circles with a mark in the centre to represent the trunk. They are drawn at their mature spread, not their initial size.

Smaller plants and bulbs are represented by more amorphous shapes.

USING GARDEN DESIGN SYMBOLS

A garden plan (below), showing the pond, the trees, shrubs and smaller areas of planting, and the path and hard landscaping all of which can be seen realised in the photograph of the final scheme (opposite). An accurate plan ensures that you'll obtain the right quantities of plants and landscape materials for a perfect result.

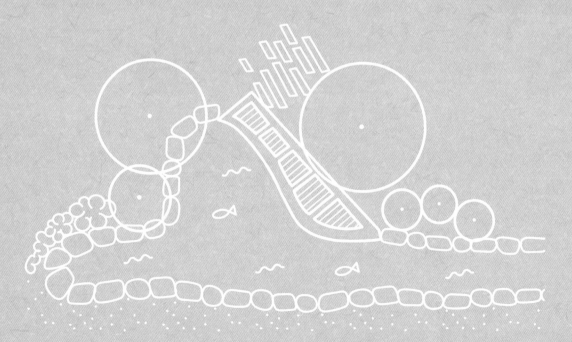

10. THE GARDENING YEAR

There are plenty of gardening jobs for every month of the year, although some periods are busier than others. You'll find yourself repeating many of them over and over (lawn-mowing, say, may be a weekly activity when the grass is growing), while others are season-specific annual one-offs.

The following pages look at the natural cycle of gardening activity and offer a broad guide to what to do when. Climate change has knocked our seasonal predictability somewhat, but even though an unusually cold, hot, dry or rainy season may push things forward or bring them back a little, our overviews and job lists will be useful in helping you to keep tabs on where you are in the garden, and what's to come, give or take a week or two.

Autumn is the real beginning to the gardening year – it's when you make plans for the growing seasons and start your preparation. Winter is a breathing space for the gardener, although it can also give you the chance to catch up on routine indoor jobs and to get ahead of the workload to come in the busy season.

Spring may start slowly but it's deceptive – by late spring, you'll probably feel that everything is happening at once and there are too many garden jobs to get through. In response, though, the garden will be starting to flourish and put on a show. Early summer is just as active, but by August, things are starting to calm down and you can afford to relax a little and enjoy the garden, before the whole cycle starts again.

EARLY SPRING

As the days get longer and plants get more sunlight, they prepare for growth. Bulbs start to come into flower before bigger plants expand and shade them out. Although still too cold in the north, in the warmer south of the country the longer days of sunshine will begin to heat up the soil ready for the early sowing of hardy annuals and vegetables, although frost is never far away. Be cautious – the soil needs to be 7°C (45°F) or warmer for at least a week for seeds to germinate successfully. The early blossom of almond and cherry trees will be out, along with swags of yellow forsythia, the first camellia and magnolia flowers, and the small early bulbs, such as crocus.

EARLY SPRING TASKS

In the garden

- [ ] Clear the lawn of debris. As the grass starts to grow, mow the lawn on the highest setting.
- [ ] Prune flowering climbers such as wisteria and summer-flowering clematis.
- [ ] Prune hybrid tea and floribunda roses.
- [ ] Prune any shrubs that will flower on new wood produced in the coming growing season. This includes shrubs such as buddlejas, ceanothus and hardy fuchsias.
- [ ] Prune shrubs grown for winter stem colour, such as dogwood and willow.
- [ ] Divide tired herbaceous perennials and replant young, healthy sections.
- [ ] Plant summer-flowering bulbs.
- [ ] Leave spring bulb foliage to die down naturally after flowering.
- [ ] Lift and separate overcrowded clumps of snowdrops after flowering.

In the greenhouse

- [ ] Take cuttings of overwintered tender perennials as they come back into growth.
- [ ] Sow summer annuals that need a warm start such as phlox, lobelia and snapdragons.
- [ ] Sow seeds of hardy perennials like campanulas and delphiniums, which can be planted out later in the year.
- [ ] Start tuberous begonias into growth.

In the vegetable patch

- [ ] Cut out all old summer-fruiting raspberry canes, tying in any loose new ones. Cut autumn fruiting raspberries back completely.
- [ ] Lift and separate tired clumps of rhubarb, or plant new crowns.
- [ ] Sow broad beans, early peas, parsnips and early shallots.
- [ ] Lettuce and carrots can be sown under some sort of protection.

LATE SPRING

As growth starts to speed up, gardeners become busier. The garden goes green again as dormant trees and shrubs come into leaf, giving a fresh backdrop to hyacinth and narcissus flowers, which give way slowly to tulips, lilies of the valley and delicate fritillaries. Camellias and viburnums will be followed by rhododendrons and laburnum, as late spring becomes early summer.

LATE SPRING TASKS

In the garden

- ☐ Mow lawns more regularly, slowly reducing the height of the cut. Apply weedkiller and fertiliser.
- ☐ Prune any winter-flowering shrubs as they finish flowering, and finish pruning roses, heathers and clematis.
- ☐ Feed and mulch all roses and shrubs. Later on, begin spraying against blackspot or apply seaweed extract as a foliar feed to ensure their health.
- ☐ Tidy up herbaceous borders and stake plants that will need support later on. Apply a mulch of compost or leaf mould.
- ☐ Clear away any spring flowers and pots as they go over. Lift and store tulips once the foliage has died down.
- ☐ If you're planning a new lawn, this is the best time to prepare the ground and lay one.
- ☐ Sow remaining hardy annuals and any new perennials or shrubs. Plant out the summer-flowering bulbs started off under cover.
- ☐ Make sure everything is kept well watered.
- ☐ Sow biennials such as wallflowers and foxgloves.
- ☐ Towards the end of this period, when all danger of frost has passed, plant out half-hardy annuals and bedding plants.

In the greenhouse

- ☐ Sow and plant tomatoes, cucumbers, peppers, chillies and aubergines in beds or growing bags.
- ☐ Sow sweetcorn, beans and squash to be planted outside in summer.
- ☐ Take dahlia cuttings.
- ☐ Prick out and pot up any seeds sown earlier. Begin to feed.
- ☐ Stop watering winter-flowering bulbs such as hippeastrum and leave to rest.
- ☐ Begin watering cacti and succulents after their winter rest.

In the vegetable patch

- ☐ Plant new trees and fruit bushes.
- ☐ Weed fruit beds, including strawberries, and mulch with straw.
- ☐ Dig over any remaining beds and prepare for planting.
- ☐ Plant early potatoes (maincrops should go in a few weeks later). Towards the end of spring, plant out squash, sweetcorn and beans.
- ☐ Weed and thin seedlings, and start new sowings of successional crops. Sow beetroot and brassicas.

EARLY SUMMER

Early summer is often the best time of year in the garden: the first roses appear, bearded irises bloom and peonies and lupins start to come into flower. Behind and above them, philadelphus, lilac, weigela and wisteria put on a stunning show of scent and colour. Everything in the garden is growing fast, and gardeners have to work hard to keep on top of jobs that need doing. In the vegetable patch, too, everything seems to be happening at once.

EARLY SUMMER TASKS

In the garden

- [ ] Keep on top of routine tasks like weeding and mowing. Mowers should be set to their lowest setting. Catch weeds early before they have set seed.

- [ ] Prune any shrubs that have recently flowered.

- [ ] Continue to spray roses in order to prevent disease taking hold.

- [ ] Remove suckers from plants on a rootstock, such as roses and plums, or those with natural suckering tendencies, such as lilac.

- [ ] Deadhead any spent flowers to ensure good second flowering.

- [ ] Plant out any remaining bedding plants and half-hardy annuals.

- [ ] Remember to water in dry spells. A good soaking once a week is essential for borders to look their best. Pots and hanging baskets will need much more frequent watering.

In the greenhouse

- [ ] Feed and water plants regularly.

- [ ] Provide shade and ventilation to reduce temperatures in the greenhouse and stop the strong sunlight from scorching leaves.

- [ ] Feed tomatoes as soon as the first truss has set, and feed regularly thereafter.

- [ ] Prick out and pot up any remaining seedlings before acclimatising them to the outside.

In the vegetable patch

- [ ] Continue to weed and thin around crops such as carrots and parsnips that have been sown directly.

- [ ] Earth up potatoes.

- [ ] Plant out winter vegetables grown from seed.

- [ ] Begin cropping broad beans and peas and watch out for early strawberries ripening.

MIDSUMMER

Herbaceous borders and bedding schemes peak now, before beginning to lose their sparkle towards the end of summer. Fewer trees and shrubs are flowering but summer clematis and strong-scented lavender will be in full flower. Pots and hanging baskets of petunias and pelargoniums bring vivid colour to entranceways and patios. By midsummer, growth is beginning to slow a little, leaving you time to enjoy the garden a little more. In the vegetable garden, peas, beans, potatoes and lettuces are all ready to eat.

MIDSUMMER TASKS

In the garden

- ☐ Continue to keep on top of weeds.
- ☐ In dry periods, raise the cut on the mower to avoid putting too much stress on grass.
- ☐ Deadhead roses and other flowering plants often. Bedding plants require extra attention to ensure they keep looking good for as long as possible.
- ☐ Prune ramblers as they finish flowering.
- ☐ Clip deciduous and evergreen conifer hedges.
- ☐ Water and feed plants in pots regularly.
- ☐ Take stem cuttings of shrubs.
- ☐ Plant autumn-flowering bulbs such as colchicum and nerine.

In the greenhouse

- ☐ Keep feeding and watering plants in pots to keep them in top condition.
- ☐ Watch for any signs of pests and diseases and take action quickly before the problem escalates.
- ☐ Pinch out the growing tips of aubergines and tomatoes, leaving the fruit that has already formed to ripen.
- ☐ Pot on any remaining spring-sown seeds.
- ☐ Take cuttings of subshrubs such as lavender, rosemary and santolina. Keep them warm but shaded from direct sunlight.

In the vegetable patch

- ☐ Summer-prune espalier and cordon fruit trees.
- ☐ Continue to sow successionally. Carrots and lettuce are good candidates. Sow spring cabbage.
- ☐ Ensure all crops receive plenty of water — this avoids them suffering from water stress and splitting.
- ☐ Harvest and lift early potatoes and shallots and store in a cool, dark place.
- ☐ Turn and water compost heaps.
- ☐ Pick soft berry fruits as they ripen.

LATE SUMMER

Herbaceous borders may begin to look tired, especially if earlier deadheading was missed. Phlox is a late-season star, as is penstemon, while many of the more tender salvias seem to come into their own at this point. In the south, dahlias will already be in full bloom and a second flush of roses is usually on show, too. Generally, the pace of the garden will have slowed. More and more vegetables should be ready to crop. As well as stalwarts like carrots and peas, courgettes and cucumbers should be ready for harvesting.

LATE SUMMER TASKS

In the garden

☐ Keep up regular watering, deadheading and weeding. Begin to raise the height on the mower to reduce grass stress.

☐ Sow hardy annuals, such as cornflower, nigella and larkspur, to flower early next year. Mark their position, so you don't forget them.

☐ Take evergreen cuttings (with a heel), and place in a cold frame for around six weeks to root.

☐ Plant early spring-flowering bulbs such as aconites and crocus.

In the greenhouse

☐ Keep feeding and watering greenhouse crops and potted plants.

In the vegetable patch

☐ Make new strawberry beds with the runners from older plants.

☐ When blackcurrants and summer raspberries have finished fruiting, prune them.

☐ Cover brassica plants with mesh to avoid problems with caterpillars.

☐ Lift and store onions after drying them in the sunshine.

☐ Start picking early apples and continue to harvest vegetable crops. Freeze any surplus, or give it away.

EARLY AUTUMN

The garden slowly begins to fade, developing autumnal hues of gold and red. Leaves begin to change colour and drop. Hydrangeas come into their own, and sedums are still in flower, feeding the butterflies. Flowering dahlias are kept company by other late performers such as asters, chrysanthemums and Japanese anemones. Rudbeckias and echinaceas are in flower, too, working well with grasses. Early autumn sees potatoes lifted in the vegetable garden, blackberries picked and maincrop carrots harvested.

EARLY AUTUMN TASKS

In the garden

- [ ] This is a good time to prepare for a new lawn, as the weather starts to cool, ready for new turf or seeding. Cut grass only when necessary.
- [ ] Repair any damage to the lawn by over-seeding or patching with new turf.
- [ ] Tie in new shoots of rambling and climbing roses.
- [ ] Lift and divide overcrowded iris to refresh them for the following season.
- [ ] As summer bedding dies back, clear the beds and prepare for winter displays.
- [ ] Sweep up fallen leaves and collect them to make leaf mould.
- [ ] Unless the autumn is very dry, this is an excellent time to plant trees, shrubs and roses, especially those bought with bare roots
- [ ] Begin planting daffodils and lilies.
- [ ] Take cuttings of tender perennials such as argyranthemums, scented pelargoniums, fuchsias and penstemons to pre-empt winter losses.

In the greenhouse

- [ ] Check that heating is in good order.
- [ ] Clean off any shading paint and move shading netting.
- [ ] Bring in any tender plants that have been outside for the summer.
- [ ] Repot cacti and succulents.

In the vegetable patch

- [ ] Lift all onions, potatoes and maincrop carrots before slugs have the chance to move in on them.
- [ ] Cover lettuces if cold weather threatens.
- [ ] Plant out spring cabbages. Check Brussels sprout plants and stake if necessary, to avoid wind rock.
- [ ] Put grease bands around the trunks of fruit trees to stop winter pests crawling up the trunk.
- [ ] Sow green manure to suppress weeds and add nutrients to the soil in spring.

LATE AUTUMN

Towards the end of autumn there will be clear signs of plants preparing for dormancy. Leaves fall, the berries on trees and shrubs ripen, grasses fade and seed heads in all shapes and sizes bring the birds to feed in the garden. It's a season for planning, and a good time to create any new borders and beds or making a new lawn, before increasingly wintry weather makes working in the garden harder.

LATE AUTUMN TASKS

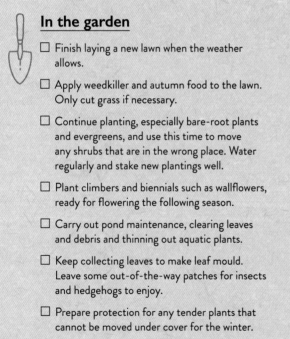

In the garden

☐ Finish laying a new lawn when the weather allows.

☐ Apply weedkiller and autumn food to the lawn. Only cut grass if necessary.

☐ Continue planting, especially bare-root plants and evergreens, and use this time to move any shrubs that are in the wrong place. Water regularly and stake new plantings well.

☐ Plant climbers and biennials such as wallflowers, ready for flowering the following season.

☐ Carry out pond maintenance, clearing leaves and debris and thinning out aquatic plants.

☐ Keep collecting leaves to make leaf mould. Leave some out-of-the-way patches for insects and hedgehogs to enjoy.

☐ Prepare protection for any tender plants that cannot be moved under cover for the winter.

In the greenhouse

☐ Store lifted dahlias after the first frost has blackened them.

☐ Store lifted begonias and other summer-flowering bulbs.

☐ Remove summer crops once harvesting has been completed.

In the vegetable patch

☐ Clear away summer plantings that have finished cropping, such as sweetcorn and beans.

☐ Harvest squash as they ripen.

☐ Dig over beds where possible.

EARLY WINTER

Tidy when the weather allows – bearing in mind that too tidy a garden is bad for wildlife – and do any necessary repairs of hard landscapes and garden structures. If it is not too wet and cold, dig over beds and borders; early frosts will help to break up heavy clods. Witch hazels, mahonias and winter-flowering heathers are among the few plants left flowering, while snowdrops may come out before Christmas if the weather is right.

EARLY WINTER TASKS

In the garden

☐ Top-dress heavy, poorly drained lawn areas with sand.

☐ Finish clearing and tidying garden beds and borders.

☐ In colder areas, begin to prune roses.

☐ Plant tulip bulbs.

☐ Check that vulnerable plants are well protected against frost.

☐ Plan and dig new borders, adding plenty of compost or manure, whenever the weather allows.

☐ Order next season's seeds and plants.

☐ Sharpen secateurs and shears and ensure mowers, strimmers and other machinery are given their annual maintenance checks.

In the greenhouse

☐ Check forced bulbs and bring them out into the light.

☐ Reduce watering for pot plants and stop watering cacti completely.

☐ Remember to ventilate when the weather is calm and not too cold.

☐ Check that stored bulbs and tubers are not rotting, and remove any that are.

In the vegetable patch

☐ Continue digging and improving the soil when the weather allows. Avoid digging or walking on wet soil.

☐ Finish pruning fruit trees.

☐ Lift leeks and parsnips and pick early sprouts.

☐ Plant shallot and onion sets and garlic.

☐ Check the pH of the soil. Add lime if it's needed but do not mix lime with compost or manure. Limed beds can be improved with humus in spring instead.

☐ Clean and disinfect the greenhouse thoroughly, along with pots and seed trays.

LATE WINTER

Short days and cold weather can make gardening at this time of year difficult, but there are always days when jobs can be started. Don't garden on wet, frosty days, as you can do more harm than good. It is still possible to plant shrubs and trees, dig over beds and tidy away debris. Snowdrops and winter aconites will come into flower during late winter, along with the winter-flowering iris, daphne, winter-flowering honeysuckle, hellebores and winter pansies. Inside, early crop potatoes can be put to 'chit' and cuttings taken of overwintering plants and chrysanthemums.

LATE WINTER TASKS

In the garden

- [ ] Begin to clear herbaceous borders, removing weeds and forking over before mulching with compost or leaf mould.
- [ ] Keep checking vulnerable plants for frost damage.
- [ ] Prune dormant shrubs and trees, removing any dead, damaged or diseased material.

In the greenhouse

- [ ] As soon as the greenhouse has been thoroughly cleaned, you can begin sowing annuals and hardy border perennials. In warmer areas, tomatoes and peppers can be sown under cover, so long as you can keep them warm through germination and the seedling stage.
- [ ] Take cuttings of chrysanthemums and overwintered plants.
- [ ] Pot up lily bulbs.

In the vegetable patch

- [ ] Sow broad beans with some protection.
- [ ] Prepare beds ready for spring and cover with plastic or cloches to help the soil to warm up.
- [ ] Dig in green manures that have overwintered in vegetable beds, this will give them time to decompose.
- [ ] Sow parsnips, shallots and onions in a prepared bed.
- [ ] Finish pruning soft fruit bushes, including autumn raspberries.
- [ ] 'Chit' seed potatoes to give them a better start. This needs to be done around six weeks before planting, so plan accordingly to take account of the last frost.

FURTHER READING

Books

100 Perfect Plants
by Simon Akeroyd
(National Trust, 2017)

The Good Gardener
by Simon Akeroyd
(National Trust, 2015)

RHS Grow Your Own Veg & Fruit Bible
by Carol Klein
(Mitchell Beazley, 2020)

RHS Small Garden Handbook
by Andrew Wilson
(Mitchell Beazley, 2013)

RHS Design Outdoors
by Matt Keightley
(Mitchell Beazley, 2019)

RHS How to Plant a Garden
by Matt James
(Mitchell Beazley, 2016)

RHS Lawns and Ground Cover
by Simon Akeroyd
(Dorling Kindersley, 2012)

RHS Shrubs and Small Trees
by Simon Akeroyd
(Dorling Kindersley, 2008)

RHS Vegetables for the Gourmet Gardener
by Simon Akeroyd
(Mitchell Beazley, 2016)

RHS Practical Latin for Gardeners
by James Armitage
(Mitchell Beazley, 2016)

**RHS A–Z Encyclopedia of Garden Plants
(4th edition)**
ed. Christopher Brickell
(Dorling Kindersley, 2016)

RHS Encyclopedia of Plants and Flowers,
ed. Christopher Brickell
(Dorling Kindersley, 2019)

RHS Pruning & Training
by Christopher Brickell and David Joyce
(Dorling Kindersley, 2017)

Botany for Gardeners (3rd edition)
by Brian Capon
(Timber Press, 2010)

The Hillier Manual of Trees and Shrubs
eds John G. Hillier and Roy Lancaster
(RHS, 2019)

Garden Design: A Book of Ideas
by Heidi Howcroft and Marianne Majerus
(Mitchell Beazley, 2015)

Planting: A New Perspective
by Piet Oudolf and Noel Kingsbury
(Timber Press, 2013)

RHS Encyclopedia of Gardening Techniques
by RHS
(Mitchell Beazley, 2008)

RHS Complete Gardener's Manual
by RHS
(Dorling Kindersley, 2020)

**The Vegetable Gardener's Bible
(2nd edition)**
by Edward C. Smith
(Storey Publishing, 2009)

Websites

www.rhs.org.uk

www.nationaltrust.org.uk

www.simonakeroyd.co.uk

www.greatbritishgardens.co.uk

www.thegardeningwebsite.co.uk

www.allotment-garden.org

www.soilassociation.org

www.gardenorganic.org

Index

Picture credits